HIDDEN Heritage
The Story of Paul LaRoche

HIDDEN
Heritage

The Story of Paul LaRoche

by Barbara Marshak

Beaver's Pond Press, Inc.
Edina,   Minnesota

Quote from Strikes the Ree, Chapters 5 and 15: used with permission from Bob Karolevitz, author of 37 books and countless articles regarding the history of South Dakota.

Information regarding Strikes the Ree, Chapters 5 and 15: used with permission from the descendants of Strikes the Ree and the Yankton Sioux Tribal Tourism Association.

Photograph of Strikes the Ree: used with permission from the South Dakota State Historical Society, 900 Governors Drive, Pierre, South Dakota.

ISBN-13: 978-1-59298-135-9
ISBN-10: 1-59298-135-6

Library of Congress Catalog Number: 2006921709

Printed in the United States of America

First Printing: May 2006

10 09 08 07 06   5 4 3 2 1

Beaver's Pond Press, Inc.

7104 Ohms Lane, Suite 216
Edina, MN 55439
(952) 829-8818
www.BeaversPondPress.com

To order, visit www.BookHouseFulfillment.com
or call 1-800-901-3480. Reseller discounts available.

In loving memory,
Irma Summers
Arlene LaRoche

CONTENTS

Foreword

When Barbara Marshak approached me about writing our story, I was filled with excitement and apprehension. Finally, a writer seemed genuinely interested in documenting our unique story in written form.

My disappointing experiences with writers prior to this meeting were all too common. Many shared an interest in the Native American culture but usually there was some hidden motive at work. All sooner or later pursued their own personal projects.

Over time, I began to wonder if our story was of any significant interest to the outside world. Perhaps what I was feeling was still the lingering effects of the initial overwhelming excitement from our reunion. Over the years, following our first return to the Lower Brule Sioux Reservation, I have observed what I call a *transformation* in many people—these transformations occurring upon hearing short excerpts of our story. Timing is critical in all human endeavors. By the time Barbara and I had our second meeting, my heart was firmly committed to revealing the full story.

It has always been difficult for me to adequately describe the feeling of being a product of two worlds. From the beginning, I have felt a combination of joy and lament. Joy from the unconditional acceptance of our new loving family, and lament as a result of instantly inheriting the plight of Native America.

It was hard, at first, to accept the situation. There is a certain guilt one carries in being removed from such an environment at birth, even though all circumstances are beyond your control. Knowing that I was brought into the comforts of mainstream America, yet my biological brother, one year younger than me, remained in the reservation system. What if the situation were reversed? It causes you to think deeply about just what is going on. Then, there is the realization and skepticism of being part of something of a spiritual nature. That is where things can get heavy. Early on, during a grant application review in Minneapolis, I was criticized for using the term "transforming." How dare I suggest that this somewhat common reunion story has a "transforming" quality. Well, the grant fell through, but the transformations continued.

I now realize that when one encounters the spiritual, you walk a fine line. The things that were programmed into you when young, the linear philosophy of mainstream America, it all goes out the window, yet you still need to function in the mainstream. Most of us, including myself, wish to maintain our credibility. I was raised in a Catholic family in white, middle-class America, yet somehow I found common ground in the spiritual philosophy of Native America. This in itself could be grounds for criticism from most mainstream religions, not to mention cause for concern from friends and family.

There seemed to be something mysterious at work here. Something always just out of reach of simple explanation. It is the timing to start with. If these events had happened a mere 30 years earlier, a blink in the course of American history, all this information would have simply been swept under the rug. Like most families of that era who were of Native American descent, that information was kept secret or even destroyed. It wasn't popular or desirable family history. It only became popular to be Native American in the past 20 years. I meet thousands of people every year who can't wait to share with me that "they have a little Cherokee in their family tree somewhere." Unfortunately, families now looking for documentation of their Native American ancestry will never find the truth. In most cases the information was lost with the previous generation.

Another enigma is the actual facts surrounding my adoption. There remains unanswered questions as to my actual departure from the reservation. I am content with the information at hand and I now believe this to be part of a universal plan of sorts. I have accepted this as something of a spiritual gift, not to be questioned or doubted.

Finally, there continues to be the overwhelming response from the many individuals who have been affected in a positive way by this story. It would seem as though I was placed here for a specific reason. As time passes, the big picture has become clearer to me.

Never in my younger days had I used or comprehended the term "reconciliation," but now I use it often. In simple terms, when I became part of these two worlds, mainstream America and Native America, I became a different person. As most of us would do, I proudly claimed ownership of both sides, having a love for both. In a childlike effort to share the two with each other, I found myself trying to bring them closer together. Within this act of love, I have found myself at work on this thing called reconciliation.

In my heart, before I could let love flow between these two worlds, I had to apply unconditional forgiveness from both sides for the wrongs of the past. Then I could feel love surround both sides. With love as the common denominator, I could see the way to infinite and unimaginable possibilities never before conceived.

This greater sense of purpose is at the core of all aspects of my life. The "transformation" occurred seamlessly in my heart, though it was a more delicate process on the exterior. I have been surprised at the medium I find to be the best conductor of the message. Most of my life I took music for granted. I was thankful for the ability to entertain others and gathered great joy from doing so. Never did I anticipate that one day I would find the true potential of music. In explaining this story, I find my vocabulary insufficient to fully encapsulate the events. Somehow, music seems to completely translate the story. It is as if music has an extra dimension not usually tapped into: a spiritual dimension.

As a result, I have been privileged and honored to be at the crossroads of what I have observed as a healing process between these cultures.

Sometimes I feel like a rogue filmmaker, following my heart against the odds, flying well below the radar of the mainstream music industry, and traveling like a band of gypsies down a nomadic trail. We have carved out a niche where one never existed. The underground circuit we initially cursed now seems like a blessing in disguise. We have learned to be self-sufficient and have come to enjoy the unconventional venues that we frequent. I feel like part musician and part minister, traveling the backroads, spreading our music and message, hoping to facilitate the healing process.

For the most part, this healing goes unnoticed by the masses and the mainstream media. It is an underground movement that appears to be gaining momentum. I believe it is meant to be an individual process, a part of each individual's personal spiritual journey, and it requires individual attention.

Even today I am a little uncomfortable with so many references to "spiritual" and "mysterious." I am certain though that we are on the road less traveled, the one that brings a sense of purpose while navigating its narrow path. I have found a good indicator for this road. Generally, the greater the negative resistance, the closer you are to being on track. This fights conventional wisdom. It is not an easy path to follow, but I have been told that the "red road" has never been easy to follow. The road narrows until it is only a fine line, thin as string. Engaging in work that puts positive energy into the world requires great mental and spiritual strength as well as outside support.

I have decided, with my family's support, to openly share our journey in progress. Barbara came along at just the right time and with the right amount of personal conviction to see the task through. She has worked diligently for many years and has demonstrated a level of commitment that even I could not match, almost as if the job were meant for her. I can only speculate that she has drawn from a part of her own personal spiritual journey as well. That is how it works.

The Lakota have a saying: *Mitakuye Oyasin*. It is actually a philosophy for living in harmony still followed by our indigenous people today. It means "we are all related." The actual Lakota translation goes deeper to mean "we are related to all things." Not only are we as humans all related, regardless of racial boundaries, but we are related to those things around us: the air, water, plants and animals. We are further connected to a higher power, the Creator. This is the "great mystery" that we will never fully understand.

I have been shown these basic spiritual laws in a dramatic manner through this personal journey, but the lessons are there for all. I share them with you in the hope of forgiveness, healing and reconciliation of our cultures. None of us alive today can change or alter the past, but we can bring love, hope, peace and unity into the future for the greater good of human existence.

Mitakuye Oyasin
—Paul LaRoche

Acknowledgements

Dear Reader,

I feel honored to be *chosen*, in a sense, to write Paul's story. Chosen not because I knew Paul personally, or because I have an adoption story, or even because of similar heritage. Rather, I believe, it's because the story called out to me, and it wouldn't let go.

On a family vacation in the Black Hills one summer we happened upon Brulé playing at the Buffalo Stockade in Deadwood. The music from this small, upcoming band of three was as captivating as the surrounding landscape. Their distinct sound initially caught my attention—the hauntingly beautiful mix of flute, keyboard, and traditional drum they're now famous for. Listening, one could immediately sense something deeper at the heart of it. Sure enough, in reading Paul's biography I realized this man's life was equally captivating.

All the way back to the Twin Cities from the Black Hills a voice kept telling me to turn Paul's story into a book. I automatically dismissed the voice, unwilling to believe I could or should do such a thing. But each time I listened to the unique music of *We The People*, the voice returned. Finally I reached a point where I knew I needed to listen to that voice and respond.

Six years and a few trips to South Dakota later, I'm happy to say it is now in written form and I'm thankful to God for prompting me to action. To me, Paul's story is one that touches the heart of the human spirit through family ties, following your dreams, bloodlines, and reconciliation.

I want to thank Paul and Kathy for trusting me to write Paul's story. I also want to thank Shane, Nicole, Heather, Fritz and Cheryll LaRoche, Yvonne Linster, Linda Thompson, Esther Spears, Mike Spears, Suzie Reinhard, Shirley Frisch, Sister Mona Kirwan, and others for opening up and sharing their family history.

I want to thank my family—my husband, John, our kids, Karli, Summer, Krissy, Emily, John Ryan, and David for their love, support, and encouragement throughout this long project. I especially need to thank John for making numerous trips across South Dakota on I-90 to Lower Brule and the Black Hills. Every trip brought a valuable piece of the story to life for me.

I need to give a special thanks to the Leonard Warren family for inviting us to the White Earth Pow Wow in June 2002. The wondrous sights and sounds of the Ojibwe gathering in northern Minnesota prompted me to make my initial contact with Paul that fall. I also want to thank Cindy Jensen, Kay Kniefel, Char Friedges and Ann Hagberg for reading the manuscript and giving helpful feedback. And a big thank you to Julie Saffrin, whose encouraging words and votes of confidence spurred me onward more than once. Thanks to Barbara Brink, Ruth Ann Cramer, Nancy Hudson, Jill LeVin, Chawna Schroeder, Tim Remington, and John Prin in my writing groups for their helpful comments.

I also need to thank Milt Adams and his mission in creating a mentoring publisher like Beaver's Pond Press. Thanks also to Judith Palmatier and Kellie Hultgren for their helpful expertise throughout the process. Thanks to all the people at the Dakota County First Judicial District in Apple Valley for their continued interest in this book. Thanks to Sharon Veden, Norma Lee, Doris Veden, Marvin Veden, and Doris Anderson for their love and encouragement. Thanks to Tom Heller and Jay Monroe for their excellent design work.

At one point early on in my writing career I prayed, "Take me on an adventure, Lord, one with gracious uncertainty and breathless expectation." God did that and then some. Writing *Hidden Heritage* has been an adventure I wouldn't have wanted to miss. And in turn, writing Paul's story allowed me to fulfill my own dream—my first published book.

Blessings,
—Barbara Marshak

One was missing.

Tiyospaye...family

"I had dreams as a young boy of a brother not here.
There was a sadness in my heart and I prayed he would come
home. And then one day he came.
I believe what God has given to Paul, he will make a way."

—Mike Spears, Sioux Falls, SD
Paul LaRoche's cousin and enrolled member
of the Lower Brule Sioux Tribe

Prologue

In late June 1955, a woman arrived at St. Mary's Hospital in Pierre, South Dakota, all alone and close to her time for delivery. She was in her mid-thirties and came from a good Indian family, highly respected in the community. The woman deeply *loved* her newborn son, but with her reasons still a secret, she made a most painful decision. With a heavy sadness in her heart, she wrote his name on the birth certificate, a name she chose with great care. Then she left the hospital, leaving her infant son in the care of St. Mary's nurses.

There was something special about the baby boy with dark hair and dark eyes. The nurses in the obstetrics unit were instantly enthralled with him. They took turns doting on him, gently caressing his cheeks, noting how his skin was as soft as silk. They held him, cradled him, and rocked him when he cried. Oh, how they *loved* him, watching over him day and night, lulling him to sleep with their favorite hymns. As the hours turned to days, and the days turned to weeks, Baby Boy LaRoche almost outgrew the tiny bassinet that was meant for newborns. The nurses fervently prayed to find a good home for him.

One day when the baby boy was about five weeks old, a couple came to see him. The first time the husband and wife laid eyes on him, they were immediately taken with him. "Oh, he fits right in our family," the woman crooned softly. "He's so beautiful." She even thought he resembled her dark-complected husband.

The nurses were reluctant to let him go, because Baby Boy LaRoche had unequivocally captured their hearts. However, they knew that the most important thing for the little boy was to have all the love and advantages a family could offer.

With great joy the husband and wife from the White world prepared to take the little boy from the Indian world into their home. The nurses could see the Hand of God at work, intricately weaving the lives of these three souls together as a family. They knew no matter the circumstance, God could bring something beautiful and wonderful out of the weave, and so the nurses let him go.

ONE

Whipped Cream Kid

At 38 years of age Paul Summers located a biological brother only a year younger than himself. Paul and his wife, Kathy, along with their two teenage children, Shane and Nicole, were planning to meet the newly discovered brother. The past couple of weeks had been a flurry of phone calls back and forth between Minnesota and South Dakota. Between the Summers' and the LaRoches—phone calls between blood brothers.

The simple drive from Minnesota to South Dakota was a journey from one culture to a new one. The Summerses left one family they'd known all their lives to meet blood relatives they'd never known. The journey uncovered long buried secrets.

. . .

Clarence and Irma Summers lived in the picturesque village of Worthington, a thriving rural community of approximately 14,000 people in southwestern Minnesota. Surrounded by farmland, the town was full of middle-class homes, tree-lined boulevards, and spacious parks. With beautiful Lake Okabena centered in the heart of the community, Worthington almost idyllically represented a midwestern Norman Rockwell lifestyle.

Clarence and Irma, now middle-aged, owned a sage green, two-story house on West Lake Avenue, directly across from Lake Okabena in Cherry Point neighborhood. Friends and neighbors liked them as two of the kindest, warmest folks around. Clarence worked as a plumber for Montgomery and Fauskee Plumbing and Heating, and Irma was the bookkeeper. In their early years they enjoyed dancing and loved going "visiting," a common form of entertainment before television invaded everyone's living room.

Childless for many years, they stayed active in church and community events and grew large flower and vegetable gardens. In 1946, the couple opened their home to Irma's sister, Verena Linster, after her husband died. Clarence even had a large addition built onto the house to accommodate Verena and her 11-year-old daughter, Yvonne.

By this time they were making a comfortable living, but their hearts longed for little footsteps to fill the big house. In May 1955, Yvonne graduated from high school and later moved to Yankton, South Dakota, to attend the x-ray technology program at Sacred Heart Hospital, leaving the three adults alone in the spacious home. Clarence and Irma were about to give up hope of ever having a baby when their prayers were answered. Word came of a baby boy at St. Mary's Hospital in Pierre, South Dakota, available for adoption. Originally from South Dakota, Irma was very familiar with the Pierre area. They made an appointment to see him and fell in love with him on the first visit. Immediately they began the adoption process. Following their attorney's advice, they filed a certificate of birth for the South Dakota Department of Health listing their son's name as Paul Edward Summers. Four weeks later, on July 30, 1955, they brought the little boy home under the temporary status as foster parents. Next came a six-month waiting period until the legal paperwork between South Dakota and Minnesota could be completed and the adoption finalized.

A few years later, the hospital called again with another boy needing a home. This little boy was over a year old and needed surgery on one of his feet. Without hesitation, they started the adoption process and named their second son Mark Joseph Summers. As soon as they brought Mark home, they wasted no time in seeing to his medical needs. Irma quit work to stay home with the boys. Always a meticulous housekeeper, she wasn't about to let children change her habits. With her home now complete, the gardens got smaller as she kept busy with two rambunctious boys under foot. Verena, a school cafeteria cook for many years, did most of the cooking for the family and filled in as a second mom, looking forward to Yvonne's occasional visits.

The extended Summers family fell into a comfortable routine. Clarence came home every day for lunch. Even at the young age of six, Paul looked forward to his dad coming home in the middle of the day. One day he arrived home carrying a box that looked like a suitcase. "Come here, Paul," he said. "I got this for you."

Paul watched as Clarence opened up the case and took out an accordion. He strapped the contraption onto Paul's small frame and loosened the bellows. As soon as Paul's fingers touched the keys, a wondrous musical sound exuded from the strange instrument, lighting up Paul's eyes. He immediately started taking lessons. By fifth grade he entered the talent show at St. Mary's Catholic School. It was nerve-wracking for Paul to walk out on stage in front of the entire school and give his first public performance, but at the same time it instilled a quiet confidence in his young, influential character.

The Summerses did their best to provide a loving home for Paul and Mark. The boys' younger years were filled with family picnics, camping, school activities, and church. The house was filled with plants, including Irma's rare African violets. Delicate glassware and antique dishes lined the shelving and hutches. Clarence turned the basement into a rec room, which became a cool hangout for the boys and their friends.

Paul and Mark always got along, even though there were five years separating them. Mark was more mischievous, which sometimes got him in trouble. One Christmas morning the two boys couldn't wait any longer to open their presents. They raced out of their bedroom and as they neared the stairway, Paul threw something over the railing into the living room, trying to beat his little brother downstairs. The sound of breaking dishes froze Paul and Mark in their steps as an entire row of Irma's teacups crashed down from the shelf. When questioned minutes later, Paul panicked and took advantage of his little brother's reputation. "Mark did it!" he cried, never owning up to it.

As the brothers got older, they enjoyed crossing the street to Lake Okabena where they could spend endless hours swimming or fishing. One year the Summers family took a three-week vacation with a pop-up camper, visiting popular destinations as they headed north and west. They traveled through the Canadian Rockies to Banff National Park and Lake Louise, then continued farther west into British Columbia and to the Pacific Ocean. From there, they followed the coastline to Oregon and back through Yellowstone into the Black Hills. Even with all the incredible sights, Mount Rushmore made a lasting impression on Paul as they stood in front of the massive monument literally carved out of a mountain. Paul and Mark loved the entire trip, viewing each day as a new adventure with exciting places to explore.

Summers Family Photo, 1980
Clarence, Mark, Irma, Paul

Paul's musical interest expanded from the accordion to the piano and organ that sat in the enclosed front porch. With a window view of Lake Okabena, Paul spent many hours practicing and making up songs. On warm summer evenings he loved to play his music, watching the moon come up over the lake, windows open, letting his mind wander. The next day Paul would often hear comments from the next-door neighbors. "Nice concert last night, Paul!"

Dabbling in every kind of genre available, Paul spent his teen years in the heart of the rock-and-roll generation, and on Sundays played the organ at St. Mary's Catholic Church. Life was good and Paul flourished under the comfortable roof of the Summerses' household. Irma was extremely proud of Paul's musical gifts and often asked him to perform impromptu recitals for company. Paul happily obliged, sitting down at the piano to play a song or two for his mother's friends. With a wink and a grin, his fingers raced across the keys, not even needing the sheet music. In Irma's eyes, Paul fit the nickname she bestowed upon him: the whipped cream kid.

Paul always knew both he and his younger brother were adopted, but both assumed they were the same as everyone else in Worthington, white. As a youngster, Paul's tall, slender frame often stood heads above other boys his age. During the summer months he tanned nicely, but the brown always faded during the winter. With a mother's protective instincts, Irma attributed Paul's deep-set eyes and dark features to French Canadian roots. That answer worked for Paul; he didn't need to know more.

Now a junior at Worthington High School, his days were filled with typical school activities. Ironically, Paul didn't make the high school band and instead poured himself into organizing his own rock-and-roll bands with friends. He was the lead vocalist and keyboard player. One such band, Scarlet Sun, played all the Top 40 songs of the early 1970s, and Paul could closely imitate any popular singer. His best friend, Matt Standafer, gave him the befitting nickname, Humms, while his other buddies called him Studley. Paul's band played nearly every school dance and all the girls knew the popular lead singer with the charismatic smile. Clarence then converted the basement rec room to a "band room" for Paul and his friends. With Jack Leslie on base guitar, Kevin DeVries on electric guitar, Craig Silver on drums, and Paul on keyboard, the four boys rattled Irma's dishes upstairs during every practice. After all, the unspoken rule for every rock-and-roll band was to be *loud*.

It was a common occurrence on warm summer days to find the Cherry Point Gang hanging out together: Paul Summers, Matt Sandafer, Greg Hegwer, and Mike Graff. A typical afternoon meant swimming and waterskiing at a friend's house on the lake. Paul kept hearing talk about a girl named "Frisch", and he wanted to meet her. When Paul showed up at the lake one day during the summer of 1972 between his junior and senior year, Matt and Mike were already playing "horse" in the water, each boy held a girl on his shoulders. Each horse and rider tried to wrestle the opposite rider into the water.

Paul watched from the dock until they came out, laughing and out of breath. A pretty girl with an engaging smile and long, blonde hair that he hadn't met before immediately caught his attention.

"Hi, I'm Kathy Frisch," the pretty blonde said.

"Hey," he answered with a shy grin. "Paul Summers."

Just then someone's little brother asked to be thrown into the lake.

"Help me swing him," Kathy said to Paul as the young boy rushed out of the water.

"Sure," Paul said, getting into position across from Kathy. "C'mon, let's go!" he said to the boy.

Paul grabbed the boy's other arm as he and Kathy began the count. "One! Two!" Paul locked eyes with Kathy and in that very instant *something* clicked. "Three!" Kathy yelled and they both let go. The boy flew several feet into the shimmering blue water sending a splash in all directions.

As usual, all the teenagers congregated in the house, looking for something to eat. An old, upright piano in the living room caught Paul's eye and he sat down and started playing.

"What are you playing?" Kathy asked, sliding onto the bench beside him.

"Just a couple Eagles' songs," he said, making room for Kathy. "Do you know how to play?"

"I actually played the violin for awhile."

"Want to learn a song?"

"Sure," she smiled. "What are you going to teach me?"

"Put your fingers right here on this key," he instructed. "And copy me." Paul played five notes and paused for Kathy to echo. "Good. This is "Color My World" by Chicago."

The hours slipped away and by the time Kathy said goodbye, Paul was hooked. He quickly found excuses to show up at her house and in a short time they were officially dating. Even on their first date, she wasn't afraid to bring up the subject of Paul's unknown heritage.

"You know you're adopted, right?" she asked. Paul and Kathy were spending a mild September afternoon hiking the trails at Camden State Park a few miles west of Worthington. Brilliant blue filled the sky overhead, the midday sun catching on the maple leaves that were just beginning to turn golden yellow.

"Well, yeah," Paul answered, leaves scrunching under their boots as they followed the trail.

"Don't ya wanna know who you are? Where you came from?" she pressed with a smile.

Paul laughed it off. It didn't really occur to him to pursue it or even give it much thought. *His* mom and dad, Clarence and Irma, loved him unconditionally and that's all that mattered. If anyone mentioned Paul's dark complexion, Irma always reiterated the French Canadian connection. End of story.

Paul and Kathy found a spot to sit along the Redwood River. A few leaves slowly filtered to the ground, some catching in the mild breeze. They spent the next hour talking and sharing their dreams for the future, holding hands as they revealed their heartfelt passions.

Something in Kathy's sparkling blue eyes melted any walls Paul might otherwise put up around girls. She was warm and open and easy to talk to. "It's music for me," he said.

"I want a family," Kathy said simply.

As usual, the afternoon disappeared far too quickly so they ended the day with plans for another date. Paul and Kathy continued seeing each other after Paul graduated from high school and began attending Northwest Technical Institute in Hopkins, a suburb of Minneapolis. He came home every weekend to see Kathy and by December of Kathy's senior year Paul knew she was the one, and officially asked Kathy to be his wife. Both the Summerses and the Frischs encouraged their son and daughter to wait until Paul was done with trade school before they married, and the young couple complied.

Deeply in love and ready to conquer the world, Paul and Kathy exchanged wedding vows at the First Lutheran Church in Worthington on May 17, 1975. Friend Bill Potts sang *The Greatest Gift*, a song Paul had composed for Kathy.

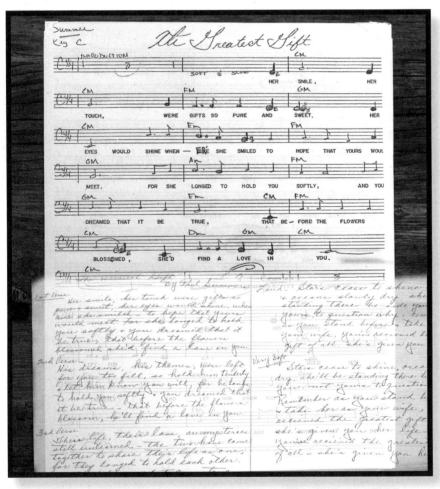

Original Music Score and Irma's notes "The Greatest Gift"

Paul got his first job in the engineering department with the City of Worthington. Even though Paul had earned a two-year degree in drafting, his intentions remained to pursue a career in music. Under the guidance of supervisor Craig Ebeling, Paul learned the city street infrastructures during the day and pursued his musical options at night. Kathy wanted to start their family soon and on August 20, 1977, Shane Michael was born weighing a whopping 10 pounds, 4 ounces. Two years later, almost to the day, August 28, 1979, Nicole Marie Summers completed the family unit. The young family of four settled into a house on West Lake Avenue, a few houses down from Clarence and Irma.

Paul & Kathy, May 17, 1975

Kathy understood Paul's passion for music and fully supported his professional musical aspirations. She knew it wouldn't be the easiest way to make a living, but firmly believed in her husband's talent and determination. Bottom line, she was willing to make choices that might otherwise be hard on a young couple with two small children if it meant furthering Paul's chances at success. Clarence helped Paul transform their basement into a music studio with various recording equipment and instruments.

As a toddler, Shane often wandered downstairs to watch his dad play music. Inquisitive and curious, it didn't take long for little Shane to earn his first nickname.

"Shane, no!" Paul shouted as Shane's unsteady feet stepped on a guitar, snapping the neck. "Shane, no!" was a common response when his sticky fingers reached for the keys. Pretty soon when someone asked Shane his name, he would answer, "Sha-no."

Nicole, too, was drawn down the steps as a little girl. With coloring books and crayons in hand, she was content to lie on the floor, draw, and listen to her daddy's music.

Throughout the early years the Summerses made several moves, always in support of Paul's career. In the 1980s Paul played at several clubs in the Twin Cities with great success. One such job was playing the piano at Howard Wong's on the "494 Strip," a section along the I-494 freeway in the suburbs of Bloomington, Richfield, and Edina where several popular nightclubs and restaurants were grouped together. For a while, the money was good and steady, but lean times always followed and for periods they had to rely solely on Kathy's income from various administrative positions.

For over a year Paul played at Prior Place, a club in Prior Lake, just southwest of the Cities. While there, he built quite a large following and became soloist for a band he formed called Interpreter. Next came a move back to Worthington where they opened a little club called Paul's Place. With the success of Paul's Place, someone suggested taking that same scenario and opening a club in Denver, so the Summerses next relocated to Colorado. Unfortunately, what worked in southern Minnesota didn't fare as well in the Mile High City. When Paul's parents' health began to fail in 1984, Paul and Kathy felt the need to return to Minnesota.

Doctors had already detected cancer in Irma and she underwent a mastectomy. Paul relied once again on his engineering background and found a job as a civil engineering technician at Maier Stewart and Associates in Minneapolis where his former boss, Craig Ebeling, now worked. The private consulting firm was well established with the municipalities surrounding the Twin Cities designing local highways, city streets, water systems, and resolving environmental concerns. Paul stayed with relatives and commuted the three-hour drive to Worthington on weekends, while Kathy and the kids stayed with Irma and helped her around the house.

Not long after, Irma suffered complications from a blood clot in her leg and doctors found it necessary to amputate her leg. Following Irma's surgery, Verena moved in with her other sister, Sylvia, so as not to create a further burden for Clarence. Watching his wife endure so many hardships, Clarence did his best to help her through the difficult days and nights. Meanwhile, Kathy's father, Dick Frisch, developed serious heart problems and was in need of a transplant.

And then, without warning, on September 28, 1986, Clarence died from a heart attack. At the funeral Irma confided to a family member, "If I ever needed him, I really need him now." Her heart forever broken, Irma passed away the following April. A mere week after Irma's funeral, Dick Frisch underwent transplant surgery. Kathy and Paul were overwhelmed with the loss of both Paul's parents and the added stress of her father's surgery. Too much, too close together.

Long before he was ready, Paul found himself at the house on West Lake Avenue sorting through his parents' belongings. He wandered from room to room, his heart aching. A sense of peaceful familiarity arose from the tiny flowers on the African violets still perched near the windows. Mark and his wife, Lori, were there as well. Both Paul and Mark picked out a few items of sentimental value, trying to split up the heirlooms between themselves and their cousins. But what would they do with all the rest? The only answer seemed to be an auction. It was sad to think at the end of two wonderful lives that their parents' life-long possessions would go to the highest bidder.

Immediately following Irma's funeral, Paul had to return to work in Minneapolis while Kathy and the kids remained in Worthington until the house was sold. With Lori's help, Kathy continued to sort through Clarence and Irma's belongings, preparing items for the auction. One afternoon Kathy sat down at Irma's desk, a kidney-shaped writing table with beautiful carved décor and curved legs. She reached in the back of a drawer and pulled out several envelopes dating back to the mid-1950s. One was dated October 5, 1955, from the Department of Public Welfare in St. Paul, addressed to Mr. and Mrs. Clarence J. Summers. A second letter dated January 26, 1956, was from a local attorney to the Division of Child Welfare in Pierre, South Dakota.

"These are about Paul's adoption," Kathy whispered, scanning the letters. She unfolded the letters and began reading. "Oh, my goodness—here's his name, *Arlen Faye LaRoche.*" She couldn't believe her eyes—she found his birth name! Kathy simply couldn't wait to call Paul that evening and tell him of her discovery. Maybe Paul would want to trace his biological family. She searched the rest of Irma's desk but didn't find anything else, nothing even about Mark's adoption.

"Have you seen these before?" she asked Paul that Friday evening when he came back to Worthington for the weekend.

"Not now, Kathy," he said. "I can't—I need time."

Losing both parents so close together took an emotional toll on Paul. As the days turned into weeks, he knew it would require a lengthy healing process. Kathy fully respected Paul's grieving, after all, she too was grieving for Paul's loss. She tucked the papers away until he was ready.

After matters were settled with his parents' estate, Kathy and the kids joined Paul in the Twin Cities. Paul and Kathy found an apartment in Eden Prairie and enrolled the kids in school, dragging Paul's makeshift studio equipment along with each move. Even though Shane struggled a bit in elementary school, he shined when it came to sports. Recognizing his talents, Kathy signed him up each year for baseball and hockey. Pitching and goalie were his favorite positions and he excelled at both. Nicole took an interest in music and began playing flute in school. Kathy set up auditions with the Greater Twin Cities Youth Symphony, which Nicole successfully passed. The next step was private flute lessons with Judy Ranheim, a well-known professional freelance musician and teacher.

As the family settled into a suburban lifestyle, Paul tried his best to adapt to life at Maier Stewart. By now drafting with T squares, rulers, and pencils had been replaced with a computer CAD system which necessitated Paul switching positions. Now as an inspector, Paul worked as a liaison between Maier Stewart and the contractors. His duties meant being at the job site everyday, serving as the eyes and ears for the engineers in the office. Even though he was at a construction site, he still needed to represent the company in a professional manner and arrived each morning in casual clothes and work boots. Paul usually started his day at the office for a short meeting and then headed to the job site. He reviewed the raw plans and used the instruments to calculate the progress. Each summer Paul inspected four to five large projects, working closely with each contractor. The Minnesota construction season ran spring to fall, leaving the winter months when he was laid off to focus on his music.

For a while things moved along smoothly. Kathy's interest in the medical field led to various administrative jobs in health care to help make ends meet. When their six-month lease was up, Paul and Kathy decided to purchase a house and found a nice modified two-story in Eden Prairie so the kids wouldn't have to change schools. Paul readily acknowledged that Kathy's strength and maturity kept the family on track throughout the ups and downs of the late 1980s. Even though he was still working at Maier Stewart, Paul was simultaneously collaborating with a musician friend, Jerry Schmidt from Minneapolis on an instrumental New Age recording project titled *Towards the Sun*.

Over the years Paul faced continual battles to survive in the real world and to survive as an artist. Although in and out of regular jobs and different bands, Paul's enduring love and passion was his music.

Paul and his family reached a low point, however, when the *Towards the Sun* project fell apart before the album's release. With his own financial and professional pressures mounting, the sinking feeling in Paul's gut told him it was time to give up the music. He simply could not carve out a career in the field he loved and provide a decent living for Kathy and the kids. He knew in his heart he had tried everything imaginable to make it work and it simply hadn't. All his resources were drained—physically, financially and spiritually—and there was nothing more to pull from. Much like the thundering crash of a cymbal marking the end of a symphony, his dream was gone, shattered in tiny pieces and reality was staring at him head on. Yet something continued to tug at the depths of his soul.

TWO

A Piece of the Puzzle

Working full-time for a few years brought a regular paycheck, but it didn't bring the satisfaction of creating sweet sounds on a keyboard, or seeing someone's eyes light up at an upbeat mix of melodious harmony.

But that was in the past...

Without music in his life, Paul convinced himself he had no choice but to cave in and do things the corporate way: education, career, retirement. He would adhere to society's rules by establishing a good home for his wife and kids. The bigger, the better, right? The more luxuries, the easier life will be. Isn't that the American way?

The economics of the early 1990s skyrocketed home prices across the Twin Cities, and an Eden Prairie zip code only added to the high cost of living. Paul realized their typical suburban home was more than they could realistically afford. They diligently scrimped and saved each month to make the mortgage payment. Before they knew it, Paul had to sell the house and move the family back into an apartment. They could only afford a two-bedroom, so Paul and Kathy gave the kids each a room and they slept on a hide-a-bed in the living room. It wasn't ideal, but they could make do.

It was getting harder for Paul to go to work every day. Running the city rat race at full speed didn't yield any personal satisfaction. Instead, it left an emptiness, a deep, spiritual void. It had been six years since his parents' deaths. Off and on Kathy brought up the adoption papers, but he simply wasn't ready. Besides, what good would it do?

Normally Paul viewed late autumn in Minnesota as one of the most beautiful times of the year, when the clumps of woodlands surrounding the comfortable neighborhoods were alive in brilliant shades of red, yellow, orange and brown. Fall reminded him of the season when he and Kathy first fell in love. But this October the falling leaves presented nothing more than a stark reminder that another cold, dark winter lurked just around the corner. Sometimes alcohol diminished the frustrated thoughts in his mind; other days even that didn't work. A depression set in that Paul couldn't seem to shake.

Outwardly nothing had changed in Paul's appearance, but as only a wife of eighteen years could see, Kathy knew he was deteriorating on the inside, leaving nothing more than a shell of the man she loved.

Hard as he tried to fit the corporate mold, he simply didn't. A part of him wanted to let his hair grow longer, but it caused issues at work so he kept it cut short. He was fighting to be himself and running into obstacles at every turn. He didn't understand any of it.

Sensitive to Paul's needs, Kathy couldn't stand to see him like this. She thought of the adoption papers again. One evening she approached Paul as he laid on the couch, eyes closed, shutting out the world around him. "Paul, we need to talk," she said softly.

Paul exhaled slowly, but said nothing.

"Paul," Kathy stressed. "I know we've talked about it before, but I think for some reason if you find your biological family and go through this process, it will help you deal with whatever you're feeling inside."

He remained silent, contemplating her words.

"You're not happy." Kathy tenderly touched his forearm. "I can see it, the kids can see it. I think it's affecting Nicole, she argues with me constantly. About school, her friends, everything."

"Nicole is just independent."

"It's more than that, Paul. She's also smart; she can see something's going on with you. We can't go on like this, watching you waste away before our eyes."

Maybe Kathy was right. He rolled onto his side and opened his eyes. "I don't know what good it will do," he said honestly.

"I don't know either, but let's try," Kathy pleaded. "What have we got to lose?"

Paul glanced up at Kathy, her eyes now moist with tears. He loved her with all his heart. She'd been there to support him all these years. He trusted her judgment. If she thought this would help, then he'd try.

"All right," he said, giving in to her persistence. "See what you can find out."

"This will be good for you, Paul," Kathy sighed with relief. "I'll start with Yvonne."

Paul's older cousin, Yvonne Linster, who had lived with Irma and Clarence before Paul and Mark were adopted, had connections with the sisters from St. Mary's Hospital in Pierre when she worked there as an X-ray technician in the 1960s. Shortly after Kathy had discovered the papers, Yvonne had approached Paul at a holiday dinner. "Come and talk to me if you ever decide to pursue this," she whispered. "I know some things."

"Really?" he half-inquired.

"For one thing, you're part Indian."

Paul heard her words, but simply shrugged them off.

Kathy pulled opened the drawer on Irma's kidney-shaped desk, now in their living room, and retrieved the adoption papers, the only piece of the puzzle they had. It would likely take years to find Paul's biological parents, but at least she could start.

Kathy dug out her address book with Yvonne's number and dialed. "Hi, Yvonne, it's Kathy. Say, Paul and I were talking tonight. Do you think you could make some calls and see if you could find anything about Paul's birth mother?" she asked.

"Yeah, I think maybe I could," Yvonne replied.

"Do you have a pen?"

"Yup, got one right here."

"Okay," Kathy said. "His birth name was Arlen Faye LaRoche, L-a-R-o-c-h-e."

"L-a-R-o-c-h-e," Yvonne repeated. "And his birthday?"

"June 23, 1955."

"Okay," Yvonne said. "I'll make some calls…I certainly know where to start."

. . .

A couple of days later, Yvonne called Kathy back. "Here it goes," Yvonne started. "I called my friend and asked her to check the records at St. Mary's Hospital. She traced Paul's name and date of birth and found the parents' names. Let's see," she said pausing. She flipped a notebook page. "Here…the mother's name is Bessie Arlene LaRoche and the father is listed as Fred Daniel LaRoche."

"Say that again," Kathy said, writing the names down as fast as Yvonne talked.

"Bessie Arlene LaRoche and Fred Daniel LaRoche," she repeated. "I called information and found a phone number for a Fred LaRoche," she continued.

"Yeah, yeah," Kathy said impatiently.

"He's in a little town called Lower Brule, not in Pierre," Yvonne advised.

"Lower what?"

"Brule, B-r-u-l-e. I called the number and talked to a woman named Cheryll. First I asked to speak to Arlene LaRoche and she told me that she died a number of years ago," Yvonne said.

Kathy glanced at Paul, hiding her immediate disappointment. *We're too late, his mother is already gone.*

"So then I asked to speak to Fred LaRoche and she told me that there's more than one Fred LaRoche."

"Really?" Kathy asked with surprise.

"I said I was looking for Arlene's husband, and she said he passed away several years ago as well."

No, Kathy's heart cried, *they're both gone!*

"We kept talking and she finally put her husband on the phone. His name is also Fred LaRoche, but he goes by Fritz. Fred LaRoche was his dad. I explained I was calling for you, to find out about Paul's birth mother. We talked for quite awhile. I asked several questions because I wanted to make sure I had the right family. It's obvious this Fred LaRoche is too young to be Paul's father."

Kathy breathed another sigh of disappointment.

"But I think it's his brother," she said.

"Really?" Kathy's heart beat faster. "A brother?"

"I want to warn you though," Yvonne said, hesitating momentarily.

"What?" Kathy asked. "What else did you find?"

"Well…they're Indians."

Kathy brushed the comment aside. What mattered was they were close to finding Paul's family. "Do you have the number?" she asked impatiently.

Kathy scribbled it down on a piece of paper and thanked Yvonne for her help.

She whirled around to face Paul. "I can't believe it! She thinks she found your brother," Kathy announced, her eyes wide with excitement. She joined Paul in the living room.

"Really?" he asked. He looked at Kathy waiting, anticipating her next words.

"I'm so sorry, hon," she said, reaching for Paul's hand. "It sounds like both your parents are gone…" Kathy sat down beside him on the couch and put one arm around Paul's shoulder, gently caressing his neck.

Paul ran his fingers through his hair and nodded in acknowledgement. "Oh, man," he whispered.

Kathy held him tightly while he absorbed the news.

An undefined feeling, a sense, passed through him. All his life he'd never known anything about his birth parents and here—in one phone call—Paul found out he would never meet them.

Paul rose to his feet and paced from the kitchen to the living room and back. *Now what?* It all happened so quickly, he didn't quite know what to do. Most people spend months or years searching for their biological family. Here it had been only a matter of days and they had a contact. It simply defied the odds.

"I think we should wait a while before we call," Paul finally said, tucking his hands in his jean pockets.

"Paaaul!" Kathy exclaimed, jumping to her feet. She could hear the doubt and uncertainty in his voice. "This is what we want! You can have some answers. Don't you want that?" She held her hands in the air, waiting for his reply.

"Sure I do," he said. But the tone of his voice belied his own words. "We've waited this long, what's a few more days?"

Kathy shook her head and started unloading the dishwasher.

Holding his thoughts inside, Paul wondered what this unearthing might mean. If anyone knew anything about American history, there was plenty to be concerned about. When the Native Americans were taken from their homelands and placed on reservations, their whole way of life was taken from them as well. The last few generations were raised on government handouts and the belief that their American Indian heritage was unimportant, even shameful. With the loss of their culture and a self-supporting lifestyle, many individuals succumbed to the negative plagues that afflicted the reservations: alcohol, dysfunction, unemployment.

It was time to make up his mind that he could—and would— accept whatever he found, good or bad. There was no guarantee what they would uncover. Yet another thought haunted him even more.

Rejection.

He was too late to meet his parents, but what if the others didn't want him to simply show up after all these years? They gave him up once before—they must've had a good reason. Family scandal? Poverty? Maybe they didn't want him back. The distressing thoughts tore at Paul's state of mind. He simply didn't know if he could handle it.

Kathy lifted the clean plates into the cupboard and closed the doors. She leaned her back against the counter and faced her husband. "Paul, I believe with all my heart this is the right thing to do. They'll want us to come back," she insisted, her blue eyes pleading for understanding. "I just feel it. And no matter what we find, we should accept that."

Paul stepped closer and kissed Kathy's forehead. "I wish I felt as confident about this as you do," he said simply. He wanted to, but the tormenting *what ifs* were stronger than her optimism.

• • •

Two nights later Paul and Kathy were alone in the apartment. Kathy finished wiping off the counters and shut the overhead light off. "Want some fresh coffee?" she asked, lifting the full decanter.

"Sure," Paul said, sauntering over in stocking feet.

"Let's call that number tonight, while both the kids are gone," Kathy suggested.

Paul took the hot mug from her outstretched hand and pulled out a chair at the table. "On one condition," he said, holding up his fore-finger. "I'm not here. Okay?" he instructed Kathy, holding her gaze with his deep brown eyes. "I'm not ready to talk," he stressed. "*Do not* let on that I'm home."

Kathy tossed her long, blonde hair behind her shoulders, nodding. "I got it," she sighed. She glanced at the slip of paper with the phone number and pressed the buttons.

"Hello," a man's voice answered on the second ring.

"Hi," Kathy began. "My name is Kathy Summers and I'm mar-ried to a man who could possibly be your brother."

"Yeah, we got a call from someone the other night," he acknowl-edged. "We've been waiting for someone to call back."

"Oh, good," Kathy said with relief. At least he appeared open to a conversation. "My husband's name is Paul Summers. We've always known he was adopted, but recently we found a letter that listed his birth name as Arlen Faye LaRoche."

"Arlen Faye? My mother's name was Bessie *Arlene* LaRoche," he said with sincere hopefulness. "But she always went by Arlene."

"According to the records at St. Mary's Hospital, the birth parents are listed as Bessie Arlene LaRoche and Fred Daniel LaRoche," she continued.

"Oh, I can't believe I have a brother!" he suddenly exclaimed. "Those are *my* folks."

The awkward conversation soon turned into a series of rapid questions going back and forth. "So your real name is Frederick?" Kathy asked. "But you go by Fritz? Okay. Uh-huh." Kathy repeated bits and pieces for Paul's benefit. "There's a sister in Pierre? Oh, uh-huh. Yes, his adopted name is Paul Edward Summers."

Too nervous to sit, Paul paced the short distance between the living room and dining room. He longed to hear both sides of the conversation, but there was still a cloud of anxiousness hanging over him.

"You must be older than Paul then?" Kathy asked.

"Let's see, my birthday is October 3, 1956," Fritz shared.

"Well, wait—Paul was born in 1955. So you're *younger* than Paul?" Kathy inquired. "That doesn't make sense."

"You said he was born in '55? I'm 37."

"Now I'm confused—wait a minute," Kathy answered, turning to Paul. "Paul, what year were you born?"

Paul's jaw dropped and he waved his hands, reminding Kathy he "wasn't there!" But it was too late.

Time stood still momentarily as Kathy locked eyes with Paul. "He wants to talk to you, Paul," she said, handing him the receiver.

Now came the moment of truth. Paul reached out a hand and took it from her. He swallowed hard and cleared his throat. "Hello?" he asked cautiously.

"Hey, bro," Fritz replied. "You're Sioux!" he announced, followed by a warm, friendly laugh.

As the realization of his words washed over him, Paul glanced down at his arms and hands. Hands that he'd watched fly over the keyboard thousands of times, hands that held his newborn children, hands that loved to caress Kathy's hair as she slept. Was it his imagination or did they suddenly look browner than ever before?

THREE

The Homecoming

"Mitakuye Oyasin...
We are all related."

For two weeks straight, Paul and Fritz talked on the telephone each night. Some nights Kathy exchanged information with Fritz's wife, Cheryll. Fritz and Cheryll invited Paul and Kathy and the kids to come out Thanksgiving weekend, believing it was the most fitting holiday for them to come home. Paul and Kathy didn't even have to discuss it. *Yes*, they would come.

Friends and family alike were happy for Paul upon learning of his recently discovered brother and sister. The initial excitement, however, died down somewhat as soon as Paul and Kathy announced they were going to visit the reservation.

"Are you sure about this?" Kathy's boss asked her one afternoon. Kathy now worked in human resources at the Minneapolis Clinic of Neurology, located in Golden Valley.

"Paul's brother and his wife have invited us to come out for Thanksgiving so we can all meet. I think it's a great idea."

"You know sometime these adoption reunions don't always turn out to be a positive experience. Why don't you just meet them somewhere halfway?" she suggested.

"They've all been so warm and open on the telephone. And some have written letters welcoming us home," Kathy explained. "I asked where the nearest hotel was and Cheryll insisted we stay with them. They're good people, I can tell."

"I'm sure they are," she acknowledged. "Just be careful."

"Don't worry," Kathy laughed, shutting off her computer. "My mom said the same thing last night."

• • •

Paul suppressed the mix of emotions constantly threatening to surface as the weekend neared. He came through the apartment door and called to the person who always held things together in a crisis, his dependable, devoted partner in life. "Kathy!"

"In here," she called from the master bedroom where they shared the large closet with Nicole.

"Do I need to put gas in the car?" he asked,

"I already filled it on the way home from work." Kathy placed a couple of sweaters in an open suitcase. "I'm packing sweatshirts, because it's supposed to snow," she advised.

"Just what we need," Paul muttered, unbuttoning his work shirt and tossing it in the hamper.

"What's wrong?"

"Bad day at work."

"Don't think about work. Just concentrate on the fact we'll be meeting your family tomorrow afternoon." She turned around, her forefinger pressed to her lips. "Oh, yeah—I don't have any tapes for the video camera."

"I'll run to Target and get a couple." Paul pulled his black jeans off the hanger and handed them to Kathy. "Throw these in for me with a couple shirts."

"Nicole wants her jeans washed so I'm going to do a couple loads of laundry," she said, pulling clothes out of the hamper.

"Do we need anything else?" he asked.

"I think we're all set," Kathy advised with a smile.

The next morning Paul, Kathy and the kids piled into the Oldsmobile, packed and ready for the long weekend. He estimated the trip would take a minimum of six hours, especially with the forecast of snow. During late November travelers in the Upper Midwest are often at the mercy of Mother Nature.

The directions were simple enough: Drive south from the Twin Cities to I-90, head west across southern Minnesota into South Dakota, turn north on Highway 47 at Reliance and follow it right into Lower Brule.

Dark, gray clouds hung low in the November sky as winter seemed to be waiting on the western horizon. The fields in rural Minnesota had been harvested the month before, leaving a rigid, barren landscape, almost pleading for the blanket of snow sure to come.

"Aren't we stopping to see Grandma Shirley?" Shane asked as they passed the exit to Worthington.

"Not this trip," Kathy answered. "This weekend is strictly about Dad's new family."

"If there's a whole bunch of tipis, we're turning around," Shane declared.

Kathy frowned at her son. "Relax," she said.

The community of Lower Brule was a mere 220 miles from where Paul had grown up and spent most of his life. It overwhelmed him to think that these people, *his family*, were in one sense so close, yet seemingly an entire world away. Just the word, *reservation,* created a sense of something different, something separate.

Soon after they crossed the state line, snow flurries swirled in the air and the wind picked up strength. Not enough vegetation to slow it down, only fence lines and an occasional tree. Paul watched the landscape pass in a blurred stream until the highway flattened out completely, stretching out before them in an endless straight line. A herd of Black Angus straddled a gravel trail that cut through a wide open pasture. In the next section of fencing, several horses galloped in circles, snorting in the chilly November air.

A slow, steady rain fell from the dark and dreary sky. The rhythmic thump of wheel against pavement allowed Paul's mind to waft and drift like the clouds hovering overhead. He wondered about these people that he'd never known before. Uncle Jiggs and Uncle Bill—the names themselves gave an impression of Wild West days.

Fritz and Cheryll said to meet them at the Squeaky Door Market, the grocery store in town. Paul smiled, remembering Kathy's comment from the other night. "Do you think it has those swinging doors like the Old West saloons?" she had laughed.

As the family neared Lower Brule, Paul silently wondered, *how do you prepare yourself to face truths that have been hidden for years?* Right now he wasn't sure if this unearthing was positive or negative, a blessing or a curse. He tried to prepare himself for it to go either way, good or bad, and in recent weeks he'd come up with a mental picture of what the reservation might look like.

One thing Paul knew for sure, he wouldn't be doing this if his adoptive parents were still alive. He couldn't betray their love and all they had done for him over the years. To him, when a child is given up for adoption the missing element isn't so much the parent, it's the love. As a kid Paul never felt a void because his mom and dad provided love through and through. Their love was fulfilling and strong, and he found comfort in having known that all his life.

It saddened him to realize that he would never meet his biological mother and father, but he was thankful there were two siblings still living. Fritz had told them their oldest sister, Fanchon, had been killed in a car accident in Ft. Pierre when she was only 26 years old. The next oldest sister, Suzie, still lived in Pierre. Unaware of Paul's birth, of course, the next child in the family was Fritz, born 13 years after Suzie. *Why was one baby boy given up for adoption and only a year later, they kept another baby boy?* Hard questions to answer, Paul acknowledged silently, especially when neither parent was alive. No doubt there was a secret his mother took to her grave.

Paul could speculate. He and Kathy had come up with several scenarios—but that was all they were, guesses. Maybe the truth was entirely different. Maybe it didn't really matter at this point. And maybe not all secrets were meant to be uncovered.

Soon the rain turned to ice, at times freezing onto the windshield. Paul gripped the steering wheel a little tighter, driving with extra caution.

"How much farther?" Nicole inquired.

"Couple more hours at least," Paul advised. "Depending on the weather."

"This'll be cool, Dad."

"Ya think?"

"Yeah. I mean, to find out about your background, your family," she said with a 14-year-old's enthusiasm. "I think it'll be neat to find out what their lives have been like. Ya know? I can't wait to meet them."

"I don't know why everyone's so surprised," said Shane.

"What do you mean?" asked Kathy.

"C'mon—look at Dad. It all adds up…adopted, black hair. Duh."

Paul grinned at his son's straightforward conclusions. "Glad you had it all figured out, Shaners." At 16 he was becoming more sure of himself. Paul knew part of that came from his participation in sports and part of it was just his character.

Just before Chamberlain, the freeway crested a steep hill and the wide expanse of the Missouri River opened up before their eyes. "Wow," Paul breathed.

"Oh, man, look!" Shane said. The highway gradually descended to a long bridge that crossed the river. The water mirrored the dark gray of the clouds, the rippled waves looking cold and uninviting. Billboards advertising Native American souvenirs to travelers and hunters heading west suddenly seemed a bit strange to Paul.

"When are we gonna eat?" Shane inquired. "I'm starving."

"You're always hungry," Nicole commented. "Your stomach is a bottomless pit."

"I haven't eaten since breakfast," he said defensively.

"Maybe we better stop here for lunch. I don't think there are too many more towns between here and where we turn off the freeway," said Kathy, looking at the map. The strong wind threatened to penetrate their outer layers as they hurried from the car to Big Al's Oasis for a quick lunch.

With food in their stomachs and the river at their back, the landscape changed dramatically, the gray sky now shedding a blanket of heavy, wet snow. "Man, it's coming down hard," Paul said.

Here the land gave way to rolling hills, interspersed with areas of gray, stony terrain. The pattern of clumps of brush and low-lying trees partially covered in the fresh snow was rustically elegant.

"Whoah," Shane said. "This looks like *Dances with Wolves.*"

"It does," Nicole agreed.

Twelve miles past Chamberlain Kathy spotted the exit for Lower Brule. "Get off here, Paul," she said. As soon as Paul exited, he had to stop the car and scrape the ice off the windshield. "Seven miles on this road Cheryll said, and then we turn again," Kathy advised. An unsettled quietness filled the car for the full seven miles, the huge, white snowflakes collecting in drifts along the tall prairie grasses lining the shoulder.

"Look!" Shane exclaimed when they made the next turn. "There's a sign for Lower Brule." The large wooden sign was adorned with teepees, a buffalo and the tribe symbol. *"WELCOME FROM THE KUL WICASA OYATE LOWER BRULE SIOUX TRIBE."*

Welcome to Lower Brule Sioux Reservation sign as we saw it on our first trip to the reservation–1993

27

"Stop so I can get a picture, Paul," Kathy said, opening the camera case.

"Are we on the reservation?" Shane asked, leaning forward to get a better view.

"I'd say we are," Kathy replied, snapping a few pictures.

Paul stared at the sign for a moment before starting the car again. As he shifted into gear and pulled forward, he knew there was no turning back.

They crested the last hill and here again the full width of the Missouri River came into view. A nearby dam downstream caused it to widen extensively, and there, protectively nestled along the river's edge, lay the tiny community of Lower Brule. A lump rose in Paul's throat and he slowed the car, pulling over to the shoulder.

"What are you doing, Dad?" Nicole immediately asked.

Paul took a deep breath, leaning forward against the steering wheel. "I need to look for a minute," he said softly. He pulled his jacket around him and opened the car door. Nicole, Shane, and Kathy got out beside him. "Wow...it's breathtaking," he said, taking in the panoramic view.

"Are you okay?" Kathy asked.

"Yeah," Paul answered.

"What do you think, Dad?" Shane inquired, watching his father's expression.

"I'm thinking this would have been my home," he said, pointing toward the small community artfully framed against the river's backdrop.

The cold wind whipped around them, but it couldn't shake Paul's desire to absorb the breathtaking view. He was flooded with emotion as he looked at the expanse of the open prairie, seeing the breadth of the Missouri River. It was magnetically beautiful, vast, and stretched to both horizons as far as the eye could see. Somehow, even the sky seemed bigger than before. In that split second, something struck a chord in Paul. It was something he couldn't yet grasp, but it was there nonetheless.

Kathy came up behind Paul and hugged her husband. "It all makes sense now, doesn't it. The questions, the wondering."

"There's a whole new world waiting for us," Paul said softly.

"I know," she whispered. "And it'll be good, you'll see."

"Wow, Dad," Shane said. "The town is so little, but look how far you can see here."

"C'mon, I'm freezing!" Nicole said. "Let's hurry and get down there."

"Let me get the video camera," Kathy said, opening the car door. "We need to get this on tape." For several moments, the others watched while Kathy filmed the scene before them. They got back in the car and continued down the hill into town. Only a few buildings lined the highway, some in various states of disrepair. Most were made of sheet metal with an aluminum roof, including the tan-and-beige building at the next intersection with a screen door entrance.

"There it is," Kathy said, pointing.

The simple sign read: Squeaky Door Market. Paul put the car in park and looked at Kathy. "Coming in with me?"

"We'll wait out here," she said with a grin.

"C'mon—there's no swinging doors," he said, pointing to the main entrance.

"You can call us the three chickens," Kathy giggled.

"Thanks," he said with a nervous grin.

Paul hurried up the walkway and grabbed the handle. Sure enough the door creaked loudly as he pulled it open. "I'll have to tell Kathy it *does* squeak," he laughed to himself. He summoned up his courage and stepped inside, brushing the snow from his shoulders. Talking to Fritz on the phone was one thing, but now they were about to meet face-to-face. How should one act? Or react? The thought was a bit odd, that two brothers, Paul at 38 and Fritz at 37, would see each other for the first time in their lives.

At 6'1" Paul was tall enough to see over most of the store shelving lined with groceries and miscellaneous items. He noticed several customers stare at him as they stood in the aisles, then quickly look away. The cashier, too, glanced at him more than once as he processed an order.

Feeling slightly out of place with everyone's gaze upon him, Paul stepped slowly down another aisle, daring only a glance at each individual. Just then a man close in age and not quite his height approached him. He was wearing a baseball cap and a maroon baseball jacket with a western shirt underneath. He had glasses and a thin mustache, and Paul sensed something slightly familiar in the curve of his mouth. "You must be Paul, huh?" the man asked with a broad grin, extending his hand to shake.

Their eyes locked as Paul took his outstretched hand. "Yes, yes, I am," he said, grasping it in a firm shake.

"Well, I'm Fritz," he replied. "Your brother." And with that he reached forward and gave Paul a big hug. Emotions surging inside, the two brothers held each other momentarily and then stepped back to get another look. Fritz was stockier than Paul, and broader across the shoulders. His face was more square, not at all like Paul's long and narrow facial features.

Suddenly a petite woman in her thirties with brown eyes and dark hair touching her shoulders stepped from an aisle with a half-full shopping cart. "Hi, I'm Cheryll," she announced, unable to hide the sparkle in her eyes. She reached up and embraced Paul in a warm hug. "It's so wonderful to meet you. Welcome home!" she stated with a smile.

"Yes, brother," Fritz said, his eyes moist. "Welcome home."

"It's kind of hard to talk in the store," Cheryll said, nodding toward a few onlookers. "I need to finish my shopping, but you can follow Fritz out to the house and then I'll be right out."

There didn't appear to be a viable business district in the center of town. Across the street was the Golden Buffalo Casino, one small restaurant, one gas station, a post office—all scattered over several blocks—but no stores lined the main highway.

Paul and Kathy followed Fritz's truck up another steep hill, heading west of town. Scattered streets of modest government-issued houses faced each other up and down in rows. The sign said West Brule. Some of the homes were neat and orderly, while others were rundown with chipped paint and broken windows.

As they passed, several kids chased each other down the gravel side road, their long, black hair flying in the wind.

"There's real Indians here!" Shane suddenly exclaimed. He pointed to the youngsters, his brown eyes wide with astonishment.

"Yeah," Kathy said simply, glancing at him. "And you're one of 'em!"

Shane was silent, letting the realization of his mother's words sink in.

Paul and Kathy followed behind Fritz's pickup past the small collection of houses before turning down a gravel road for another full mile.

"Man, how far are we going?" Shane asked, looking at the open grazing land sporadically dotted with a few homes here and there.

"Don't worry, they're all wearing jeans and shirts, just like us," Kathy teased.

"Guess what?" Paul asked.

"What?"

"The door really squeaks!" They all giggled, still not sure what to make of the unusual circumstances.

"Are we staying overnight at their house?" Shane asked.

"They've been gracious enough to ask us, so we're staying," Kathy answered. "And remember—Cheryll pronounces her name, *Sha-rell.*"

It was almost dusk when both vehicles turned into a long driveway that curved around a stance of woods. Finally a small red house with white trim came into view. Large, round rolls of hay were stacked along a fence line, now covered in snow. A horse trailer and tractor were parked next to each other near a shed. On the fence post near the house a wooden sign boasted, "LaRoche Ranch." It was obvious that Fritz and Cheryll had a sense of ownership with their property. Lights warmed the window facing a deck that led to the front door, offering a welcoming appearance.

Fritz directed everyone inside. "C'mon in," he insisted. "Take your coats off and get comfortable."

Fritz had explained they were part-time ranchers, as well as helping Cheryll's parents, Vernon and Violet Rekow, run the grocery store in town. Cheryll was also the realty officer for the Bureau of Indian Affairs (BIA) in Lower Brule. Keeping up with all their obligations was hard work with huge time constraints, but it provided a decent living for their family.

Once inside it was immediately apparent that Cheryll was a collector and purple was her favorite color. The ranch house was family oriented with photos and lavender, violet, and plum-colored mementos perched everywhere. By the time Paul and Kathy got their bags inside, Cheryll pulled into the yard. She started to put away the groceries just as four boys entered the kitchen. "These are our boys," Cheryll said. "Harlee, John-John, Jeremiah and Frederick." John-John was the tallest of the boys.

"Nice to meet you," Paul and Kathy said, acknowledging each one individually.

"And this is Shane," Paul said, resting his hands on Shane's shoulders. "And Nicole." The six teenagers grinned and nodded, exchanging a variety of greetings.

Smiling, Cheryll touched Jeremiah's arm. "Look how much Nicole and Jeremiah resemble each other. Oh, I can't get over it!"

"They do," Kathy agreed.

"And Shane and Fred look a lot alike, don't they?" Paul asked, looking at the two young boys standing next to each other, unsure what to make of this unusual family gathering.

"To think we didn't even know about each other all these years, and look how much our kids look like one another. It's amazing," Cheryll said. She had a natural enthusiasm that exuded smiles and tenderness from her small frame.

Surprisingly, all the doubts and fears Paul had before coming to Lower Brule vanished in the wintry-white South Dakota wind. It was obvious they were sincerely thrilled to have him back. The atmosphere inside was warm, welcoming, and wonderful, all wrapped up in the confines of one small reservation house. He wanted to absorb everything about their initial encounter and capture it in his memory forever.

"Look at this picture," Fritz said. He pointed to a framed picture on the living room wall. "This here is our mother, Arlene."

Paul bent his slender frame to get a closer look at the photo, slightly aged, and studied the woman he would never have a chance to know. She was young in the photo, with beautiful, dark hair and deep set eyes, and a long, narrow face. *His mother.* The thought was still hard to grasp, after all, *Irma* was his mother. But this woman's smile seemed to speak to Paul's heart, and yes, he could see it: an unmistakable resemblance.

Indescribable feelings ran through his blood. *Indian blood.* Who'd have ever imagined?

"Here's Fanchon and Suzie when they were little," Cheryll said, pointing to another framed photograph from the 1950s.

Cheryll poured coffee as they gathered around the kitchen table, the conversation relaxed and comfortable. Complete darkness had set in and despite the cold outside,

Early picture of Arlene, Paul's biological mother.

the mood inside the tiny house was warmer than anything Paul had ever known.

"We'll drive up to Pierre on Friday so you can meet Suzie," Fritz said.

"Oh, she's so excited to meet you," Cheryll said.

"We don't have copies of the actual birth certificate yet," Kathy interjected.

Fritz and Cheryll glanced at each other, their expressions revealing their emotions. "You don't need to show us a piece of paper to prove anything," Cheryll said simply. "We don't doubt it for a minute. One look at our kids tells us that."

Paul glanced out the darkened window, trying his best to process all the aspects of this night at once. Fritz and Cheryll were eager and ready to accept this news without documentation. But what if there was a mistake somewhere along the way? A wrong name listed? Shouldn't it be confirmed?

The two couples couldn't talk fast enough, trying to unravel 38 years of family history in a matter of minutes. All six kids listened intently for awhile before retreating downstairs to the family room. Similar in age, Jeremiah and Nicole paired up, striking up a conversation. Harlee was so happy for Fritz to meet his brother that he practically trembled with excitement. The youngest, Frederick, took out his cars and played while the older kids talked.

Fritz and Cheryll tried their best to answer Paul and Kathy's myriad questions. "Yup, there's 13 years between Suzie and me," Fritz explained. "No one in the family ever knew about Paul."

"No one?" Kathy asked.

"No, we've talked to her sisters and no one knew she was even pregnant then," Cheryll said.

"I wonder why she chose to give him up," Kathy said.

"Ever since we got your call, I've tried to figure out why she did what she did," Fritz said, his voice filled with tenderness rather than anger. "But I don't have an answer."

"Maybe no one does," Paul said.

"I can tell you this," Fritz said, tapping his finger on the table. "She was a good person, don't ever doubt that." The room was quiet for a few moments. Fritz cleared his throat and broke the silence. "Well, she must've had a good reason."

"Yes," Paul nodded in agreement. "Maybe we have to leave it at that."

"Didn't you say Paul's birth name was Arlen Faye?" Cheryll asked.

"Yes," Kathy said. She leaned forward, glancing at Arlene's photo a little closer. "I wonder if she dropped the 'e' from Arlene to leave some sort of a trail, a connection," she suggested.

"That's what I thought," Fritz said, sitting up straight. "It would make sense."

Paul's soulful expression matched the emotion showing on Fritz's face. It was almost too much to absorb at once. "Whew!" Paul finally said, exhaling. "Lots to contemplate; lots to think about. I'll be honest—it's a bit overwhelming." He folded his arms across his chest and smiled at Kathy.

"Take your time," Cheryll said. "We know there's a lot to deal with, and it's so unexpected and all."

Paul nodded and looked at Fritz. "So tell me about your life," he said.

Fritz leaned back in his chair, his gaze fixed on his mother's photograph. "Let's see…when I was about five years old, the folks, Arlene and Fred, got divorced. Sometime later, Mom married Leo Bush from Porcupine, South Dakota, and we moved down to Pawnee, Oklahoma, while I was in elementary school." Fritz talked in short, unhurried sentences. "While we were living there Mom discovered a mole on her right shoulder and went to a doctor to have it checked out. They removed the mole and sent it in for an examination. By the time the results came back, the cancer had already spread through her whole arm. Doctors tried to cut some of the flesh on her shoulder to get the cancerous cells, but they didn't get it all. From there, it spread like wildfire." He paused, his voice soft. "I was pretty young so I don't remember much, but she became extremely sick from the treatments and lost all her hair."

"Oh, how sad," Kathy offered.

"By then Mom wanted to come back to Pierre, to be near her family. She asked to be flown back to South Dakota, so we chartered a medical plane and I flew with her on the plane to Pierre. I had to bring all my things 'cause I wasn't going back, you know? She had asked Uncle Jiggs to raise me, after…she was gone. Even brought my bike in the plane," he said with a grin. "Mom's older sister, Aunt Esther, was in the hospital room with her the night she passed away. After that I went out to Uncle Jiggs's ranch on the Little Bend. It's quite a spread on the inside of a big bend in the Missouri River," Fritz said with a wave of his hand. "We'll show you tomorrow. So, from age 12 to 18, I lived on the ranch with J.W., or Uncle Jiggs as he's called, even though our dad still lived in town."

"Really?" Kathy asked with surprise.

"Yup," he said, nodding. "I saw my dad all the time though. One summer he even worked for Uncle Jiggs and lived with us on the bend. But he never remarried. He lived right here in Lower Brule until he died in 1975."

Paul glanced at Kathy and her eyes registered his reaction. Why would Arlene ask J.W., rather than the father, to raise Fritz? It was another secret that may never be resolved.

Paul stood up to fill his coffee cup.

"I had a lot of good years, you know, growing up on the ranch," Fritz said, reflecting. "It was hard work…we spent the summers chasing cows, breaking horses, hauling hay, swimming in the river down there." He paused for a moment, the words catching in his throat. "But I never had a *brother* growing up," he lamented, his voice full of emotion. "There's a lot of little things that Paul and I missed out," he said to Cheryll and Kathy. "Something we'll never get back. It's just so great to have him here now. And it's great to know, too, there's another brother through his adoption, Mark Summers."

Cheryll stood up and clasped her hands together. "I think this is the perfect time," she said, unable to hide her excitement. "C'mon into the living room. We have something for you."

Cheryll called the kids to join them. Paul and Kathy glanced at each other and politely followed their hosts into the next room. The living room contained the usual household belongings, TV, couch, and comfortable chairs with a touch of Indian décor. Kathy noticed a beautiful quilt folded on the end of the couch.

"Oh, there's so much to tell you," Cheryll said, folding her hands across her chest. "I hardly know where to begin." She smiled and clasped Fritz's arm, always using hand gestures as she talked. "We have something for you, but I need to explain the meaning behind it first. Even though we live on the rez, both Fritz and I were raised with contemporary customs rather than the traditional Lakota ceremonies. That's just how it was. But we do know that the star quilt is especially important in the Lakota culture," Cheryll said, lifting the quilt. "It represents the Morning Star. There are seven tribes in the Sioux nation and the Lower Brule, our tribe, is the smallest of the seven." She held

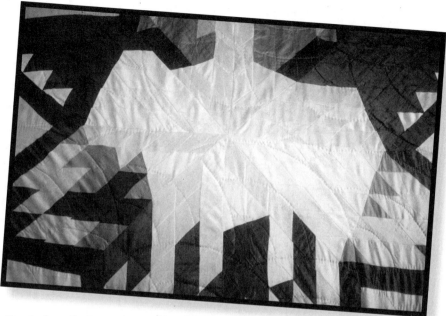

***Design on Lakota star quilt, gift from Fritz
and Cheryll, homecoming 1993***

up the edge of the full-sized quilt and let it fall open to display a large, single, eight-pointed star in the center of the quilt top. The light pink background was offset by the dark burgundy outline of the star.

Fritz pointed to the three symbols accentuated inside the star in sections of blue, brown and white. "Here's the eagle right here," he indicated. "And the white buffalo, and here is the peace pipe," he finished, running his hand along the outline. "Can you see it?"

"Yes," Paul answered, with Kathy nodding.

"Yup, I can see it," Shane added.

"Me too," said Nicole.

"All three have significant meaning to the Lakota," Fritz advised.

"Today, star quilts are one of the most valued gifts of the Lakota people," Cheryll continued. "Having you come home, Paul, along with Kathy, Shane and Nicole, it means so much to us. We are so delighted to have you in our home and we want to express our sincere love and say 'welcome home' by giving you this quilt."

Kathy squeezed Paul's hand, tears springing to her eyes.

"The way we do it is to wrap it around you, so that's what our family is going to do for your family," she said, ushering them to the center of the room.

Fritz took one end of the quilt while Cheryll took the other and along with their boys, wrapped it across Paul and Kathy's shoulders as they stood with Shane and Nicole. "May this quilt always be a reminder of your true heritage and the Lakota culture," Cheryll said, her voice on the verge of tears.

"And always know you have a home in Lower Brule," Fritz finished, embracing Paul once again.

Overwhelmed, Paul was at a loss for words. They had only known each other for mere hours and he was already being bestowed with something so significant, a gift of *honor*. It was 38 years in the making, but the welcome home was more than he could ever have imagined.

FOUR

A Special Gift

Lakota Forever...
           Have Thine Own Way, Lord

Thursday morning Fritz whipped up a large batch of pancakes and two skillets of sausages before the kids even roused from their sleep in the adjoining living room. Paul and Kathy soon joined him in the kitchen, helping Cheryll prepare Thanksgiving dinner for the large gathering expected in a few hours. One by one the kids started waking up, still rolled up in blankets, and resumed their conversations.

Nicole sat up on the couch, yawning, and pulled the blanket around her. Her eyes looked tired and her long brown hair fell in all directions.

"How ya doing?" Paul asked, sitting down next to her.

Nicole slid over, a soulful expression filled her face. "Oh, Dad..."

"What?"

"I had the strangest dream last night," she said with a hint of excitement. "It was so different than anything else I've dreamed."

"Really?" he asked with interest.

"It was so vivid and real..."

"Tell me," he said.

"Well, we were here, in this house. Mom came upstairs and said, 'C'mon, let's go.' So Mom and I got in the car and started driving down the gravel road out there," she said, pointing. "I saw this large black horse that took up the whole sky and I could hear it galloping. And then suddenly there was a big moon that took up half the sky and the horse was running in front of the moon." Nicole spoke very animatedly and precisely, using her hands to describe the unusual scene. "But Mom couldn't see it and we started arguing. Then I heard these big gusts of wind pushing us toward a plateau straight ahead, and I'm like, 'Mom—don't tell me you can't see it!' All of a sudden there was a big eagle that stretched from the east over to the west, across the whole sky. Mom still couldn't see it, then whoosh—it dropped behind the mountain. Oh, this is weird," she said, looking at the empty couch across the room.

"What?" Paul asked.

"Last night I fell asleep over there," she said, pointing. "And now I'm over here." She looked up at Paul, her brown eyes beaming. "What happened?"

Paul grinned and rubbed his hand on her head. "I don't know, sweetheart. Must've been some dream."

"It was, Dad," Nicole nodded with exaggeration. "I don't think I'll ever forget it."

•   •   •

A few hours later the LaRoche kitchen counter was filled with turkey, potatoes, and all the trimmings. Several of Cheryll's twelve siblings and their families came over for Thanksgiving dinner. There were too many people to fit around the table, so everyone filled their plates buffet-style and found a place to sit. It seemed they couldn't run out of things to share.

Later in the afternoon some of the boys decided to go pheasant hunting. "Hey, Shane, wanna go with us?" Harlee asked.

"Sure," Shane said. As a kid growing up in Worthington, he'd always dreamed of hunting in the great outdoors. The small town and manicured yards didn't yield much wildlife, but with a young boy's vivid imagination he took his BB gun and ran around the shrubs and flowerbeds pretending. This, however, was for real!

"C'mon, follow us and we'll get you set up." The boys dressed in layers of outerwear and headed outside to the nearby fields and pastures. Shane couldn't believe his eyes—within an hour, the boys had gotten 13 pheasants.

"Over here," John-John said. "I'll show you how to clean 'em the quick way." Shane watched while John-John grabbed one of the birds. "You shove your fingers in, right by the thighs," he said, demonstrating. "Give it pressure and rip away the skin." He grabbed a knife and continued. "Make a few cuts by the wing and the whole breastplate slips right out." John-John tossed the breast meat in the cooler and grabbed the next pheasant.

"Cool," said Shane, impressed with the instant demonstration. All the years of Shane's hunting in southwestern Minnesota had never yielded as great a bounty as the rez.

. . .

Simply being in Lower Brule certainly affected the Summerses. Nicole was having vivid dreams and Shane had renewed enthusiasm for the outdoors. Surrounded by a new family and a new culture, Paul's mind was unable to process all the new information and emotions. That night, in Harlee's bedroom downstairs, Paul closed his eyes and tried to go to sleep on the "rez." But what exactly was a reservation?

It was clearly more than simply Native American land without fences to distinguish its boundaries. Although there were no obvious indicators that a reservation is a different sovereign nation, one can feel a powerful sense that life is not the same there. The change is silent and unspoken.

History declared that current day reservations came into existence through several signed treaties in the nineteenth century between the Tribes of the Great Sioux Nation and the United States. The word "Sioux" was not part of their vocabulary and was originally derived from the spelling of an Ojibwa word, Nadowisiwug (Nadowe—small, thus little snakes or enemy) applied to the Santee in the mid-1600s.

Paul and Kathy had recently learned the Great Sioux Nation was in fact made up of three tribes of Siouan speaking people.

Dialect	Tribe	Original Area
NAKOTA	*Ihanke-Towan* (Camps At the End)	South
	Hohe (Stonies)	North
included 3 bands: Yankton, Upper Yanktonai, Lower Yanktonai		
Dialect	Tribe	Original Area
DAKOTA	*Isanyeti* (Knife Makers)	Eastern Dakota
included 4 bands: Mdewakantonwon, Wahpeton, Wahpekute, Sisseton		
Dialect	Tribe	Original Area
LAKOTA	*Titonwan* (Dwellers of the Plains)	Western Dakota
included 7 bands: Sicangu, Hunkpapa, Oglala, Mnikoju, Itazipco, Siha Sapa, Oo'Henumpa		

The seven subtribes of the Lakota, or *Oceti Sakowin* (Seven Council Fires) were

Seven Bands of The Lakota	Current Reservation
Sicangu (Upper Burnt Thigh)	Rosebud Reservation, SD
& *Kul'Wicasa* (Lower Burnt Thigh)	Lower Brule Reservation, SD
Hunkpapa (Camps At the Edge)	Standing Rock Reservation, ND & Canada
Oglala (Scatter Their Own)	Pine Ridge Reservation, SD
Mnikoju (Plants By The Water)	Cheyenne River Reservation, SD
Itazipco (Without Bow)	Cheyenne River Reservation, SD
Siha Sapa (Black Feet)	Cheyenne River Reservation, SD
Oo'Henumpa (Two Kettle)	Cheyenne River Reservation, SD

Rosebud was the site name for the federal agency designated for the *Sicangu* People in 1877, so named because of the abundance of wild rosebuds that grew in the area. Even more interesting was how the *Sicangu* became known as the Burnt Thigh. According to oral history the name originated when a sudden prairie fire destroyed a Lakota village. Many children, men and women on foot some distance from the village were burned to death. People who could get to a nearby lake saved themselves by jumping in. Many were badly burned about the upper legs from running through tall burning prairie grasses, which led to the name *Sicangu*, which the French later translated as Brule or Burnt.

The Kul Wicasa Oyate was first designated reservation lands along the Missouri River in 1865. The Lower Brule Sioux Tribe was further defined and the boundaries expanded by the Act of March 2, 1889, which identified all the reservations in present day North and South Dakota. The Lower Brule Sioux Reservation was just one of the seven Lakota reservations scattered throughout North and South Dakota. Legal documents were then created that established the boundaries and recognized the rights as sovereign governments. The tribal governments maintain jurisdiction within the boundaries of the reservation, operating under a constitution consistent with the Indian Reorganization Act of 1934.

The construction of the Big Bend and Fort Randall dams on the Missouri River flooded the land along the river, forcing the entire community of Lower Brule to completely relocate to higher ground. The reservation now covers an area of about 404 square miles. Over 90 percent of the population live in the district known as Lower Brule. The number of enrolled members is about 2,500 with a reservation population of approximately 1,400. That was the official, condensed version of the facts, but what would the people say? Would they tell a different story?

• • •

On Friday the two brothers and their families followed the gravel road all the way to Pierre, about 60 miles, to meet Paul's only living sister. Paul and Kathy followed Fritz's vehicle as the ribbon of gravel curved in and around the endless miles of rolling hills. Cattle grazed in the large pastures along the road that followed the winding route of the Missouri River.

"What are those sticks in the water?" Shane asked. In several places along the way there were numerous tree stumps poking through the top of the water.

"Fritz said it's from when they flooded the area with the dam. The water covered the big cottonwood trees that were growing along the river's edge."

"It's so eerie…like a graveyard," Kathy commented.

"In a way, I guess it is," Paul said. "The water took away much of their land, their homes and even the town, forcing everyone to relocate."

After a good hour they turned onto the highway that led into Pierre. "No wonder Fritz asked if we had plenty of gas," Paul said. "There's nothing between the two towns!"

The capital city is situated in the center of South Dakota, with a mere population of approximately 12,000. Centered along the Missouri River, the small city displayed a clean and neat appearance. Residents of Lower Brule had to travel to either Sioux Falls or Pierre to do any major shopping.

Suzie Reinhard, a pretty woman with dark hair and deep-brown eyes, welcomed both families into her home. "Hi, Paul," she said, reaching up to give him a warm hug. Her hair was styled in short curls and her pastel pink sweater accented her cheeks in a rosy glow. "Oh, I'm so glad to meet you."

"I feel the same way," Paul shared, holding her close.

"I can just feel you're family," Suzie said. "I know it for a fact."

Frederick and Jeremiah automatically went up to Suzie and gave her a hug. "Hi, auntie," the boys each said.

Kathy noted the sincere closeness between family members as Cheryll helped Kathy and Paul with the rest of the introductions. Suzie had three children, Mark, Cherylyn, and Fanchon, named after their sister who had died so young.

The families visited for the full afternoon and once again, the conversation returned to days and times of the past.

"Well, when I was growing up," Suzie said, "Fanchon was five years older than me, but we still played together. First we lived in Brulie, then we moved to Fort George."

Paul and Kathy noticed the locals referred to Lower Brule as Brulie.

"We passed Fort George on the way to Pierre," Fritz explained to Paul and Kathy. "There's not much left, just the old church and the cemetery. Uncle Bill lives in the main house now. The other houses are all gone."

"Dad ranched in those days," Suzie continued, "had to take care of the cattle, you know, open their water holes in the winter, haul feed. During the summer, Dad's brother's kids came to stay with us so we had six kids living in the house. Dad had a huge garden, so we'd help pull weeds, haul water, pick potato bugs," she laughed. "Whatever needed to be done. Mom had a schedule: Monday was wash day; Tuesday she baked; Saturday we went to town but us kids had to take turns because there were too many to ride in the car. The boys could go one Saturday and the girls got to go the next. And Sunday was always church. Oh, and Mom could sew anything…she could look at a dress in a catalog and make her own pattern."

"This is so interesting," Kathy commented, eager to find out everything about Paul's family.

"Some years I went to public school and other times I went to the Indian boarding schools. The folks liked to travel in the summer, go visiting, so then I stayed with Unci and Lala, Grandma Ruth and Grandpa Ben. They lived in a house right across the road. Ooh, that was special, staying with Unci and Lala."

"I love those names," Nicole said. "Unci and Lala."

"I was 13 when Fritzie came along," Suzie said, glancing at her younger brother. "Dad sold the cattle and a few years later the folks broke up. Mom moved to Oklahoma and got married again. By then I was already married and living on my own. I never knew about Paul. No one did. Mom was a large woman, tall…maybe 5' 11". I guess she was able to hide it." Suzie looked directly at Paul. "We're so glad you made it home."

"It's too bad we can't get a nice photo of the three siblings," Cheryll said.

"Say, there's a photographer set up at the Kings Inn for holiday photos," Suzie said. "We could head over there and get one taken."

Everyone agreed the occasion should be recorded so Paul, Fritz, and Suzie all trekked to downtown Pierre to get a formal photograph. The deep smiles on all three evidenced the importance of the moment.

Just like the night before, the adults gathered around the kitchen table, talking and sharing highlights of their lives. "Hey, Paul," Fritz said. "Kathy said you're into music. Is that right?"

"Yeah…yeah, I am," Paul said, nodding.

"Our dad was a good singer," Suzie said.

"Really?" Paul asked, somewhat surprised.

"Yes, he had a beautiful tenor voice."

"Uncle Jiggs told me that Grandma Ruth—our mother's mother—loved to sing and dance," added Fritz.

A tiny flame flickered inside Paul, igniting his deeply buried passion.

"Oh, yes, Unci had a real gift for music," Suzie said, nodding. "She always played the piano for us kids. There was music in the house all the time. She played the organ for many, many years at the church in Fort George. She played the old hymns over and over."

Paul, Suzie, Fritz (Paul's brother and sister) Pierre, SD, homecoming 1993

Kathy's eyes lit up. "This is so neat to find out all these things. I can't tell you how much it means to us." She looked at Paul. "Now we know where you inherited your musical gift."

"Grandma Ruth could play the piano by ear," Suzie said.

"Paul plays by ear too," Kathy added.

"In fact, Grandma Ruth had to play a tune before every meal. You could sit down but you couldn't eat until she finished the song!" Suzie laughed. "And our Grandpa Ben's mother, Mary Little Elk, had a beautiful voice and loved to sing hymns in Lakota. Looks like some of that was passed along to you, Paul," she said. "The gift of music."

It was late in the evening before the LaRoches and Summerses took the long drive back to Lower Brule. The night sky was crystal clear, stars dancing brightly in place. A large, full moon enveloped in a whitish glow inched its way above the horizon. The moonlight reflected brightly against the snow-covered ground, highlighting the quiet beauty of the night. Despite the late hour, the outline of the bluffs and rolling prairie was clearly visible in colorless shades of bluish-gray hues.

"Look—there's some deer," Shane said, pointing to four whitetail standing in a field, heads cocked on alert. "This is cool out here, Dad. Can we come back and go hunting sometime?"

Paul smiled, noting his son's enthusiasm for the wide open spaces. Very few vehicles traversed the rural road at that hour, and a comfortable silence filled the car. Suzie's comments lingered in Paul's mind. *Grandma Ruth had a real gift for music; Great Grandma Mary had a lovely singing voice.* It was in his blood—he'd inherited it.

Paul's eyes settled on the silhouetted landscape, echoing an eerie glimpse of days gone by. He wondered what the voices of the past would tell him if they could speak. Ancestors such as Strikes the Ree, a Yankton chief, Red Leggings, Elijah Quilt, Appearing Cloud, Hotanka, and Mary Little Elk. The names themselves spoke of great character. What would they say if they could talk to him now? What would they share about the days of long ago, when they too had seen the moon grace the night in such splendor.

FIVE

Hunkas Iyaya
The Ancestors Speak

In the year the Whites called 1804, the Great Sioux Nation was made up of Lakota, Dakota, and Nakota tribes, and it covered a vast majority of the Northern Plains. The Yankton Sioux, one of the Nakota bands, were camped near the mouth of the Jacques River, in the month of Wasutun Wi, When All Things Ripen, the hot, dusty days of August.

One morning smoke from a distant fire was spotted and the chiefs sent several young boys to investigate. A short while later they returned to the village with three White men, one of whom could speak their language. The White men requested the chiefs and warriors come for an important council with the Corp of Discovery at the river bluff.

The Yankton chiefs first held their own council over the course of several days to discuss their options. Many of the women and children were destitute and the leaders recognized the need to protect their people. They were concerned about their lack of firearms and ammunition, and the changes in their world already transpiring. Finally, about 70 chiefs and warriors dressed in their finest buffalo robes, painted leggings, moccasins, and war shirts decorated with porcupine quills and feathers, journeyed to meet the Corp. Carrying their bows and arrows, they arrived on the opposite side of the river bluff from the White men and set up a temporary camp. Down below, a keelboat rested along a sandbar. The White men sent over gifts of corn and tobacco.

The next morning a heavy fog hung over the river. The chiefs waited for the dense cloud to lift before crossing the shallow river as requested to hear what the White men had to say. Their two captains, Meriwether Lewis and William Clark, stood next to a flag flying high on a staff and delivered a lengthy speech in grandiose fashion.

The chiefs could tell these White men were different from the English and French traders already traversing across Sioux Territory. Through an interpreter they were told the land now belonged to the United States, and that a man far in the east, President Thomas Jefferson, was their new Great Father. To those who had lived on the land for countless generations, there had never been a line on the earth to distinguish that the land belonged to one and not the other.

The Corp gave the Chiefs peace medals and a flag, and instructed them to make peace with enemy tribes. The atmosphere was festive with much music and food, and the Corp even performed a kind of parade. At night the Yanktons sang and danced as they gathered around three fires. During their time together the warriors proudly displayed their hunting skills for the White men.

Word came that a baby had just been born in the Yanktons' village, a boy named Pa-la-ne-a-pa-pe. Lewis asked to see the infant and swaddled him in an American flag, baptizing him as an American. Despite the celebratory mood, Chief Weuche kept his focus and explained the desperate conditions of his people and the need for a reliable trading partner. Instead Captains Lewis and Clark extended an invitation to send a delegation to see the Great Father in the east and continued on their journey.

At that time much of the northern plains of North America was unmistakably a Lakota world. A little farther north and west along the Great Muddy, the nomadic lifestyle of the Sioux was rich and rewarding as the small bands followed their lifeblood, the tatanka (buffalo) across a vast majority of the plains. The families used dogs and horses to pull their possessions on a travois from one camp to the next.

When the tatanka were spotted, an entire camp could be packed on travois and be on the move in twenty minutes. Individual tipis were set up in less than 15 minutes and taken down in three. Everyone had an important role within the tribe, which in turn, supported the village as a whole.

The people of the Great Sioux Nation maintained a lofty wisdom given to them by Wakan Tanka, the Great Spirit or Great Mystery. To them, the Creator—who made the world and everything in it—gave to all breath and life. A reverence for life was evident in the physical, intellectual, and spiritual dimension that carried through to their daily lives.

Every aspect of their existence revolved around their relationship with the Great Spirit. The tipi represented the universe with the entry facing the rising sun and the circular home emulating the cycles of the moon and sun given by the Creator. Inside belonged to them, but the space outside belonged to the Great Spirit. The simple lodge brought humility and a willing dependence upon the Great Spirit.

Even the winged ones made their nests in a circle. The sun came forth and went down again in a circle. The moon did the same—and both were round. The wind, in its greatest power, whirled in a circle across the dust-covered plains.

The dances were conducted in a circle, carefully paced and usually sunwise. When the elders and chiefs gathered, they sat cross-legged in a circle, and smoked the pipe. Tobacco was mixed with sumac leaves and the dried inner bark of trees, like the red willow. Sometimes in rare supply, it was usually saved for ceremonies. Such tobacco smelled pleasant and did not harm its users.

Like all young boys, it was an honor for Palaneapape to walk in the path laid out for him and learn the lessons of his father and grandfather. Palaneapape was on his way to becoming one of the great hunters and warriors. The elements were closely related, so the providers and protectors of the village took time to show young men like Palaneapape how to carry the bow. Through much practice and patience he learned how to shoot an arrow straight, and, equally important, how to care for his prized tool.

Palaneapape was often gone for extended periods and no one worried, since the hours in the day were not measured into minutes or seconds. Instead it was commonplace for a young warrior in training to come home after the lesson had been learned. Palaneapape proudly wore a quiver of arrows across the small of his back as he set out on foot to search the creek bottoms for elk, hare, whitetail, and black tail deer. He enjoyed time away on his own, tracking along the river bottoms, taking cover in the shade of a cottonwood grove, or simply walking the ridge of the river bluffs. Whenever his arrow connected with a whitetail or an elk, Palaneapape offered a bundle of prairie sage to acknowledge the gift of life for the animal killed as he had been taught. He also thanked the animal for giving his life to give food, clothing and tools for the people.

As Palaneapape matured and took on more responsibilities, he looked forward to when the tribes assembled for the grand buffalo hunts. In the warm summer months other encampments joined together for a time of social interaction. Plans for the occasion brought great merriment among the people, their hearts singing with thoughts of visiting friends they had not seen in a long time. Chores were shared in the large encampments, and there was a constant exchange of gifts.

During the winter the bands broke up again and moved to locations that offered better protection where they could remain in one place until March or April. The people enjoyed the prospect of quiet times and rest when the storytellers gathered the younger ones around the fire in the warmth of a tipi, repeating words and actions until the stories were memorized.

As a warrior, Palaneapape was often required to protect his band. On one such encounter he traveled north of the Yanktons and became involved in a battle against the Arikaras, who were also called the Rees of the Upper Missouri, beyond the Brule territory. In the midst of the skirmish, Palaneapape avenged his brother's death by killing an Arikara with a spear. Because of the encounter, from that day forward, Palaneapape was known as Strikes the Ree.

Strikes the Ree was painfully aware of the presence of the White man and the inevitable changes being thrust upon the entire Sioux Nation. Word spread that almost the entire village of the Mandan to the north had been wiped out with a sickness from the White man in 1837. There was plenty of reason to be concerned—not only did the Whites kill people with long rifles, the chiefs surmised, but also with spots that cover the skin.

Nearby, in another Yankton band, a young boy named Red Leggings was also learning the ways of a hunter and warrior. He too spent hours learning from his father and grandfather, keeping his eyes and heart in tune with all of nature surrounding him.

No matter where the many bands roamed on the vast, open prairie and rolling grasslands, the Sioux had one thing in common—Paha Sapa, a place of great spirituality. Located in the center of the Great Sioux Nation, the dark, pine-forested bluffs of Paha Sapa rose unexpectedly from the enveloping prairie.

The craggy hills jutted out in a wilderness shrine where the physical beauty equaled the powers of the spirits. The music of the streams called out to those who came in search of guidance from the Creator. Known as "the heart of everything that is," a warrior could come to Paha Sapa alone, seeking further clarification for his purpose and calling through intense prayer and fasting.

The Lakota lived in close accord with the animals, believing the Creator put them on earth to teach valuable lessons. The animals had abilities worth desiring—bravery, craftiness, and endurance—proficiencies they'd received with grace and power from the Almighty.

The winged ones, the four-leggeds, the finned ones, all contributed to the fullness. It was well known that the wanbli, the eagle, was a very special winged one, the only earthly being to ever see the Creator.

In the spring the prairie came alive; the hosi cekpa was the first flower to emerge from the dormant soil. Beavers, snapping turtles, and prairie dogs were among the critters that made their homes among the grasses, rushes and sedges. By summer, the colorful prairie flowers politely nodded to each other in the warm breezes, while soft clouds cradled the setting sun each evening.

Strikes the Ree and Red Leggings, just like all the members of the Sioux Nation, participated in a spiritual lifestyle in a personal way. From their waking up to their going to sleep, Wakan Tanka was acknowledged through sacrifice, petition, and thanksgiving.

Both Strikes the Ree and Red Leggings were well aware the tatanka was the main source of livelihood, supplying tasty, nourishing food year round for all ages. Mothers gave their infants choice pieces of meat to suck and toothless old people sucked the juices in the same way. A favorite dish was a soup made of buffalo fat, buffalo blood, and berries.

When meat was plentiful, large quantities of the lean flesh were cut into long, thin strips, dried in the sun on racks of poles, then packed in parfleche, envelopes made of buffalo rawhide. Dried meat was made into pemmican, the meat was cooked, then pounded with a stone hammer and mixed with boiled marrow grease and sometimes berries. It was then stored in bags made from buffalo rawhide.

The task of butchering and skinning the buffalo usually fell to the women. After scraping off fatty tissue, they stretched and dried buffalo hides by pegging them to the ground with stakes. The women tanned the buffalo hide with a mixture of buffalo brains, liver, grease, and soaproot. Sometimes it took as many as ten days to prepare one buffalo hide.

Life on the prairie produced a healthy productive society. Men and women alike had strong bodies and clear minds because there was always something to do. Children mimicked adults in their play, thriving in their carefree, yet secure environment.

As the midpoint of the century neared, the Yanktons strived to continue their ways along the now-named James River. Through his experience as a warrior and a negotiator, Strikes the Ree became chief of his band. Many respected his foresight and continuing interest in preserving the surrounding natural resources. Men enjoyed spending time in the council tipi, sitting around the flickering fire, listening to stories he shared from long ago, when only a few of the White men had been seen.

Now their conversations were of a much more desperate tone because of the precarious circumstances intruding upon their beloved lands. "The White men are coming like maggots," Strikes the Ree announced to the leaders in the council lodge. "It is useless to resist them. They are many more than we are. We can not hope to stop them." He looked at their solemn faces; expressions that revealed the inevitability of ominous changes. "Many of our brave warriors would be killed, our women and children left in sorrow, and still we would not stop them. We must accept it; get the best terms we can get and try to adopt their ways," Strikes the Ree stressed. He had been to the east; he'd seen firsthand how many Whites were there, and how many more were coming.

A cold silence ensued as the men in the tipi listened to the troubling discussions. Some didn't want to believe it and exited, shaking their heads. Others nodded in understanding, the words cutting straight to their hearts, knowing the truth they held.

Across the great Dakota Territory, the White man's ever increasing presence brought a deep uneasiness. Stories reached Red Leggings's band that many wagons and White men were headed west, following the corridor along the Shell River. By 1847 the Long Rifles in blue coats demanded that the travelers along the corridor be protected under the Great Father in the east.

The Whites referred to it as the Oregon Trail, and it cut through the southern part of Sioux territory, bringing a steady stream of emigrants moving east to west. Curious young boys lay in the grass on the hilltops, watching the wagons and horses pass, wondering what would come to be. The Sioux surmised it must be a Holy Road, to have such protection, and had given their word to the officers that they wouldn't bring harm to the White travelers.

Shortly after, a council gathering of some 5,000 Plains Indian representatives signed a treaty at Fort Laramie in 1851 to guarantee safe passage to the westbound travelers. Another 3,000 women and children were present to exchange and trade goods. In return, the Sioux leaders requested that Paha Sapa, their sacred land, remain off limits to the Whites.

Throughout the 1850s the Plains Indians tried to hold fast to the lifestyle they knew, always waiting, watching for a sign of tatanka. They moved their encampments from place to place, desperate to find the tatanka that were disappearing in vast numbers.

Strikes the Ree remained active in his quest for peace. He was greatly concerned for the safety of his people as more conflicts ignited between settlers and factions of Indians. Other Whites talked of a peace treaty, with promises of food and annuities for the Sioux. Seeing the desperate conditions of his people, Strikes the Ree struggled deeply to make the right decision. If they didn't sign the treaty, the thought of war with the U.S. Calvary and their long rifles presented a bleak picture.

How many more Yanktons must die? he wondered. With heavy hearts, the chiefs tried to foresee the impending future for their descendants. After much deliberation the chiefs and elders felt their options dwindling.

Strikes the Ree then traveled to Washington, D.C. His name was the first of 14 Yankton Sioux representatives listed on the Yankton Sioux Treaty of 1858. In the end, the Yankton Sioux gave up their lands in return for trade goods, retaining their annuity rights from the Fort Laramie Treaty of 1851. The treaty intended to end the Indian wars and establish protection of the American Indians by the U. S. government. Within a few months over 2,000 tipis crowded the 40,000-acre tract of land, and soon they were out of wildlife to hunt within the restricted borders. The traditional foods, like berries or roots, were also gone. Suddenly the tribe was solely dependent on government rations.

Strikes the Ree, a Yankton Chief

Strikes the Ree went one step further than any other American Indian had at that time. Maybe his chance encounter at birth with Captains Lewis and Clark foreshadowed his future. At 55 years of age, he became the first American Indian citizen of the United States. He then requested an American flag for the First Indian Agency at Greenwood, South Dakota, never giving up on the idea of peaceful solutions.

For his continued efforts in pursuing peace, Strikes the Ree received medals from three U.S. presidents: Franklin Pierce, Ulysses S. Grant, and James Garfield.

The peace, however, was short lived.

In 1862 the Homestead Act unleashed a flurry of settlers across the plains. Although hated by some of his own kind, Strikes the Ree continued his efforts to quash the conflicts. In that same year he advised his militant young warriors not to join the ill-fated Santee uprising to the east where the Dakota bands were facing starvation. His main goal was to save their lives and at the same time protect some of the innocent white settlers.

Meanwhile, a few years later, Red Leggings moved north and west to the Lower Brule encampment of his wife, Many Husbands. She'd earned the name because she had outlived several husbands. Early one morning in the year 1863, she gave birth to a baby in the women's tipi.

The women attending Many Husbands then cleaned the tiny infant and carried him to the encampment to show Red Leggings his new baby, a son who would carry the promise of strength and great character.

As Red Leggings held his son up high to thank the Creator for this gift of life, the baby cried out. Because his voice was so loud, he was named Hotanka, meaning Big Voice.

In accordance with Sioux tradition, every adult in Hotanka's extended family circle contributed to his development as he grew and matured. Some acted as teachers, others nurturers and caregivers, and still others taught him the ways of a skilled hunter.

Isolated conflicts were now commonplace as wagon trains, army patrols, and civilians all pushed their way into Indian territory. The seven bands of the Lakota had no way to know they were on the cusp of such dramatic changes. Red Leggings and the other warriors fought hard to protect their villages, but the U.S. soldiers were better equipped with rifles and ammunition.

Through dangerous and often deadly encounters, the tribal leaders came to the realization that some of the officers were determined to crush the bands of people into submission—and nothing would stop them from doing so. The mere image of a man dressed in the dark blue of the U.S. Calvary with the gold buttons and trim, and the distinctive navy cap with two gold swords crossed on the front, brought a sickening fear for the women and children.

By now the Iron Horse smoked and roared across the plains, and the buffalo herds had shrunk drastically. Red Leggings and his people were devastated to see thousands of tatanka killed and left to rot on the open prairie. Why, they wondered, would someone do such a thing?

To calm the fears of settlers, the government ordered the Army to force the Indians who remained onto small reservations. Many had no choice but to submit. Red Leggings joined the discontented conversations in the council lodge. Some of the neighboring tribes had fled north, to Canada. Others wanted to keep fighting. Some though, were happy to take the trade goods offered by the officers, coveting the items, content to let the wool blankets replace the buffalo robes as the preferred winter garment. During the harsh months of Tiobeyunka Wi (Frost in the Lodge) and Cannanpopa Wi (Popping Trees), January and February, the days were bitter cold and the food supply ran low. Yet the promises of food and rations were not fulfilled. With spirits crushed, many Lakota consented to go to the reservation.

In 1874 when Hotanka was only 11 years old, word came to their camp that Pehin Hanska, General George A. Custer, was leading an expedition into Paha Sapa. Known for his shoulder-length blond hair, the Sioux referred to him as Long Hair. Brash and high-spirited, Custer brought a thousand troops with him under the pretense of looking for a place to build a fort. The truth, however, was much different. They were looking for gold.

Suddenly a stampede of fortune hunters and prospectors descended on Paha Sapa, breaking the Fort Laramie Treaty of 1856. The Army and government did nothing to keep the miners off the sacred spiritual lands of the Sioux, as they'd promised. The Sioux watched as more and more men arrived to chase after the yellow dust in the hills.

A Senate commission created to renegotiate the treaty prepared to offer $6 million for Paha Sapa. Sitting Bull, Crazy Horse, and other defiant warriors refused to participate, unwilling to discuss a sale of their most sacred place. No price was high enough. After all, Ina Maka, Mother Earth, belonged to all and could not be bought or sold.

Within two short years all the Indian bands were ordered to return to their reservations or be considered "hostiles." The Seventh Cavalry under General George A. Custer was ordered to bring the Sioux bands in and place them on the reservation lands. Great Sioux leaders like Sitting Bull and Crazy Horse refused to be permanently confined to reservations. They were prepared to defend their hunting camp against the U.S. Army and Long Hair, launching one of the most memorable conflicts with the United States Calvary.

The Lakota Nation, along with their Cheyenne and Arapaho allies, gathered at a place called Greasy Grass. Sensing the enormity of the impending battle, Sitting Bull desperately prayed to Wakan Tanka to save his people.

Rather than let his men rest after their long journey, Custer pushed his weary troops to a place called Little Bighorn, Montana, where his scouts had spotted the Sioux. Wearing his trademark buckskin uniform, Custer wasted no time and immediately attacked, unknowingly outnumbered four to one.

Warriors were waiting and ready. The Sioux forces joined together with Sitting Bull in the lead and headed straight for Long Hair. In a relatively short time, the Sioux Nation of 2,500 warriors won a major victory over Custer and his Seventh Cavalry.

The victory was short lived.

Once word got back to Washington that warriors with such strange names like Low Dog, Crazy Horse, and Sitting Bull defeated such a decorated soldier, the Whites demanded more action. It wasn't long before an even bigger army of blue coats relentlessly pursued the Indians. In retribution, Congress took back the Black Hills despite the treaty and—in addition—took another 40 million acres of Lakota land. The Great Sioux Nation then scattered, some to Canada. By 1877 the United States government formally demanded that the Lakota Nation move to the reservations. Between the allotment acts and other government policies, the reservations were carved up and cut back dramatically in size.

Missionaries and boarding schools sprung up as a way to "civilize" the hostiles. Hotanka was now a young man in his teens when the White men came up the Missouri River to Chamberlain, offering to take Indian children back east to the Hampton Institute. Red Leggings was afraid for his son because of all that had taken place, and told him not to go.

Fifteen-year-old Hotanka knew the Indian way of life was gone forever, and he understood the pain in his father's eyes. Something inside Hotanka told him that his only chance was to keep up with the new ways of the White man. Hotanka snuck away one night and got on the riverboat, despite his father's pleas.

Many days later Hotanka arrived at the Hampton Institute with other Indian children in a faraway place called Virginia. The instructors in charge asked him to give his name and he proudly said, "Hotanka, Big Voice." The instructors shook their head disapprovingly and asked for his father's name. He answered, "Red Leggings."

They shook their heads again. "Pick one of the English names, so we can pronounce it," they ordered.

Hotanka listened as they read the names he could choose from, and he picked Thompson. From that day forward Hotanka, Big Voice, was known as Joseph Thompson.

Next the staff looked disapprovingly at his shiny black hair that fell down his back. Joseph, along with all the other young boys, was taken into a small room where men with sharp silver blades cut their hair short, like the White men. All the students were given uniforms to wear and their soft moccasins were replaced with hard shoes.

Joseph had come to the institute for far bigger reasons than clothes and shoes. He could no longer hunt the buffalo like his father: he was here to learn a new trade. For half the day, the boarding school teachers taught formal academic subjects. The other half of the day was spent on vocational skills. Since the federal government never provided enough money or staff, Joseph and the other students often spent more time cleaning, cooking, sewing, and laundering than they did in the classroom.

In his three years at the institute, Joseph learned five trades in all, bookkeeping, tinsmithing, blacksmithing, carpentry, and wheelwright. He returned to the Lower Brule area after finishing school. The traditional village was gone, but those who remained strived to keep a sense of the Lakota spirit, hosting frequent gatherings, dances, weddings, and giveaway feasts.

When he was 21, Joseph married Mary Little Elk, only 17, a beautiful young woman who was half White and half Lakota from Lower Brule. Her father was a soldier in the Calvary and sometimes she was called Akicita Winyan, Soldier Woman. She was so beautiful, in fact, he had to pay two horses for her, instead of the usual one. Joseph was happy to be back on the gentle, rolling prairie. He and Mary settled in Fort George. Although the actual fort was gone, the name stuck to the area about 20 miles from Fort Pierre and Pierre.

Joseph and Mary did their best to adapt to the new ways, sensing a bright dawn of better days ahead. Mary never learned English, but she loved to sing hymns in Lakota on Sundays at Holy Name Chapel, the tiny Episcopalian church in Fort George.

In the early years, Joseph made furniture and went in search of a place to sell his goods. Sometimes he brought them to the riverboat and headed south on the Missouri River. He tried to be an example to other Indians, demonstrating how his education helped their family and could lead others to a better way of living.

Joseph also worked as a Pony Express rider and mail carrier on the trail from Oacoma to Fort Pierre. One time he was carrying the payroll on his route and a small band of robbers started chasing him. Outnumbered, he guided his horse into the deep river and swam to the other side. In doing so, he lost the outlaws and continued his ride into Fort Pierre from the other side.

In 1890 Joseph Thompson and the others heard of the horror against Chief Big Foot's band, then camped at Wounded Knee Creek on the Pine Ridge Reservation. In an attempt to disarm the band, the Calvary massacred over 300 Indians, mostly women and children, on December 29. To add to the terror, a blizzard struck the next day, freezing many of the bodies into horrifying positions.

Life on the South Dakota plains was harsh for many of the White settlers unaccustomed to the barren conditions and long winters. Since wood was scarce on the treeless prairie, homes were made with blocks of prairie sod for walls, with earth roofs, and dirt floors. Another option was to build tarpaper shacks that sometimes sprouted up near the railroad. Either way, the bare structures were often erected in the middle of nowhere, leaving the women and children isolated while the men were off hunting game. The most constant companion was the wind, blowing up dust, dirt, or snow throughout the lonely months. The only fuel readily available to hold off winter's frigid chill was cow and buffalo chips or twisted strands of hay.

Life was good but not easy for Joseph and Mary. As the five children came along, there were times of great sadness. Baby Esther died as an infant, and her sister Josephine died when she was only 12. Bessie grew up and married, but died as a young mother. Joseph and Mary then raised Bessie's children, Meta and Henry Goodface. Only sons Harry and Benjamin were left to carry on the Thompson name. Joseph rode his beloved horses until the age of 75, when his son Ben told him it was time to quit.

When Ben was a young boy, the schools were run like a military academy, with strictly enforced rules. He was instructed to forget the Indian ways and learn everything about the White man's ways. For example, students were forbidden to speak Lakota. If they did they faced severe punishments.

Many of the surrounding reservations were changing—physically, mentally, morally, spiritually, socially, and economically. It was a new era for the American Indian. Around the country the general consensus was that the Indians were a "problem." No jobs were available, so many continued to hunt and fish and gather what they could, but it was not enough to sustain them.

The Indian families looked forward to Issue Day because it was a chance to visit friends and relatives and trade items. Blankets, yards of cloth, shoes, and farm equipment were also available. They often stood in long lines to collect their rations at a time when Congress slashed funding, resulting in shortages.

Ben Thompson grew up and married Ruth Walton, a young woman who came up from Peoria, Oklahoma, to work at the boarding school. They too settled in Fort George in one of the little houses that lined the creek. There they raised their eight children—Ben, Arlene, Joe, Muffet, Esther, Bill, Majel, and Winona—while enduring a different type of struggle throughout the 1920s and 1930s. Life at home was simple, but good. Piano music could often be heard coming from the tiny frame house and all the kids knew the Missouri Waltz was their mother's favorite song. Faithfully, every Sunday, Ruth played the organ at Holy Name Chapel.

Ben raised horses and became well known for having teams and wagons for sale. Sometimes he was paid in gold for his fine teams. "Look at these, kids," he'd say, rolling the shiny nuggets in his palms. Ben chose to dress more like a cowboy than an Indian, and became skilled at branding cattle. During roundup, ranchers came from all over to help, bringing their own pup tents along for nightly cover.

As the years went by, Ben ended up with a herd of 1,400 horses. When the time came, he took only three men on horseback to drive all 1,400 head from Fort George to Presho to sell the horses to the Army. Those who saw it say it was a beautiful sight to see the whole drove of mustangs galloping and kicking up dirt, coming over the hills, racing toward the Missouri to drink. The horses came in all shades of white, tan, brown, spotted, and painted, streaming over the hills like pouring sand, heads raised high, manes and tails flying. Magnificent and majestic, they galloped at full speed, their muscled legs carrying them in harmonious motion. Some of the open-range horses belonged to neighboring ranchers, so they had to be branded. Ben picked out the ones that would make good saddle horses and team horses before continuing down to Presho.

Sometimes Unci (Grandma Mary) and Lala (Grandpa Joseph) took the grandkids with them on a trip down to Lower Brule to trade and purchase supplies. With a team and wagon the distance required an overnight stay, so they'd spend the night at John Small Waisted Bear's house about halfway. Little Esther and Meta danced for the adults while John played the skillet, the only available musical "instrument." Joseph made tin cups to sell and usually brought several gunny sacks filled with shaved willow tobacco. When the wagon was full coming home, the kids could count on walking up Cedar Creek hill to lighten the load up the steep incline for the horses.

Joseph and Mary Thompson

Unci Mary also took Arlene and Esther along digging for wild turnips in the spring. She showed her granddaughters how to make patties from wild chokecherries. After the berries were picked and washed, she'd put them in a leather bowl and pound them up real fine, seeds and all. Next they'd form the patties and dry them on a screen in the sun before storing for winter.

The girls loved to reach in the basket for a piece of fry bread and cover it with the red berry sauce, their favorite afternoon treat.

"Mmm! Delicious, Unci!" they cried in unison. It was well known that Unci Mary's chokecherries made the best wojapi sauce.

On lazy afternoons, the kids played with bone horses, pieces of bones that were shaped like little horses. Matches and string made the fence to keep the "horses" in the corral.

In the winter, Ben harvested ice from the river, cutting big blocks of ice. He'd get sawdust from the neighbor who ran a saw mill, Tom Somers. Tom and Ben then packed the sawdust around the ice blocks in an icehouse built into the side of a hill.

In their later years, Ben and Ruth moved near Chamberlain where Ben worked as manager of the farm program for the tribe. Eventually they returned to Fort George, where the older children were now young adults.

By now Arlene was an outgoing young woman, not at all afraid to take charge in a situation, just like deciding as a little girl to go by her middle name Arlene, rather than her first name, Bessie. Following high school, she attended the Haskell Indian Training School in Lawrence, Kansas. After completing a business course, she returned to Lower Brule and worked in the tribal office.

A handsome young man with a charming smile caught her attention and before long, Fred LaRoche proposed to

Ben and Ruth Thompson

Arlene. Fred was a great baseball player and even had a chance to play semi-pro ball in Minneapolis. But he missed the rolling prairie and open lands and came back to South Dakota.

The young couple liked to dress up and go out on special occasions. Arlene's favorite photo was taken one night at a carnival. She was wearing her best dress with a string of pearls, and her hair was curled perfectly; Fred looked most stunning with his black hair slicked straight back, his distinct jaw set in place. Their cheeks almost touched as the flash recorded their special moment. Unlike some couples, they could at least afford a car, so family or friends often accompanied them on trips to town.

Fred joined the Navy during World War II and served his stint aboard a Navy vessel as a firefighter. Later Fred and Arlene moved to Fort George where Fred tried his hand at ranching. Just like her mother, Arlene was a wonderful seamstress and cook as she and Fred started their own family. Two little girls, Fanchon and Suzie, came first, both adorably cute with round cheeks and sweet smiles. Fred loved singing to the girls when they were little, while Arlene sewed calico print dresses with the cap sleeves and round collars.

Before long the girls started school, first at the Cheyenne River Sioux Boarding School and later the Pierre Indian School. Arlene stayed busy running the home because it seemed there was always a cousin or aunt or uncle living with them, along with three or four of their kids.

The years passed and late one evening Arlene headed to Lower Brule from Fort George all alone, a route she'd traveled numerous times. On this November night Arlene's thoughts were in turmoil. She had a difficult decision to make and she simply could not confide in anyone, not even her mother or her husband.

The reservation road was desolate on the wintry evening, and the cold easily penetrated the crack next to the starter on the floorboard. All around her moonlight flooded the prairie, reflecting on the light dusting of snow that covered the pasture grasses. Her eyes were drawn to the full moon rising just above the rounded edge of the distant bluff. Amber in color, it shone clear and bright, silhouetting the rolling prairie.

The single pair of headlights caught a rabbit as it scurried across the road and disappeared into the ditch. Arlene slowed her speed and stayed in the middle of the gravel road to avoid the rigid ruts along the side as the old Chevy bounced along. She knew she only had a few more weeks before the baby inside her would begin to grow. The girls were getting older, Fanchon was 16 and Suzie 11, but they were mostly away at school.

So many things had changed. If only the answers were as clear as the moon above. Like a valuable ornament of gold, it exquisitely adorned the night sky. The prominent sphere boldly declared on this night that no clouds could hide its precious light.

Hide...the thought crossed her mind with newfound meaning and she blinked back the tears. Maybe no one would have to know.

SIX

A Different Person

*In an instant life changes and you
come back a different person.*

—*Paul LaRoche*

"Interested in a tour of the rez?" Fritz asked after breakfast. Dressed in a brightly colored Western shirt and Levis, he took one more swig of coffee.

"You bet I am," answered Paul.

"Let's go, bro." Fritz put on a jacket and black cowboy hat and waved a hand for the rest to follow.

The four adults piled in Fritz's pickup and turned onto the highway toward town. Fritz slowed his speed as they came to a group of homes. "This is West Brule," he explained. "It started out as one little street of houses. Every year there's a housing project and they keep adding more. Now it's almost as big as Lower Brule."

"How do people get their land?" Paul inquired.

"By going through the council. See, this is all tribal land," he said, motioning toward a large section of land.

The highway followed the hill into town, offering a full view of the community below. "You'll notice the streets don't run north and south or east and west," Fritz said. "It's more of a wagon wheel layout." They continued down the hill and turned left on a gravel road. Fritz pulled up near a circular arena with brightly painted bleachers in red, yellow, white and black. "This whole area right here is the center of activity in August."

"Why is that?" Kathy asked.

"Rodeo grounds, Pow Wow grounds, and softball diamond. This here's where we have the annual tribal fair and Pow Wow. It's the second weekend in August every year. All the grounds around here will be full of campers. The little buildings are for the vendors. It's quite the exciting little weekend," Fritz said with a chuckle.

He turned on a side street and drove through the heart of Lower Brule. They passed a small building with a sign reading, *Friendship House, Sober Social Center.* Paul noticed several small churches: Bible Baptist, St. Mary's Catholic, Assembly of God, and Holy Comforter Episcopal Church. All the houses were similar in size and structure. Some had plastic covering the windows, some were boarded up and sprayed with graffiti. Broken furniture, old appliances, and even a few wrecked cars were strewn about in several yards. The shell of a burned-out house caught Kathy's eye, but on the same street there were several homes in excellent condition, lights warming the windows on the cloudy, cold afternoon.

"Here's the main part of town," Fritz explained. "The post office, a bank, the Squeaky Door Market. And right there, the casino—that was our old high school," he said, pointing to a two-story brown building. "Last year when they legalized gambling, they turned it into a casino because we had already built a new high school down the street."

"What's that building?" Paul asked with interest.

"That's where all the offices are for the tribal council and social services," Fritz explained. "Plus there's the Bureau of Indian Affairs, which is the federal branch, and the departments that take care of the land operations. The realty office oversees the trust tribal land."

Fritz drove slowly, taking his time as they turned down one street and then the next. In a matter of minutes Paul and Kathy had pretty much seen the entire town. "We can head out to the bend and I'll show you where the Thompsons have their land, where I spent my years with Uncle Jiggs and Aunt Helen."

Paul smiled. He loved seeing the community and area, poking along the gravel back roads. He couldn't wait to see it in the summer.

"That's called Little Bend up there, it's the river bottom on the inside of the bend. The Big Bend is the outer perimeter on the other side of the river. Did you see how close the river was on that end?" Fritz asked.

Paul and Kathy nodded.

"It forms a big bend and comes back around and away it goes again. There's 3,500 acres up here in this little loop. If you look at a map, the river forms an S. It's a local people's term. They say, 'Ah, he's up in Big Bend,' then we know what he's talking about. Or 'she's over in Little Bend.' I don't think it's on any map though. Just over that hill right there," Fritz continued, pointing south, "the river is on the other side, maybe a quarter mile. That's how close it is right here. You'd never know it's over there. They call this area the Narrows 'cause the river's so close on both sides."

Fascinated, Paul smiled and listened to his brother talk about the reservation. So this is how the people survived—cattle ranching, farming, a few small businesses, government commodities. But what about the traditional ceremonies? How much of the true culture was still alive?

.   .   .

On Sunday morning Paul and Kathy packed their suitcases, knowing their visit to Lower Brule was nearing an end. All three days had been an absolute joy, a temporary escape from the pressing world back home. An invisible heaviness settled on Paul's shoulders as he thought about going back to the Twin Cities.

Kathy felt it too. "It's so peaceful here," she declared to Paul from the edge of the bed.

"I know," Paul said, sitting down next to her.

They were downstairs on Harlee's bed, a room perfectly designed for a young boy who loved the outdoors. "They're all so giving...I can't get over it," Kathy said. "It's like I don't want to leave."

"We don't have a choice," Paul moaned. "We'll come back, you can count on that."

There was a tap at the door and Kathy stood up to open it.

Cheryll stepped into the room with Fritz close behind. "We're not ready for you to leave!" she half cried.

Paul and Kathy locked eyes and smiled. "We were sitting here saying the same thing."

"We were so looking forward to you coming, everyone in town knew all about your visit," Cheryll said.

Fritz chuckled and slid his fingers in his jeans pockets, shrugging his shoulders. "I didn't tell you yesterday, but everyone at the Squeaky Door on Wednesday was there just to get a peek at you. They weren't really shopping!"

Paul let out a deep laugh. "I wondered about that, man! I felt like everyone was watching me."

"Oh, yeah, they all wanted to see Fritz's brother. You're big news!" Cheryll laughed.

"That's so funny," Kathy said.

"Ooh, I think you should move out here," Cheryll insisted.

Kathy didn't know quite how to respond. They loved everything about the visit, but *live* in Lower Brule? "Oh, we'd love to," she sighed, "but we have to get the kids through school and stuff. Shane's only in tenth grade and Nicole's in ninth." Kathy certainly felt at home with Fritz and Cheryll, but she didn't know what the school system on a reservation was like. Maybe *someday,* after the kids were out of school, the family would relocate.

· · ·

Back in Eden Prairie, the days dragged. Paul and Kathy couldn't wait to tell all the doubters how incredible the trip had been. Now that they'd been to the reservation once, they couldn't get it out of their minds or hearts. Paul and Kathy both agreed it was important to contact St. Mary's Hospital and obtain copies of his birth certificate, adoption papers, and hospital records. Just to be sure.

"I spent my whole lunch hour making phone calls," Kathy said. "I found out we have to get a judge to order the release of information from the hospital. We can't just go out there and ask for it directly."

"I suppose," Paul said. "So now what?"

"I've got it arranged for next week. We have to stop at the Hughes County Courthouse in Pierre with your adoption papers and have a judge sign the release order. Then we take that to the hospital and they can release the records. I've already talked to both places, so they know we're coming."

"Good," Paul said. "Thanks for doing all that, Kath."

"For me, I'd like to know your family's medical history in case there is something that affects you or the kids. Look at Arlene, she was only 50 years old when she died from malignant melanoma."

"I agree," Paul said, nodding. "We won't be able to spend much time."

"I know. I can't take many days off work right now anyway."

"Just a quick trip."

Kathy wrapped her arms around Paul's neck and kissed him. "But worth it."

The following Friday Paul and Kathy made the long drive back to South Dakota, this time directly to Pierre. It took only a few minutes for the judge to review the adoption papers and sign the release order.

They drove from the courthouse over to St. Mary's, now a large health care center right near downtown. "The receptionist told me to go to Records in the Administration wing." They walked down a long hallway toward the Records office in the Administration wing, where they handed an older woman behind the counter the release order.

She turned around to a big file drawer and thumbed through the papers. "Here's everything we have in his file," she said. "We have a record of your husband's stay in the hospital from the time he was born until the day his adoptive parents took him home," she finished, spreading out the sheets.

Kathy picked up the Newborn Record. "Oh, Paul, look at this." She held it up for them both to read. "This is wonderful!" The log started at 3:00 a.m. listing all of the infant's care.

Name: *Baby Boy LaRoche. Date: 6-23-55. Time: 2:38 a.m.*
Sex: *Male.*

Baby Boy, 9# 3oz; admitted to nursery from delivery room in apparently good condition—crying. Routine care given. 7:00 a.m. Condition appears good. Routine A.M. care. Cord cleaned.

The log continued for 11 full pages, with observations from the nurses on duty in 1955, denoting his around-the-clock care. There were columns for Medicine, Nourishment, and Remarks along with Date, Time, Pulse, Temp, Urine, and Stool, with a varied range of notes and comments.

Sleeping. Good night. Formula taken well. Awake and fussing. Tub bath. Resting quietly. Seen by Dr. Jahraus.

The last day's entry was July 30, 1955:

7:00 a.m. Good night. Formula taken well. Routine A.M. care with tub bath. Dr. Jahraus in. Weight 11# 15 ½ oz. Good day. 7:00 p.m. Discharged with foster parents.

"This is priceless," Kathy commented. "The adoption must have taken a while."

"I think about six months," the woman advised. "And here's the Certificate of Live Birth," she said, sliding another paper over to Kathy and Paul.

Paul picked up the certificate and held it so they could view it together.

"Look, Paul," she said, pointing. "There's your name with both your parents names listed."

Child's Name: *Arlen Faye LaRoche*

Father of Child: *Fred Daniel LaRoche, Indian, 44 years old, Birthplace, Reliance, South Dakota, Occupation, Laborer.*

Mother of Child: *Bessie Arlene Thompson, Indian, 37 years old, Birthplace, Reliance, South Dakota.*

There it was in black and white. His birth name, right along side his parents' names. Something about the "officialness" of the document cemented what was before a likelihood or possibility. The reality of the printed information hit Paul harder than he expected. He wasn't simply Paul Edward Summers from Worthington. He was a LaRoche. Ready or not, the transformation into a completely new line of ancestors was about to begin. He studied the document, handling it as if it were made of gold.

"This is interesting," Kathy noted. "Where it asks how many other children are now living, she answered two. How many children were born dead, she answered one. She evidently lost another baby."

"And here's one more," the clerk said. "It's the Newborn Admission Form, but it has basically the same information."

"Thank you," Paul said. He smiled and scooped up the papers. "Let's go make copies," he said to Kathy. "I'd like to give one to Suzie and Fritz. Not because we have to, I just want to."

"I think that'd be nice," she said.

A few blocks from the hospital they found an office supply store and made three sets of copies, one for each of Paul's new siblings and one for themselves. Following the emotional day Paul and Kathy found a hotel to spend the night. The next morning they stopped at Suzie's to give her a copy before leaving Pierre. They only had time for a short visit before continuing on to Lower Brule to make a brief stop at Fritz and Cheryll's. Once again, Mother Nature made driving treacherous across the prairie from South Dakota to Minneapolis.

By the time they made the last turn into the apartment complex, both Paul and Kathy were mentally and physically drained. "I'm beat," Paul said with a yawn. "But I feel good about what we did."

"So do I," Kathy smiled.

SEVEN

A Glimmer of Hope

"I'm not surprised…
just look at my dad."
—Shane LaRoche

Meeting his biological family and discovering a new heritage was rewarding in many aspects, but it didn't come with a magic wand to erase all of Paul's problems or a crystal ball to point him in a new direction.

"Paul, get up or you'll be late for work," Kathy called from the bathroom. She'd heard him hit the snooze alarm twice already.

"I'm up, I'm up," he mumbled with a big yawn.

"I need to leave in about five minutes," she said, tucking in her blouse. "Can you make sure Nicole gets to school?"

"She said what's-his-name is picking her up again."

"If that's who I think it is, I'm not so sure I like that. I don't have a good feeling about him," Kathy said.

"I hear what you're saying, but this is Nicole, remember."

"That doesn't mean we should give in."

"It's another phase, that's all."

Kathy grabbed her sweater and headed to the kitchen to make a lunch. "Oh, yeah, we have conferences at the high school tonight and two of Nicole's teachers have requested a meeting, plus there's a parents' meeting for baseball. Shane says we *have* to be there."

"Great," Paul muttered, pulling himself out of bed. Maybe a hot shower would wash away some of the frustrations. Then again, maybe it would take a whole lot more.

• • •

Shane claimed to his friends he had it figured out all along. "I mean, take one look at my dad. Number one, he was born in Pierre," he said, counting on his fingers, "number two, there's reservations all around, he was adopted, he's got black hair. It doesn't take a rocket scientist, ya know?"

"What was it like?"

"Was it weird?"

"No, it was really cool out there, normal even. I went pheasant hunting with my cousins and we got thirteen just like that!" The group of boys was clustered around a table in the high school commons. Hundreds of students were headed in all directions as another school day wound to a close.

"Your cousins? That makes you a half breed," another kid joked.

"Hey, Shane…ya gonna grow your hair long and braid it?"

"Whatever," Shane said.

Typical teenage boys, it was their duty to give Shane a hard time, but most of the questions and comments were good natured.

Grabbing his backpack, Shane said, "I gotta get to work." He hurried from the high school over to Pizza Hut for his afternoon shift. Shane gave up hockey after eighth grade in order to play baseball year round. The only way he could afford to be on the Gopher State Baseball League was to work all school year to help pay the expenses. Designed for serious players, the league competed for regional and national rankings and had a summer schedule that equaled the majors. For now, baseball was his life.

. . .

A few weeks later Paul strode through the door about 6:30, jean jacket in hand. "Hey, hon."

"How come you're so late?" Kathy was reading the newspaper at the table, feet resting on an empty chair, her empty plate pushed back.

"Sorry I didn't call. I wanted to talk to Craig about an opening for a new position at Maier Stewart," he said, tossing his jacket onto the couch. He pulled off his work boots and began snitching bites of the coffee cake on the counter. "We ended up talking quite awhile and I didn't realize it was so late."

"I made spaghetti for supper," Kathy said, pointing to the sauce simmering on the stove.

"Mmmm," Paul said, wiping his fingers on his shirt. "Sounds good." He dished up a plate of noodles and sauce and sat down at the table.

"What kind of job?"

"Can you reach the salt and pepper?" he asked, pointing to the end of the table.

Kathy yawned and handed him the seasonings, along with a napkin.

"The job title is Marketing Director, someone to design a logo, create promotional material, and stuff like that."

Kathy listened with interest. "Paul, you have a real flair for marketing."

"I asked around a couple of weeks ago about it and everyone said, 'oh, nobody from engineering can get into marketing.' Kinda like, 'you're nuts for even trying.'"

"Look at all you've learned from marketing your music over the years."

"Well, that's what I thought. Craig and I go way back to my days with the city in Worthington, so we ended up having a nice discussion tonight. He knows what we've been through. Craig said they like to hire from within, which is promising to hear," he said, taking a bite of spaghetti. "Mmm, this is good."

"I opened a jar and heated it on the stove," Kathy said dryly.

"Maybe I'm just hungry," he grinned.

"Let's put together a resume or whatever they need, Paul. I think it would really fit you." She got up from the table. "I'm going to change out of my work clothes. Last one at the table cleans up," she joked with a wry smile.

"I...hear ya," he said with a mouthful.

Within the week, Kathy helped Paul create a well-drafted package that highlighted his marketing skills, computer and graphics knowledge, drafting experience, and music software proficiency. He printed several layouts and a color brochure to submit during his interview.

Two weeks later Paul called Kathy at work. "Good news!" he announced.

"Did you get it?" she asked immediately.

"I did," he said. "Just found out."

"That's great, Paul! You deserve it," she said with enthusiasm.

"Time to hunker down."

"Are you okay with it?" she asked, knowing where her husband's heart still stood.

"Yeah, I mean it in a good way," he said, sounding confident. "I think I can get into this."

Paul followed through with his intentions and dove head first into the new position. The first order of business was to design a marketing brochure for Maier Stewart and Associates, including a company logo. The creative side of the position was good for Paul's soul, and he poured everything he had into it.

· · ·

Over the next several months Paul and Kathy went about life as usual, working full-time and keeping up with Shane's and Nicole's high school events. With Mark and Lori Summers and their three kids living close by in another Twin City suburb, the family was busy with holidays and gettogethers with the Summerses and Frisches, but now also the LaRoches as well, still meeting new relatives on each trip to South Dakota.

Every so often, Fritz and Cheryll and their boys made a visit to the Twin Cities. Cheryll wasn't shy to admit her favorite place was the Mall of America, a mere 15 minutes from Paul and Kathy's apartment. Fritz insisted the Summerses come out to Lower Brule for an old fashioned roundup, an annual event in late spring when ranchers on horseback round up beef cattle for branding.

The marketing job was a good fit for Paul for almost a full year. Inevitably though, things started unraveling at work. "You'll never guess what," Paul said to Kathy on the way to a baseball game across town.

"What?" Kathy asked.

"They're not happy with the amount of time I'm taking on the newsletter and stuff. They want it done pronto, quick. They're thinking of hiring some girl just to do the newsletter so I can do more sales."

"Yeah?" Kathy inquired with hesitation.

Paul shrugged his shoulders, merging in traffic. "Word must've gotten out about Lower Brule and everything. They want me to hit the Indian casinos in the Twin Cities for our business. Like I have an 'in' or something," he said with frustration. "There's a lot of construction going on at both Treasure Island and Mystic Lake, lots of opportunities out there. It'd probably be a good place for Maier Stewart to get in, but I don't want to do sales," he grumbled.

Another month passed as the tensions at Paul's office mounted. One Friday evening he came through the apartment door and closed it harder and louder than necessary.

Kathy whirled around and frowned at Paul. "Now what?"

"Nothing," Paul grumbled.

"Paul—talk to me."

He grabbed a bottle of beer from the fridge and leaned against the counter. "My supervisor called me into his office this morning," he started, taking a swig.

Kathy squelched the sinking feeling in her gut and swiveled on her chair to face him. "Yeah?"

"They're all down on me because... You know..." He took a deep breath. "I'm not *there*, even when I'm there. How can I say it? My heart's not in it anymore. I tried, Kathy. Really, I did. The truth is I'm not doing a good job."

"Drinking certainly doesn't help, Paul. You need to cut back."

"What am I supposed to do? I can't concentrate, my mind wanders, thinking about all this other stuff, and it shows at work. I can't hide it, for crying out loud." The tone of his voice gave away his inner frustrations. "And they keep putting pressure on me to let it go. I can't stay there, Kathy. My priorities have changed, my focus...."

"Did they fire you?" she asked quietly.

"Not yet." He took another deep breath and shrugged his shoulders. "There's a meeting set up next week to discuss it."

• • •

Just being home for the weekend eased Paul's frame of mind. By Sunday afternoon he felt relaxed and in a better mood. He slid the balcony door open, watching a steady spring shower coming down.

"I'm glad they canceled the game," Kathy said, breathing in the sweet smell of fresh rain. "Shane's worn out from working the late shift last night."

"Yeah, he needs to be careful he doesn't overdo it." The Twins and White Sox game flashed across the television screen, but Paul had the volume turned off as he slowly turned the pages of a book about Lakota history. "Man, there's so much to learn. You know, in an instant my life changed and in my heart I came back a different person. But it takes a while to put in all in perspective. Especially when I think about my lineage and actually realize I'm part of a line of people I know so little about."

"We'll just take it one step at a time," Kathy said reassuringly. She started browning hamburger for an early dinner. "Last time we were in Lower Brule, Fritz and Cheryll gave us a copy of that newspaper,

Indian Country. Remember? They ordered a subscription for us and the first copy just came."

"Great," he said, taking the publication from her outstretched hand. The newspaper based in Rapid City, South Dakota, covered current Native American issues and events nationwide.

"I picked up some more books at the library. I think that's the best way to start," she said, glancing at Paul. "It's fascinating material. I've been taking them to work and reading on my lunch hour."

Just then Nicole came through the door.

"How was your weekend?" Paul inquired.

"Great. Just hung out with some friends." She let her backpack slip off her shoulder onto the floor.

"Nicole, the school called again on Friday," Kathy said. She took a large platter of nachos out of the microwave and put it on the table.

"So?" Nicole asked, legs crossed, staring at the melted cheese.

"You missed another test in Civics." Kathy put napkins and forks on the table before sitting down across from Nicole.

"Mom! You know I have trouble with tests. I don't mind the class, I just never do well on the tests. Why can't the teachers understand that?" she questioned, her voice frustrated and angry.

"Everyone has to take tests, Nicole. They're not trying to pick on you." She slid some of the hot food onto her plate and opened a Diet Coke.

"I know that, Mother," she said without looking up, arms folded across her chest.

"Where were you during Civics?" Paul asked, taking some nachos and opening the taco sauce.

"I was in the art room. The teacher knew I was there. They're cool with that. I've got some projects in there to work on." Nicole took a portion of the nachos and covered it with a scoop of sour cream.

"That's fine, Nicole. But you can't drop your regular classes," Kathy said with a mother's authority.

"Sure. Whatever," she answered with an edge in her voice and retreated to her room, dinner in hand.

. . .

Paul reached a mutual decision with Maier Stewart to step down. Both sides agreed it was the right thing. But if he wasn't employed with Maier Stewart, what would he do for income? Paul and Kathy talked it over with the kids, explaining the need to cut back on things as they discussed Paul's career options.

"Oh, I can see it in your eyes, Paul Summers," Kathy said, crossing her arms. "You're thinking about music again."

"Is that so bad?" he asked with a half smile.

Kathy looked into her husband's eyes—they held a glimmer of hope she hadn't seen for a long time.

. . .

Ralph McKinney, one of the doctors at the Minneapolis Clinic of Neurology where Kathy worked in 1993, was particularly fascinated with Paul's new discovery. He subsequently introduced the family to his friend, Ed McGaa, a well-known Native American author. Ed then invited Paul, Kathy, and the kids to meet Morgaine Avalon, a close friend who was studying the American Indian culture, so they could all hear more about Paul's story.

Paul and Kathy arrived at Morgaine's home, situated along the pristine St. Croix River valley dividing Minnesota and Wisconsin. The property hugged the wooded bluffs in a beautiful area—a treasure that time forgot. Quaint antique and gift shops filled Main Street in the picturesque river towns on both sides.

Ed McGaa, also known as Eagle Man by his people, was an enrolled member of the Oglala Sioux band in South Dakota. Born on the Pine Ridge Reservation, McGaa had his own interesting and varied background that included a law degree, and experiences as a fighter pilot for the Marine Corps and as a historian of his tribe.

Ed proved to be a colorful character who spoke his mind with ease. With one look at Paul's dark hair and features, his first comment to Paul was, "Good grief, man! How could you *not* know you're Indian?" which immediately brought laughter all around the room. Once the laughter subsided, Paul and Kathy were thrilled to spend time with someone who had learned the sacred Sioux ceremonies from holy men such as Chief Eagle Feather and Chief Fools Crow.

Shortly after their first visit, Morgaine held "a gathering of women" that featured different cultures and backgrounds and invited Kathy and Nicole to attend. It seemed new doors were opening all around.

. . .

An old contact from the music industry had gotten in touch with Paul to discuss a good-sized musical collaboration called *LA Cowboy*. Paul thought the project had real possibilities and immediately reassembled his studio in the living room, the only area available in the small apartment. Quite often Kathy fell asleep on the hide-a-bed with Paul still plunking away on his equipment late at night, producing tracks for the new album. Thus began another phase of Paul's musical endeavors.

Kathy kept her job to keep the family going. One afternoon she rushed through the front door of the apartment. "Paul!" she exclaimed out of breath.

"What?" he asked, surprised by the urgent tone of her voice. He got up from the computer and met her in the kitchen.

"Look at this!" she said, handing him the latest issue of *Indian Country*. She tossed her purse and keys aside and spread the copy across the table. "Here's an article about a guy with a story similar to yours. He's Indian too and was actually abandoned at birth, left in a dumpster, if you can believe it. But anyway, he went through several foster homes and ended up with a family who eventually raised him. His name is Tom Bee and he's in the music industry." Kathy pushed her long ponytail behind her shoulder and turned the page for Paul. "I think you two would click. I mean, your stories, your backgrounds… and you're both in music."

"Give me a minute to read it," Paul said with a grin.

"I can't help it," Kathy said, her blue eyes bright with enthusiasm. "It's exactly what we've been looking for—someone in Native American music who understands what you've been through personally."

Paul began reading the article. "Who is this guy?" he mumbled. "It says here he's best known as founder and featured artist with the popular 1970s Native American group XIT, which led to a contract with Motown Records." Paul arched his eyebrows and glanced at Kathy in acknowledgement of a record deal with such a large label. He continued reading out loud to Kathy. "Bee had released two acclaimed albums entitled *Plight of the Redman* and *Silent Warrior*. The political overtones of Bee's lyrics kept them from ever achieving superstar status in the United States, but the group developed a cult status in Asia and Europe, which allowed their music to thrive. In 1989, Bee formed Sound of America Records (SOAR) in the garage of his home in Albuquerque.'" Paul leaned back in his chair. "Hmm, it's certainly interesting. He's had some success in the business. What'd ya think?"

• • •

By midsummer, life seemed to be holding steady for Paul and Kathy. Shane was between his junior and senior years at Eden Prairie High School, and into another packed season of competitive baseball. This year's team was ranked seventh in the world and traveled around the Upper Midwest in a full-sized tour bus. Paul and Kathy were unable to travel to those games, but always attended the home games at Parade Stadium in Minneapolis. If the team held their world ranking, Shane announced they'd be flying to the Far East for the playoffs scheduled in Japan, Taiwan, and Guam.

Unhappy with the whole suburban high school scene, Nicole defiantly quit school. She had, however, agreed to try a different school setting. Kathy searched for a school better suited for Nicole's artistic and creative talents and found a small private Christian school with an opening. All in all, the family was adjusting to the most recent changes.

"I'm going to send for this," Paul said, holding up a sheet of paper.

"What is it?"

"It's an application to become an enrolled member of the Lower Brule Sioux Tribe," he said with pride. "I just have to fill this out and include a copy of my birth certificate, which I happen to have."

Kathy smiled and squeezed his shoulders before sitting down beside him. "I'm proud to be your wife."

Paul's initial conversation with Tom Bee went exceptionally well, and Paul was seriously considering a record deal with Tom's company. In the meantime, Paul also became involved with the newly formed American Indian Theater company in downtown Minneapolis. A brand new project called *Black Elk Speaks* was in the works. It was a theatrical interpretation of the famous book published in 1932 that became a major source of information about nineteenth-century Plains Indian culture.

In the book, Black Elk, a holy man from the Oglala band of the Lakota Sioux nation, told of his boyhood participation in battles with the U.S. Army, becoming a medicine man, and joining Buffalo Bill's Wild West Show in 1886. A few years later he returned home to find his tribe starving, diseased, and hopeless on the Pine Ridge reservation in South Dakota.

Thrilled to be working on a project with such an important message, Paul wrote all the music for the play. Operating on a shoestring budget, it stretched out to almost six months of hard work before the first performance was held at the Walker Church in the Phillips Community of Minneapolis. Nicole joined Paul on her flute, and together they performed in the show, which ran for two weeks.

The satisfaction of seeing the music and story come to life on stage with a message that held a purpose lifted Paul's spirits. He absolutely thrived in the environment that now blended both facets of his life—music and Native American history and culture. He thought again of Lower Brule and his feelings in that first moment when they arrived.

Two worlds, two cultures, two distinct sounds.

With the opportunity to produce his own music interpretations at SOAR Records, Paul's creative senses were in overdrive. He enlisted Kathy's help in organizing a Native American theater company in the

Twin Cities, requiring her to quit her job. Paul and Kathy explored many avenues, working closely with the director of *Black Elk Speaks*. A husband and wife team, Graydon Kori had extensive theatrical experience, and his wife, Nancy Kaine Kori, had American Indian heritage and connections.

Throughout the subsequent months Paul and Kathy flew to Albuquerque to meet Tom Bee and visit SOAR Records. They discussed contract negotiations and made the final revisions via telephone after returning to Minnesota. Paul could see the contract certainly favored Tom's interests over his own, but at the same time it gave him a chance when no one else would. At this point he was willing to concede a better contract simply for the opportunity.

Between the play, the *LA Cowboy* project, and preliminary work with Tom Bee, Paul began compiling tracks for his own music. These nudgings often kept him up all night. Nicole offered suggestions about unique and creative sounds to include.

Unable to obtain further grant money, however, the theater company began losing momentum. Paul then turned his focus back to producing an album in Albuquerque. Kathy, meanwhile knew she needed to find a job in order to support herself and the kids through the next several months while Paul was in New Mexico. Through a temp agency, she found employment at an American Insurance office right in Eden Prairie.

Sometimes Paul and Kathy felt their marriage was like a cat with nine lives, disguised as a long-hair calico with multicolored fur. Some years were comfortable and content, purring and affectionate in style. Other years were skittish and wary, always on guard. Regardless, this furry feline posing as their marriage was poised on all fours, ready to pounce to the next life.

EIGHT

Albuquerque
We The People
A tribal gathering of music

Paul's spirits soared nearly as high as the 727 transporting him to Albuquerque, New Mexico, in mid-October 1995. With Kathy's blessing once again, he was free to create music. This time, however, he was not merely composing. He was trying to combine two worlds—two cultures—and musically meld them into one. The image of Lower Brule and all it represented had captured his heart the very moment he first laid eyes on the little community nestled along the shore of the Missouri River. Right there and then, the idea evolved in his mind to mesh part of the Native American culture with pieces of mainstream America and transform them into a musical adaptation—like notes written separately on the treble and bass clef coming together to achieve a harmonious whole. He knew enough about the music industry to realize there wasn't a genre for this unique sound, yet he felt compelled to pursue it. In one sense it was an untouched musical frontier.

Paul glanced at his carryon bag tucked underneath the seat in front of him. Inside it he carried the precious beginnings of his forthcoming album, key songs and project ideas that laid the foundation for his new music. He looked forward to the chance to work in a professional studio with a team of musicians, anticipating a smooth collaboration. Tom had already asked Paul to produce several other projects while he was in Albuquerque, so Paul knew he had a lot of work ahead of him.

Paul stared down from his window seat at the first images of New Mexico unfolding before him, a mix of brown, mountainous terrain mixed with patches of green landscape. At times it was hard to grasp everything that had happened since his first visit to Lower Brule. And now, a mere two years later, he was about to begin a brand new phase in his musical career—one final shot. He collected his bags from the luggage console, stepped into the brilliant sunshine, and flagged down a cab.

"Downtown," he told the driver. Dressed in faded blue jeans and cowboy boots, Paul figured he would blend in well enough with the crowd hanging around the downtown music scene. He caught his reflection in the side mirror. His hair was nearing his shoulders now, and it felt *right*.

• • •

The new school year was in full swing for Shane and Nicole as October painted another mosaic of vivid colors across the Upper Midwest. But fall colors were the last thing on Kathy's mind. The end of the month was nearing and she knew she had to find somewhere for the three of them to live. Without Paul's income they couldn't afford the rent. Someone suggested moving back to Worthington to live with her mother, but Kathy didn't feel right about that since it was Shane's senior year at Eden Prairie High School. She was making a decent wage at American Family and couldn't exactly walk away from that, but it wasn't enough to cover all their expenses each month.

"What about Morgaine?" Nicole asked Kathy one evening. "I heard that her guest house will be empty in a couple of weeks."

"I don't know," Kathy said with hesitation. "We've only been out there a couple of times. I barely know her," she stressed to her daughter.

"Mom—we have to be out of the apartment in two weeks!"

"I know that, Nicole. Trust me." Tears welled up in Kathy's eyes and she retreated to the bathroom for privacy as Nicole's words echoed in her mind.

Kathy agonized over the decision for three days before she found the courage to call Morgaine and explain the situation. Thankfully Morgaine said she'd think about it and eventually called her back with an answer. "Let's give it a try," she offered.

Even though it was about an hour's drive for both work and school, it seemed the best temporary answer. Rather than make the long commute, Shane often arranged to stay with friends in Eden Prairie. Kathy and Nicole rode into the city together each morning so Kathy could drop Nicole off at school on her way to work. Kathy set boundaries for the kids as best she could, but soon Nicole insisted on staying with friends as well. Eventually Kathy compromised, making sure she was aware of their whereabouts each night.

. . .

Paul's taxi driver spoke minimal English, but he knew Albuquerque like the back of his hand. He exited the freeway and began making sharp turns along the busy side streets of downtown. Watching the city skyscrapers pass by, Paul knew he couldn't go back to Minnesota without a finished product. He couldn't afford to fly back and forth, so he was here to stay until he had something concrete in hand. Paul paid the driver and stepped onto the curb in front of SOAR, bags in hand.

Eager to get started, Paul entered the front doors. Tom Bee, a tall man with long, lanky legs, greeted him. "Hey, man," Tom said. "Welcome back to Albuquerque!"

"Thanks," Paul said, shaking hands.

A broad smile stretched across Tom's face. "Ready to make some music?"

"Feel like I've been waiting my whole life for this," Paul said with honesty.

Tom escorted Paul into the front office. "Have a look around," Tom said proudly. Framed photos and various musical accomplishments lined the hall. "I can open the studio so you can get set up in there."

"Great," Paul said with a wide grin.

Tom unlocked the door behind the office, motioning for Paul to go in. "Here it is!" he announced proudly. "Just like we talked…your studio."

As Paul's eyes scanned the room he quickly recognized the studio had not been maintained. Located at the back of the building, the small, windowless room had only one door providing access in or out through the office. Paul had envisioned a recording studio in good working order, certainly not *this*. Even the main console hadn't been covered and the whole unit was covered in thick layers of dust.

"So," Tom said with a half smile and wave of his hand, "if you can make it work and come up with a record, we'll distribute it for you."

Standing eye to eye, Paul had the sense it was almost a dare. As soon as Tom left the room, Paul took a closer look. He knew enough about recording equipment to recognize the dilapidated state of the supposed studio. "Oh, man," Paul sighed, tossing his duffle bags into a corner. Challenges aside, he glanced around the cramped, dusty room and declared under his breath, "By hook or crook I'm gonna do this, if it kills me!"

The temporary "home" Tom Bee had set up for him turned out to be an old Route 66 motel room. Rooms rented for $17 a day at the DeAnza and Paul was aware that some of them rented by the hour as well. Regardless, he'd made a commitment to his family and to himself to go through with this, and he wasn't going to let a rundown studio or a crummy motel steal it from him. The arrangement with Tom allowed him about $5 a day for food, so there was literally nothing extra.

Paul spent the entire first month just getting the recording studio operable. First all the equipment needed to be cleaned and tested. Tom enlisted the help of a consultant from California who knew how to rewire a studio of this sort. He arrived with new parts and supplies and spent two weeks helping Paul rebuild the whole studio. Tom's adult son, Robby, was also involved in music, and he helped solder the connections. What seemed like miles of cables and wires had to be connected to ensure the proper signal path as it flowed through the studio. The men worked seven days a week for a full month doing the grunt work. Finally all the pieces were tested, working, and up to technical specifications. Maybe now he could start making music.

Tom Bee suggested using famed Native American artist J. D. Challenger to design the CD cover. Considered America's leading painter of American Indians, he was known for depicting the story of a people rich in heritage and tradition. Paul had seen several sketches and really liked Challenger's work. After several telephone discussions, he told J. D. to go ahead and get started on a drawing.

Within a few days Paul could easily see he didn't have much money in the arrangement, but he certainly had time—and he was committed to take advantage of every minute. SOAR's front office was open every day from 8 a.m. to 5 p.m. Paul made sure he was there at 8 a.m. sharp every morning, ready to work. But when the doors were locked in the evening, he found he wasn't ready to quit for the day. There was nothing to do back at his room and he certainly wasn't down here on vacation.

"I'd just as soon keep working," Paul said to Tom one afternoon just before Tom locked up for the day.

"How long do you need to stay?" he questioned.

"I don't know. There's nothing to do back at my room," Paul said, his expression pleading for understanding. "If it's all right with you, I may as well keep going until nine or ten every night."

"Well, I can't leave the doors unlocked," Tom said, stiffening slightly.

"I could lock up for you," Paul offered.

Tom folded his arms and shook his head. "No, I don't think that would work. Tell you what—if you want, you can stay in the studio but I'll have to lock the door."

"Lock me in?" Paul scoffed, his eyes darkening.

"The neighborhood isn't trustworthy. If you want to stay…" Tom shrugged his shoulders and waited for Paul's response.

Tom had him in a tight spot and Paul knew it. "Fine," Paul said, throwing up his hands. "As long as I can keep working."

"I'll come back around ten and let you out," Tom said, turning to go.

"That'd be great." Paul shook his head as the lock clicked behind him. A rather uneasy feeling settled over him as he glanced at the locked door. "What he's really saying is *I'm* not trustworthy," Paul muttered under his breath. *Don't think about it, Paul...let it go.*

• • •

"How's it going?" Kathy asked on one of her weekly phone calls.

"Oh, man," Paul sighed. "It's rough, Kathy. Really rough." He didn't dare tell her how bad it really was.

"I could say the same thing," Kathy sighed. "The kids don't like the commute—and I can't blame them. It's at least an extra hour in the morning. Shane's willing to take out a loan so he can get a decent car."

"That might work. He won't have all the expenses with Gopher State this year since he's only playing high school ball."

"You know Aaron and Seth Kamholz? The twins?"

"Yeah," Paul answered.

"Their parents told Shane he is more than welcome to stay with them. All the boys hang out at their house anyway," Kathy shared. "I think that'll be better for him than staying way out here."

"I agree. Then why don't you go ahead and help him get a car."

"Okay.

"How's Nikki?" It was harder than he anticipated being away from his family.

"She likes the new school much better...it's smaller and better suited for her," Kathy said.

"Hey, that's good news."

"Yeah, but I'm still worried about some of her friends. I'm sorry, we don't need to rehash that again. Let's talk about something else."

Kathy took a deep breath and exhaled slowly. "Did you see we had seven inches of snow here on Tuesday? Don't even tell me how beautiful it is there," she ordered.

"About 77 and sunshine," he teased. "Warm...blue sky."

Kathy envisioned the grin on his face. "You're pushing it," she threatened with a laugh.

"Remember last time we talked about what to use for my recording name?" Paul asked, switching subjects.

"Yeah, we wanted to take something from Lower Brule."

"Exactly. There's so much French Canadian influence in Lower Brule, I was thinking of taking the word *Brule*, and adding the little dash to make it French, *Bru-lay*. One of the elders said that was the original pronunciation. *"*

"Bru-lay?"

"Yeah. What do you think?"

"Bru-lay," she repeated. "I like it. It has a nice sound."

"Think about it for a day or two," Paul said. "Since this music is all about my heritage, my bloodline, I want to use LaRoche as my last name on the CD.

"You are keeping 'Paul' though, aren't you?"

"What's wrong with Arlen?"

"*Paul* LaRoche," she said. "I can deal with that."

"Thanks," he teased.

"You've been Paul Summers my whole life."

"*I've* been Paul Summers my whole life!" he laughed.

"Paul Summers or Paul LaRoche—I'll keep you either way," she said with the kind of deep love that twenty years together brings.

He paused and then added softly, "I miss you."

• • •

Starting out fresh, Paul put on the headphones and began experimenting with different blends, mixing Native American sounds with a piano or flute melody. As much as he had come to respect the traditional Native American and Pow Wow music, he was well aware that many people in mainstream America would not listen to that for an entire CD. Traditional Native American music can be hard to digest because it sounds very tribal and repetitious. The words are hard to understand and it often doesn't have a recognizable melody, yet it certainly has its place and value within the culture.

Paul pushed up the channel fader and ran his fingers over the keyboard, testing the volume. In studying American Indian musical genres, he had found Native American groups playing traditional music, contemporary sounds, rock and roll, jazz, and even blues. So far no one was mixing good old rock and roll with traditional Native American music except for a few foreign music producers and several non-Natives disguised as Native Americans.

Paul took his key songs and added chants from the SOAR archives and special effects to the contemporary music he had composed at home. Bits and pieces from the past two years—thoughts, emotions—came at him from all directions as he strived to flesh out the right blend.

White America. Native America. Mainstream America. Indigenous America.

The story is the focal point, he concluded. *I want people to hear a pure and unadulterated musical recounting of my journey. Living in one culture, yet within the soul, another lies hidden. Thirty-eight years in a known culture, generations of a hidden heritage.*

He took his time, listening over and over to the different compilations. It didn't take long each morning before the cramped room became hot and stuffy with the equipment running continually through the day and evening.

One thing he'd learned in studying the syncretic nature of the Northern Plains traditional music was the importance of the drum and the flute. Lakota elders told how the traditional wood flute is the essence of the wind as it rustles the grasses and leaves, scales the buttes and mountains, and skims the surface of the lakes and streams. The traditional handmade cedarwood flute had only seven notes: four notes to represent the four directions, two to represent heaven and earth, and the seventh note to represent the heart—the place where the six come together.

Paul closed his eyes, envisioning Lower Brule and what it must have been like generations ago, imagining the sounds of the people gathering for a ceremony. He had also discovered that circular symbols in the Native culture have meaning both spatially and socially. The drum occupies great cultural and symbolic power at Lakota gatherings. Simultaneously a spiritual guardian and a musical instrument, it references a past way of life. In essence, the drum actually represents the heartbeat of Mother Earth and demands great respect. Tobacco and prayers are offered to it before playing and it must be covered when it is not in use. In the Northern Plains style, the drum changes rhythm often, alternating between a steady, pulsing rhythm and a complete stop.

One week in particular Paul made especially good progress, and he was excited to feel the first Brulé CD coming together. He tweaked the percussion slightly and played the first track again. The melody flowed seamlessly from the cut. "Ah-hah!" he said jubilantly. For the first time since coming to Albuquerque he felt a sense of true accomplishment. "At least I have something to tell Kathy this week," Paul whispered to himself, making sure it was backed up in multiple places. Sticking to the pattern he'd developed since coming to Albuquerque, he took Sunday off to relax and unwind with some of the guys he had met.

Monday morning Paul returned, his spirit renewed and refreshed. Eager to pick up where he left off, he tossed his jacket on a stool. "Okay, let's play this again," he muttered under his breath. "The second one still needs a little polishing."

He hit Play on the recording decks but only eerie silence greeted him. Paul held his breath and cued up the decks, trying it again. He waited and listened, but no sound came out. Nothing. "What is going on?" he demanded, staring at the console in disbelief.

Again, stone-cold silence.

Paul spent the next hour trying everything imaginable. Every single track he'd produced the previous week was lost. Gone. Forever. Paul was sick to his stomach. It was like hitting a brick wall. Again. "How can this keep happening?!" he cried.

All the frustrations since arriving in Albuquerque built to this painful defeat—a lost or stolen composition. Despite the sometimes tense and uncomfortable relation with Tom Bee, Paul knew no one at SOAR had tampered with the console. Rather, the opposition seemed to be invisible, somehow preventing him from making any progress. He had no choice but to start over, knowing full well he could never come up with the exact same composition.

That night Paul copied his tracks and brought backup copies home with him. But when he came back the next morning, he was stunned to find several of the tapes corrupted with digital errors despite their delicate care. In the middle of a recording session the next afternoon, he watched, mouth ajar, as the equipment turned off and on again without reason. Weird, unexplained things were happening far too often and they weren't the kinds of things he could share with just anybody.

In between working on his own music, Tom had requested Paul's help on numerous projects for SOAR, including a collaboration with Tom's son, Robby Bee. Paul didn't mind necessarily, and sometimes it resulted in unique opportunities.

"Hey, Paul," Tom said just before leaving for the day.

"What's up?"

"I've got some Comanche elders coming to record some old songs. They're driving down from Oklahoma; I think they're supposed to get here around five or six. Can you cut about ten tracks for them?"

"Sure," Paul said. "No problem. I'll be here for a while yet." He went back to work, forgetting about the expected guests. Late that night, around 11:30, he heard a knock on the door. Paul peered out the front window to see a group of 70- and 80-year-old men and women with grins from ear to ear spilling out of a large van. Without a key, Paul had to call Tom and wait for him unlock the front door.

"We're gonna make a record!" one of the ladies giggled as they came inside.

Paul grinned and politely escorted the jovial group back to the studio and put on a pot of coffee. It was going to be a long night.

The elders brought 10 selected songs from the Numuhuviyanuu songbook, a collection from two Comanche Indian churches in Oklahoma. Paul got them situated and instructed the group on the recording procedures.

"Oh, this is a thrill," said an old man with white hair and high cheekbones. His eyes held a glimpse of a deep, inner joy.

The impromptu choir of aged voices in the middle of the night lifted Paul's spirit beyond words. Between recordings, laughter filled the tiny studio. The elderly singers appeared to be having the time of their lives. Even though he couldn't understand the words, Paul recognized some of the Christian hymns from his days playing the church organ. As he listened, a wave of goosebumps rushed up his spine. *How priceless and beautiful to hear their voices.* Despite the session running until 4 a.m., the late night venture turned into a true blessing.

With newfound meaning and purpose, Paul's desire for alcohol diminished greatly and before long, he had given it up completely. He wanted his mind fresh and alert, able to capture every sonata calling to his heart.

By now he was back at the console, composing and creating. Paul kept the tunes simple, a flute or keyboard melody, and experimented with acoustic and electric guitar, percussion, chants, and the drum. He could feel an artistic force deep within gathering momentum. *Keep at it, Paul.*

. . .

After a couple of months in Albuquerque, Paul had gotten to know several individuals with various Native American heritages. "Come to a sweat with us this Sunday, Paul. The guy running it is from South Dakota too."

The sweat lodge ceremony, known as the *Inipi Ceremony*, is a sacred ceremony in Lakota culture. The participants pray in traditional ways and sing sacred songs. Paul had joined the prayer circle for three Sundays in a row, and he immediately felt a release of his spirit.

The bizarre issues at the studio were weighing heavily on his mind. Finally Paul pulled his friend aside and described the troubling incidents. "And just the other night," Paul explained in a hushed voice, "I could distinctly hear someone running across the roof. I was in the studio alone. I called Robby on his mobile phone and he was right outside the studio. He flat out said there's nobody on the roof. Yet I could still hear it! After that, a picture that was hanging on the wall came across the room and hit me in the back." Paul shook his head in a helpless gesture. "I know it sounds weird, man, but I swear it happened. I don't know what to do."

His friend listened intently, knowing Paul spoke the truth. "I'll tell you what I would do. Get some tobacco, any kind. It has a connection to our people and our culture, and to our elders and the spirits of those who might be looking over you. Spread it around the room, however you want, and then say a prayer." He looked Paul in the eyes and held his gaze. "I won't tell you how to pray, that's up to you. And always carry some tobacco with you."

Paul listened carefully but with hesitation. He could tell that his friend genuinely wanted to help him. Still, Paul wondered. Come Monday morning, however, something inside prompted him to give it a try. He brought some tobacco to the studio and without a word to anyone else, sprinkled pinches of it here and there. He felt a little funny spreading it around the room, but he was ready to yield to his spirit and give it a try. Transferring his thoughts into a prayer, he began. "God, I give thanks for the opportunity to be here, for my good fortune, my health, my family..." Paul took a deep breath and released it slowly, shutting his eyes. "Today I ask for Your help in my musical endeavor, I ask for assistance in finalizing this and moving it along in a manner free from problems." He took his time, communicating with God and acknowledging Him through sacrifice, petition, and thanksgiving.

Paul cautiously worked through the day, waiting and watching as everything proceeded smoothly. No weird phenomenas. The next morning Paul used the tobacco and went through more prayers, and again everything went smoothly. And the next day. Alone at night he tried to sort it out. For now, he kept the experience private. Besides, how could one share something like that?

Within a week of Paul's new routine, he had produced the complete song list of 12 instrumental cuts for the first CD. Aware of the distinctions between sacred songs and social songs, and out of respect for the culture, he had carefully excluded sacred and spiritual elements.

Paul purposely opened the album with a prayer song titled "Sacred Praises," which started out slow and soulful with a soft chant in the background. Next he overlaid the voice of a man speaking in Lakota before rolling into a lush, rhythmic arrangement. The constant and unusual drumrolls and stops built to a crescendo before a slow fade to a piano solo.

Soothing and soulful, the next track, "Brave Hearts," started with an immediate drum beat, an attention getter, going right into an emotive flute melody, offering a precarious balance of old and new. The unique mix carried an innovative depth and exemplified the art form. For the third arrangement, "Buffalo Moon," Paul used a catalog of chants that Tom had provided and inserted a stirring chant. It melded perfectly with the drum and melody, beckoning the listener to return again and again. To Paul, it was a beautiful and descriptive soundscape of the Lakota homeland.

Song number five came to mind the first time Paul witnessed the colorful sights and sounds of a Pow Wow. He tried his best to capture all the stimulating images and sounds of the festive gathering in an up-tempo track titled "Dancing Feathers."

Paul also had access to a collection of old hymns sung in the Lakota language. He thought of the Comanche singers not long ago and how rich and soulful their hymns sounded. He selected one of his own favorites, "Have Thine Own Way, Lord," as a peaceful way to close the album. The track started with a simple piano rendition and brought in the elders singing in the traditional dialect. Paul thought it appropriate to translate the Lakota message in "Sacred Praises" into English and verbalize the overall concept of the entire album.

When all else fades away, Faith, Hope, and Love will remain.

Those feelings that are so strong, so mysterious.

I think of you my relatives, and I thank you.

The song closed out with the piano again. Although only 2.54 minutes in length, it was a track that spoke volumes to him.

In order to make the package complete, Paul inserted a prayer song entitled "Spirit Horses" for track number six. He chose the songs with both purpose and apprehension in order to achieve what was in his heart: the accumulation of the journey home and the musical process. It opened with prayer, ended with prayer, and had a prayer carefully placed in the middle.

Paul leaned back in his chair, eyes closed, and listened to the finished set of instrumentation and rhythms. A sense of peace filled his soul as the tracks played from beginning to end.

Now for the all important title. He consulted with Tom, who came up with *We the People*: *A Tribal Gathering of Music*. It fit perfectly.

An envelope arrived right on time from J. D. Challenger. Paul opened it to see his sketches for the first album. The background was an antique print of the United States Constitution with the title in large letters, *We the People*. Forefront were five Native Americans in colorful regalia, three seated and two standing. In J. D. Challenger's unique style, their faces stood out painted white with stripes of color, and each had long eagle feathers in their hair. *Brulé* was painted in bright red in the bottom right corner. The cover was both eye-catching and stunning.

Now things were really on a roll. As part of his agreement with Tom to coproduce material, Paul went right to work on another CD titled *Lakota Piano*, a reworked version of Tom's XIT material. A tranquil and meditative recording, Paul added his own beautiful, haunting piano melodies with soft instrumentation to the classic songs. Within the next three weeks he composed and produced another full CD, *One Nation,* a set of up-tempo arrangements with heavy Native American vocables. One step beyond *We the People* in world flavor, *One Nation* promised driving dance and club rhythms, new ground for contemporary Native American music. Timing was crucial in the industry, so Paul and Tom planned to hold *One Nation* for a later release.

Tom then approached Paul regarding another project with Robby. Paul agreed, and came up with another concept in the blending of the two worlds: a Native Christmas CD. The collaboration between Paul and Robby is technically known as *Red Nativity,* without the Brulé name on the cover. Together they composed and produced another composition of Christmas hymns, rewritten with a Native influence. They titled the 12-track CD *One Holy Night,* a beautiful collection of contemporary and traditional sounds preserving the integrity of the season.

Despite the many ups and downs between Tom and Paul, things always worked out for the best. As Christmas Eve neared, Paul felt a real sense of aloneness without his family. He was comforted by Tom's invitation to join his family for a holiday meal at the Bee residence.

With all four projects wrapped up, Paul handed them over to Tom for manufacturing. Equally exhausted and excited, the past four months had been more than trying. Half were moments of struggling and opposition, and half were spent crafting a rhythmically pure and beautiful sound.

Now it was time to go home.

*Summers family
1959 Irma, Mark,
Paul, Clarence in
Summers home in
Worthington, MN*

*Paul signing SOAR
contract, 1995*

Fritz and Cheryll's ranch home on the Lower Brule Sioux reservation

Paul with tribal elders Johnny and Bessy Estes

Altwin Grassrope teaching children songs and dance, Altwin is the tribal elder who conducted Paul's Naming Ceremony

Reliance 1
Lower Brule 15
Big Bend Dam 17

The I-90 Interstate sign for the reservation Paul passed many times over the years before the reunion

Fritz and Cheryll LaRoche family homecoming weekend, 1993 (L-R) Frederick, John John, Cheryll, Jeremiah, Fritz, Harlee

Jam session early days of Brulé. Frederick, Nicole, Paul, John Estes, back yard of Paul and Kathy's home on Little Bend

Basketball game on the rez at Paul and Kathy's home on Little Bend

Squeaky Door Market, Lower Brule
where Paul and Fritz first met

Paul and Kathy's
home on the
Little Bend of
the LBST
reservation

Paul and Shane
jammin' on guitars
at Brule house on
Little Bend

NINE

Going Home

*"I think we are supposed to go home
to the rez."*

—*Kathy Summers*

Even the freezing temperatures and snow-packed roads couldn't dampen Kathy's spirits. Paul was coming home! The minute she laid eyes on his tall frame and beaming brown eyes, she raced to greet him.

Paul welcomed her with a deep, passionate kiss. "I love you," he breathed into her ear.

"I missed you so much," Kathy confided, loving the feel of his strong arms around her. "How 'bout a lunch date?" she asked, her blue eyes sparkling.

"I'd love it," Paul replied, holding her close.

Kathy drove to Galleria, an upscale retail center in Edina, not far from the airport. "Let's indulge a little," she said. "I think we deserve it."

Paul and Kathy found a secluded table at one of the restaurants and talked the afternoon away. "So what happened at Morgaine's?" Paul inquired.

"It worked great for a while, but I could feel it was time to move on," Kathy said, taking a sip of Diet Coke. "You remember Lana, my other good friend?"

"Sure."

"She offered to let us to move in with her a couple weeks ago and it's working out just fine."

"What about Lana's husband? Weren't they having some issues?" He touched Kathy's fingers as they talked, happy to have her close.

"Yes," Kathy sighed. "They're going through with the divorce. It's been a little rough for her, but Lana's such a sweetheart, she wouldn't hear of us not coming. It's a nice house in Elko, just south of the Cities."

"How 'bout Nikki and Shane? Are they okay with it?"

"Yeah, I mean Shane's doing fine. He's happy with his little red sports car," Kathy said.

"Hey, what 18-year-old guy wouldn't be! I talked to him shortly after he bought it when he was living with Aaron and Seth. He said sometimes he'd just go sit in his car and look at it and smile. Can't you just picture him?" Paul laughed.

"Yes, totally." Kathy leaned back in her chair imagining Shane in the driver's seat, a grin from ear to ear. "The drive from Elko isn't much better than it was from Prescott. He should leave a little earlier to get to school on time, but he won't listen to me. He's close to max-ing out on tardies this quarter. He gives me his famous, 'Don't worry, Mom!' Nicole is still at the movie theater and living in that apartment. So far that's going okay. One day at a time," Kathy said. "Right?"

"Isn't that the truth." Paul took a deep breath as the server placed refills on the table. "Oh, it feels good to be home, Kath."

"Shane has to work after school, then he'll be out. Nikki said she'd come out too. They're both eager to see you. And everyone wants to hear the music."

Paul squeezed her hand. "I can't wait to hear what you think about it."

"Let's go out to Lana's." Kathy glanced at her watch. "No one else is home right now."

Paul's face lit up with a big grin. "What are we waiting for?!"

. . .

Paul put the tape player on the coffee table in the family room and put in the demo tape of *We the People*. As soon as he hit Play, "Sacred Praises" started off with a soft and slow chant in the background. Then the Native voice spoke in Lakota as it moved into the drum beat.

"Oh, Paul," Kathy whispered, still listening. Her eyes sparkled as she absorbed her husband's unique composition. The flute melody came first, then the keyboard solo. As it faded to an end, she hit Stop. "It's beautiful! Awesome," she said, overcome with emotion. "It's like our whole life in that song. How did you do it?"

"Do you like it?" he asked gingerly.

"Like it?" she scoffed. "I *love* it."

"Listen to this." Paul hit Play again, and "Brave Hearts" started. He held Kathy in his arms, humming along to the melody as they listened to the entire song.

Tears welled in Kathy's eyes. "It's beautiful," she whispered.

The next song, "Buffalo Moon," started out with a catchy drum beat and flute tune. Paul let all 12 tracks play, and something in the music begged the listener to pay attention as if to say, *I have something special to share.*

"It's absolutely incredible! Each song, Paul—it's stunning, honest. I can tell you've captured all your thoughts, what you've been through."

"What *we've* been through," he corrected.

Paul was right—this journey, good and bad, involved the whole family. She glanced around Lana's family room, her own furniture packed in storage until…until when, she had no idea. She thought about the incredible homecoming they had experienced, now over two years ago. The family, so giving in nature. The culture, so embracing. Cheryll's words echoed in her mind. *Why don't you move home? Come back home.*

"Kathy?" Paul asked, nudging her back to the present.

"Sorry, just thinking, wondering where we go from here." Kathy picked up the cassette and studied the dramatic images from J. D.

Challenger. "This is so different than anything you've ever played before."

"Exactly," Paul said.

"You know why?" she asked, looking into his eyes.

"Why?" He held her gaze, waiting for her answer.

"It's genuine—pure. It's from the heart."

The seventh direction.

. . .

Hints of spring filled the air, lifting their spirits and spurring those who had endured another Minnesota winter toward a period of newness. Lana's backyard bordered an open field where cottontail rabbits had tiny young hidden in nearby nests. The pond in view was nearly free of ice as the hours of daily sunshine steadily thawed the once solid surface. Shrubs burst forth with green buds, flirting with hints of summer.

Throughout the days and weeks, Paul shared his new music with family, friends, and anyone willing to listen. Facial expressions showed enthusiastic responses each time. Encouraged by their comments but unsure how to promote it, Paul and Kathy sorted through their options.

"What are we going to do now?" she asked.

"Number One, we need to figure out how to sell it," Paul said simply. "Secondly, I think we should have a concert."

Kathy almost choked. "A concert?"

"Why not?"

"We're not ready for that, Paul." Her eyebrows pulled together in a frown. "We need to take it slow, in small steps."

"You know you're cute when you're mad," he said with a grin.

"Paul, I'm working full-time. This is going to take time to learn," she continued, unmoved by his flattery. "You've always been into music, but it's always been live. We've never had a product like this to sell. And what genre does it fall into?"

"Nothing you'd find at Best Buy, that's for sure," he admitted.

• • •

"Paul, it's almost seven a.m. I need to leave now if I'm going to make it to work by eight," Kathy said, grabbing her sunglasses and keys.

"Wait up two seconds," Paul said, throwing on a pair of jeans and a T-shirt. "I'll give you a ride because I need the car this morning. I'm going to meet a couple of guys I know and brainstorm with 'em at that music studio downtown Minneapolis."

"Now I'm nervous," Kathy muttered, waiting for Paul to get his shoes on.

Morning traffic was light well south of the Twin Cities, but as soon as Paul crossed the Minnesota River bridge, all three lanes on I-35W were stop-and-go, jammed with morning commuters. "Remember, tonight is Shane's prom. All the kids are meeting at one house so the parents can take pictures ahead of time," Kathy instructed. "We have to be there at 4:30, prompt."

"Got it," Paul replied, checking the mirror before switching lanes. "494 is a mess, I'm going to take Crosstown."

"Slow down just a hair, Paul. You always get too close."

"Who's driving?"

"Never mind," she said. "By the way, Mom said she might drive up to—"

Suddenly brake lights flared brightly in both lanes of cars ahead of them. "Paul!" Kathy cried, but it was too late.

Screech! Crash!

Paul slammed on the brakes, but could not avoid the car in front of him. Tires squealed. Metal hit chrome. Fenders crunched. Smoke billowed around the vehicles involved in the multiple chain-reaction accident.

"Are you okay?" Paul immediately asked Kathy.

"Yeah, yeah," she said, her voice shaking. "I think so."

He leaned back against the headrest. "Unbelievable," he moaned. "Why us and why today!" Paul stepped out to survey the crumpled front end. The hood was bent up in an A-shape. Soon sirens neared the accident scene. Police began sorting through the damaged vehicles and checking for injuries. Paul provided his driver's license and insurance information and waited to be cleared from the scene.

"Thank goodness no one was seriously hurt," Kathy said. "That's what the EMT just told the woman in the car ahead of us."

"That's good." Paul turned the key and the engine started up. "At least it still runs, Kath. We won't have to have it towed."

"What a mess!"

"I pushed the hood down. We'll have to be careful until I can get it tied a little better."

Kathy let out a long sigh.

"What?"

"It's not like we already don't fit in with the whole Eden Prairie image," Kathy said, "and now we have to show up for prom tonight in this?"

"Oh, c'mon," Paul growled. "I've never quite fit in. Maybe we're not supposed to. Maybe we're supposed to stand out."

"Yeah," Kathy said with sarcasm. "The Mercedes, BMWs, Porsches...and here come the Summerses in a cracked up Olds."

Paul chuckled under his breath.

"It's not funny," Kathy said, lifting an eyebrow.

. . .

Paul sat at his computer in Lana's family room, pouring over some promotional options for Brulé. His cell phone rang. "This is Paul."

"Hi, Paul. My name is Linda Thompson, one of your cousins from Lower Brule."

Immediately Paul's mood lightened. "Hello, Linda."

"We met at my dad's funeral," she said in a soft-spoken voice.

"Yes, I remember," Paul said, "Uncle Jiggs." Linda's father, J. W. Thompson had died that March, and he and Kathy had gone out to

Lower Brule for the funeral. At every family gathering, they were still meeting relatives.

"I just had to call you…I bought a cassette of *We the People* and listened to it driving back to Lower Brule for Memorial weekend," she said. "I need to tell you it moved me so deeply. It's so…emotional, unlike any other music I've ever heard. It's like you *understand*, Paul. You need to come home and learn about your people."

Paul could still see it clearly in his mind—the wide Missouri, the rolling prairie, the people. *His* people. "You think so?" he asked half-heartedly.

"It's like the Indian inside you is waiting to come out, Paul."

• • •

They had no choice but to keep driving the Oldsmobile. The front grill was bent and the driver's headlight smashed. Paul had tied down the hood securely so it wouldn't fly up when they were driving. Kathy glared at the car as she walked from the office door to the far side of the parking lot. It was embarrassing to work for an insurance agency knowing they couldn't afford the deductible to get their own car fixed. Kathy slid into the front seat just as her cell phone rang.

"Hello?"

"Mom! Guess what?"

"What, Shane?"

"On my way to school this morning the cops pulled me over for speeding in Lakeville. Red sports car, ya know."

Kathy held her breath, waiting for the rest of the story. He would be paying for his own ticket! "I bet you didn't leave in time," she scolded.

"Listen to this. When the cop came up, I said, 'Sir, if I'm late for school one more time I have to repeat all my classes.' I told him I was commuting all the way to Eden Prairie and all's he said was, 'Better get going then!' and he let me go. Awesome, huh!"

"You got lucky, Shane."

"I made it, Mom. I'm graduating!"

A smile formed at the corners of her mouth and she breathed a sigh of relief. One down, one to go. Without their own place to hold an open house, Kathy arranged to celebrate Shane's graduation at a motel in Edina. It would have to do. Even though Lana made them feel more than welcome, nonetheless it was stressful to be living in someone else's house.

A couple weeks later Kathy approached Paul as he lay on the bed watching the ten o'clock news. "We need to talk," she said softly.

"Hmm? What is it?" he asked, sliding over to make room for her.

Kathy climbed onto the bed beside Paul, scrunching a pillow underneath for support. "Lana's not been feeling well. Her cancer is getting worse. I don't think we should stay here much longer. It's too hard for her. It's hard on the kids," she sighed. "We need our own place."

"Hold on," he said, and pressed Mute with the remote. President Clinton's face flashed on the screen while KARE-11 newscaster Paul Magers mouthed the day's headlines.

"I agree with you, Kathy, but we don't have the money for an apartment. They always need two months for a security deposit."

"Paul, what I'm trying to say is I think we *are* supposed to go home to the reservation and start all over." She leaned on her side to face him, resting her head on her hand. "A fresh start."

Her words fell silent as Paul contemplated a thought he'd considered but never dared share. "Do you mean it?" he finally asked.

Kathy looked her husband in the eyes. "Yes, I mean it. I think we're supposed to *go home.*"

. . .

Within mere days, things were in motion to move to Lower Brule. Cheryll and Fritz were thrilled beyond words when Paul and Kathy announced they were "coming home" and offered to find a house in Lower Brule. Friends and family in Minnesota initially questioned the move. Was it necessary to *live* out there? On a reservation? Doubt and uncertainty rang loud in their voices, but gradually they accepted Paul and Kathy's decision. Kathy advised her supervisor at American Family that she'd be leaving in a few weeks.

In mid-July the truck was loaded with all their belongings, or more accurately, with what was left of their belongings. Between all the moves and living with friends, Kathy had had to get rid of many things along the way, but in the big picture somehow it didn't matter. What mattered was the undeniable sense that this was the right thing to do. Grandma Shirley bought a few essentials to give them for the trip. Some good friends pitched in and donated extra money to rent a truck. After a 41-year separation, the time had come for Paul to reclaim his heritage.

For now, Shane decided to stay in the Twin Cities and had already moved into a townhouse with a friend. He was working full time at Burnsville Buick-Nissan and appeared situated for the summer. Nicole wanted out of her apartment and agreed to move to Lower Brule with Paul and Kathy, ready for something new and different.

July proved to be hot and sticky as the U-haul rolled along I-90 across Minnesota and South Dakota. Fritz and Cheryll had arranged for Paul and Kathy to move into an empty house in the heart of town. It was small, just like all the others in Lower Brule, with neighbors nearby.

There was no comparison between the tiny reservation community and the comfortable, upscale trappings of suburban Eden Prairie with its abundance of retail shops, restaurants, and upper-middle class homes. It was a contrast in every way imaginable. But when Paul turned the truck onto a narrow street and pulled up in front of the gray rambler, it spoke volumes to see Fritz and Cheryll and the boys, all smiles and open arms, waiting to welcome them *home*.

After a round of hugs, Paul and Kathy followed Cheryll and Fritz up the steps. Nicole and the boys chatted outside while the four adults went inside to take a look. "It's been empty for a while," Fritz said, walking into the small living room. Just then a roach ran along side the baseboard.

"Oh, no!" Cheryll squealed.

Kathy moved into the kitchen and cautiously opened a lower cupboard. "Oh, look—there's more in here," she said, seeing a few more scatter in the unexpected light.

"What's that smell?" Paul asked, looking around. The upstairs needed a good cleaning, but there was nothing visible to cause such an unpleasant odor.

"I don't know," Fritz replied. "But I smell it too."

Paul followed Fritz toward the stairway leading to the basement. "Oh, I think it's coming from down there," Fritz said. The two men retreated down the steps to inspect.

The cement floor near the drain was covered with a layer of muck. "Oh, man, look at that. The sewer is backed up!" Paul said with disgust, covering his mouth and nose.

"What a mess," Fritz said, shaking his head. He patted Paul on the back. "Don't worry about it, bro. We'll get this all cleaned up. Don't sweat it. It happens sometimes. People move out and leave it in a mess. We'll take care of it."

"What is it?" Kathy asked when Paul and Fritz came up the stairs.

"The sewer," Fritz said. "I can call a guy I know to get it cleaned up. Don't worry."

"We can't move our stuff in with all the roaches upstairs," Kathy cried. "They're everywhere!"

"Just leave it in the truck for now and stay with us until we get it cleaned up," Cheryll said, putting an arm around Kathy. "That's what family is for."

Exhausted, Paul and Kathy crawled into Harlee's bed that night. "I don't get it," Kathy whispered in the darkness. "Here we can't even move into our house because of the condition, and it still feels right to be here."

Paul kissed her cheek. "Have I told you lately that I love you?"

Three days later the house was completely debugged and the basement decontaminated. With the help of the LaRoches, Paul and Kathy moved their belongings into the house and settled into the community.

Paul and Kathy made a visit to the tribal leaders to introduce themselves and share their story. "Hello, I'm Michael Jandreau," the tribal chairman said. "We heard another brother found his way home. Welcome back." Paul shook hands with Mike and in their ensuing conversation sensed an immediate friendship.

Daily, it seemed, neighbors and residents came by to wish them well. "Welcome back to your people," a middle-aged woman said to Paul with a hint of her native dialect. "We heard you were gone for many years but now came back." Barely five feet tall, she reached to give Paul a hug. "What a wonderful thing to celebrate."

One afternoon Paul walked downtown to the Squeaky Door Market. Just as he reached the corner, an older man approached him. "We heard your story," he said, grasping Paul's hand. "We're glad to have you home, son."

"Thank you," Paul acknowledged. "I appreciate that."

"When a family member is lost or taken away, it's a very important thing to have them come home." Tall and slender, the man spoke softly, but with great conviction. His face was leathered and wrinkled, and his gray hair nearly touched his shoulders. "We cherish each one of our people."

Paul returned home with a few groceries. "It happened again," he said to Kathy.

"What's that?" she asked from the kitchen table. Bank statements and folders covered the table as she tried to organize their finances after the move.

"Another welcome home from a complete stranger," Paul said, putting the butter and milk in the refrigerator. "Have you noticed each time they say it with such sincerity? It's not a casual, hey, glad you're here. They really mean it."

"Yes, I have noticed," Kathy said, nodding. "I just hope and pray it's right for Nicole."

. . .

A strong breeze helped cool the hot July air hanging over the South Dakota prairie. Kathy had all the windows pushed open as far as she could get them. Money was running low and each day passed with the added pressure of establishing a source of income.

"It's obvious the record company isn't going to do this for us," Kathy said, gathering up dirty towels in the hallway. "We have to get it going ourselves."

"I hear what you're saying," Paul acknowledged. "But if we place an order from SOAR, number one, we have to come up with the money to pay for them, and number two, we have to find someplace to sell them."

Kathy put down the laundry basket and placed her hands on her hips. "Listen, we're in this together, right?" she asked. "I believe in you. In *this*." She turned to the end table and picked up *We the People*. "If you put some money together for the first order, I'll find a place for you to sell them. Deal?"

Paul nodded. "Consider it done," he replied. "Start making some phone calls."

Kathy spent the entire morning looking through the phone book and making calls. "Paul," she said. "Come here!"

Paul scrambled from the back bedroom to the kitchen in two seconds. "What is it?"

"There's a craft show at the civic center in Rapid City this fall. I rented space for you for Friday, Saturday, and Sunday. You used to work solo back in the Twin Cities when you first started, I'm sure you can do it again," she said with confidence.

Paul planted a kiss on her lips. "Way to go, hon."

"We're on our way."

Without warning, three little kids, somewhere between three and six years old, swung open the front door and stumbled into the house. "Hey, lady," one brown-eyed boy called. Bare-chested and wearing stained cutoffs, he looked up at Kathy. "Lady, do you have any samwiches?"

Surprised by the bold entry Kathy got up from the table and approached the kids. They were busy looking around the house, not at all intimidated to be inside a stranger's home. "Yes, I do. But aren't you supposed to be home for lunch?"

The kids wandered past her into the kitchen, their eyes fixed on the cereal and Pop-Tarts sitting on the counter. "We don't have any lunch."

"What do you mean?" she asked, glancing at Paul. "When do you eat then?"

This time the girl answered, a bit more shy than the boy. "We just eat whatever we can find. Do you have some sandwiches?"

"We're hungry," the boy said, rubbing his bare tummy.

"Hun-gee," echoed the littlest girl.

"Well, have a seat then," Kathy instructed, grabbing the fresh loaf of bread. "Let's see if we can make some sandwiches."

All three kids climbed onto chairs at the table, smiles showing through their smudged faces in anticipation of a satisfying meal.

As soon as their lunch "guests" were finished, they ran out the front door, resuming their play. "Wasn't that strange," Kathy commented, cleaning up. "It's a different world here, that's for sure."

"I agree," Paul said, glancing out the window. "Look at Fritz and Cheryll—they've taken in kids who don't have a good home or aren't being taken care of properly. I think that's how it works. If someone isn't taking care of their kids just right, another family will step up to the plate and help out."

"I guess," Kathy said. "I'm just not used to it."

"Nikki seems to be fitting in okay, don't you think?" Paul asked.

"Yeah, so far so good. It's a big change for her," Kathy admitted. Then she added, laughing, "Who are we kidding? It's a big change for all of us. For a half second this morning I thought of running to Target."

Now Paul laughed out loud. "Yeah—right up the road, only 170 miles or so!"

* * *

Nicole enrolled at the small alternative school in September, determined to get her high school diploma after all. Her desire to learn about her father's culture gave her an added eagerness she hadn't felt before. The small high school in Lower Brule offered just the right setting for her to fit in and make it work.

Two months later Kathy was getting used to the young children coming and going through the front door, but it left them with little privacy. The intense heat of summer had softened, leaving a warm, beautiful autumn in its wake.

One evening Paul, Kathy, and Nicole sat on the front steps, watching the sun gradually lowering in the western sky. The angled rays caught the tall prairie grasses up on the hill, turning the tops a stunning bright gold as they rippled in the warm breeze. Down the street a pickup squealed its tires and spun out. It raced down the street, followed by a loud barrage of profanities aimed at the careless driver.

Paul glanced up and down the block. A South Dakota reservation might garner up romantic images, but there was certainly another perspective of a reservation town as well. Like a photographer with camera in hand, depending on which angle you point the camera, you could capture two totally different images while standing at the same spot. One beautiful, one sad. It depends which image you want to send out to the world.

The usual group of little kids began running toward the Summerses' house. Suddenly it turned into a race to see who could sit closest to the "popular" new family. They tumbled and pushed and ended up all around, laughing and out of breath. "Whoa, slow down," Paul instructed, protectively grabbing a little girl as she slid onto the cement step.

The littlest girl looked up at Kathy. She had a sweet round face with two crooked pigtails. "Can we pretend...like we're with you guys?" she asked innocently, leaning against Kathy's legs.

Kathy smiled, unsure how to respond. "Oh, sweetie," she began.

"Just pretending?" the girl reiterated.

Nicole gathered her into her arms. "You are a doll!" she exclaimed. "I'll pretend with you."

Maybe it was Kathy's long blonde hair, unusual in the small community, that attracted the kids, or maybe the inviting atmosphere of their home. Whatever the reason, the small children were constantly drawn to the Summerses' house.

Later that evening Nicole curled up on a loveseat in the back porch. She still liked to draw and sketch out her ideas on paper.

"Coming in?" Kathy asked.

"I might sleep out here tonight, Mom. I'm really into my writing and I want to keep going," she explained, tapping the pen on her notebook. "It's too hot inside anyway."

"Okay. Dad and I are going to bed."

"Goodnight."

Nicole kicked off her sandals and shut her notebook, her eyes fixed on the multitude of stars that filled the night sky. With only a sliver of a moon, the black sky came alive with millions of stars. Dancing and sparkling, they captured her imagination. The Milky Way was clearly visible as it streamed across the center of the immeasurable darkness. She'd never seen the sky so alive back home and she relished in its beauty. Another hour passed and Nicole picked up her notebook and started writing again, the peaceful setting stirring her inner thoughts.

At dawn Nicole woke up in time to see the deep reddish sun edge its way over the horizon. The fog from the river rolled across the town, covering the backyard in an eerie blanket of vaporous haze. She loved to experience such new and exhilarating moments.

Suddenly a figure, only in silhouette, jumped across the fence and cut through the yard, walking right by her on the porch.

"Hey!" the young man said with surprise when he noticed Nicole.

"Yeah?"

"Aren't you the new girl?"

Upon hearing his voice, Nicole recognized him as the brother of a good friend. "G'morning," she said, still sleepy.

He joined her on the porch, dropping into a lawn chair.

"What's up," she asked, sitting up.

"Not much. Just hanging out with friends..." Nicole listened as he began telling stories of the rez, absorbed in the chronicles of a way of life she didn't yet know.

• • •

"Linda Thompson called. She heard about this house getting sold," Paul said. "Her daughter's house out by the Thompson place is still sitting empty and she offered it to us. We can move out there in a couple weeks. Fritz will be here any minute to take us out there." After Uncle Jiggs passed away, Linda didn't want her mother living alone. She too felt called *home*, and moved back with Aunt Helen on the Thompson home place.

"Oh, good," Kathy sighed. "Paul, we should have Shane come out and help with the move. Fritz is so busy between the store and harvesting in the fields. He won't have time to help us."

"You're right. I'll call him tonight and see if he can take some time off work."

"It'll be nice to live out of town." She didn't mind relocating again so soon as long as she could have a little privacy. "I can't wait."

"You won't have to worry about that out there," Paul laughed.

The Thompson house sat on a large section of land along the bend in the Missouri River where it wound around and made a large U-turn. Seven miles from town down a gravel road, it offered an abundance of quiet, solitary moments that downtown Lower Brule couldn't provide. Linda Thompson and her mother, Helen, lived another mile farther, almost to the end of the bend. Only a few houses were scattered across the 3,500 acres termed "the Little Bend." When famed explorers Lewis and Clark made their way up the Missouri River to this area, the two men crossed the narrow section of land on foot and then had to wait three days for the keelboat to meet up with them. The land was relatively flat and much of the pastureland from Fritz's days as a kid was now irrigated farm fields.

Fritz drove through the Narrows to the Little Bend, a huge ball of dust rising behind the truck. As usual he drove down the middle of the

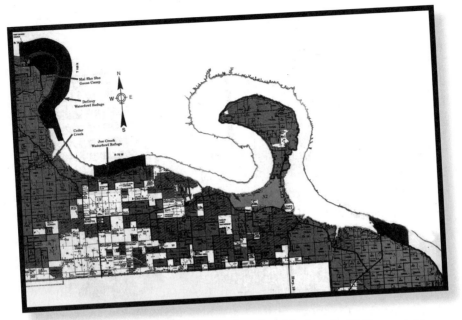

Lower Brule reservation map showing big bend of Missouri River

gravel road and only rarely needed to move to the side when they met another vehicle. Fritz slowed the truck and turned up another long gravel driveway with grazing land and prairie grasses lining both sides. On the distant horizon, the ground rose up, colored in various shades of brown and gray, indicating that the river lay in front of that hill, yet completely hidden from view.

The house itself was nothing special, another small split-entry rambler that sat among some trees and shrubs. A hedge of lilacs bushes lined a fence around the house with a few cedar trees mixed in. This house had at least been well kept and looked neat and orderly. Brown brick accented the pale green siding and white trim.

"Let's go inside," Cheryll said to Kathy. "No roaches or sewage in the basement this time," she laughed, opening the front door.

"Thank the good Lord!" Kathy added, following Cheryll inside and up the half-stairs to the main level. There were three bedrooms, a bathroom, and the usual kitchen, dining, and living room all together. Downstairs was a clean but unfinished basement.

Paul and Fritz took a walk around the yard where the grass was slightly overgrown since the last mowing. "One of the Thompson's cousins owns the pasture," Fritz continued. "He's letting Bill Long Turkey rent it out right now. He's got a herd of beef cattle out here now and sometimes he'll keep some horses too." Fritz motioned to the acres of land beyond the fence line. Behind the house, huge bales of hay were stacked along the fence line. "So if you don't mind having a few four-legged neighbors, you can move in next week."

"That won't bother us," Paul replied.

"C'mon," Fritz said, waving Paul toward the fence. "There's something I want to show you."

The brothers took turns spreading the barbed wires of the fence apart for each other to crawl through. They walked across the dry, uneven grassland where the cattle stopped grazing for a brief moment to watch them pass. Clumps of short bushes and small trees were spaced here and there as they neared the river's edge. The rolling, uneven bluff rested a good 50 feet above the water before gently sloping toward the river below. Paul saw a fish jump in the clear water, reflecting a bright blue from the October sky.

"Wow," Paul breathed, surveying the stunning yet calming landscape in every direction.

The two men stood quietly, not saying a word. In time Paul became more aware of the wildlife surrounding them. Scores of pheasants, wild turkey, deer and other small game were nearly invisible, but present. Meadowlarks sang their pretty songs as redwing blackbirds soared from a low-lying branch to the next shrub. Others hopped along the ground in search of nourishment.

"What'd ya think?" Fritz asked, hands on his hips.

Paul took a deep breath, soaking in the simple beauty all around. "This…is perfect," he said softly.

TEN

The First Gig

"I'll go with you, Dad"
—Nicole LaRoche

The move went smoothly. At last the house in town was empty and clean for the next family. The intent now was to settle in and stay put for awhile. Shane was unable to get time off work to help his parents. Knowing his dad needed him, Shane quit his job in the Twin Cities and moved out to Lower Brule.

Softball was the number one form of entertainment for boys his age. In tenth grade when he had come out for a summer visit with his cousins, they asked if he could play. Shane nodded and they put him at shortstop. It only took a few pitches before a ball came his way. He picked it up and threw it as hard as he could to the first baseman.

"Wow!" the kid exclaimed, catching the bullet throw.

From that moment on, Shane was "in" and never had any trouble with kids on the rez. He got a part-time job at the Squeaky Door and slowly developed an appreciation for their new lifestyle.

One day after work, Shane gave another boy a ride home. "Man, what you driving so fast for?"

"I don't know. I always drive this way," Shane said, foot pressed on the gas pedal.

"You're not in the city anymore, man. Slow down." The kid shook his head. "No need to hurry out here; nowhere to go, man."

· · ·

"Hey, Shaners," Paul said, stopping at the Squeaky Door. "Still need a ride home?"

"Change of plans," Shane advised. "Some of the guys stopped by and said they're putting together a softball game. Want to give me a ride to the field?"

Paul and Shane drove the few blocks down to the softball field. The diamond was completely empty, only some dust blowing across the base paths. "There's no one here," Shane said with disappointment. "I don't get it."

"Well, maybe it's not starting quite yet," Paul offered, looking up and down the street for any sign of the boys. "Run over to Fort Thompson with me. I have a quick errand and then we'll come back."

Slightly bigger than Lower Brule, Fort Thompson was straight east about 14 miles. It was on the opposite side of the Missouri River at the point of the dam. As usual, Paul ran into a few locals who had time to chat. Shane glanced at his watch and motioned to Paul. "Hey, Dad. It's been a couple hours. Want to check back at the field?"

"Sure, let's try it again." Paul drove back to the softball field and again found it deserted.

"It's not like this is the wrong field," Shane commented, looking around. "It's the *only* field." The nearby Pow Wow and rodeo arenas were also bare. Only a young mother pushed a stroller toward the health clinic.

"Maybe we missed it," Paul answered. "Could've been a quick game."

The next afternoon, the same group of boys showed up at the Squeaky Door. "Hey, Shane. You comin' down to play ball?"

"Well, yeah, but…"

"What? We told you we're playing ball," one boy said, cocking his head. "I thought you said you'd play."

"I thought the game was yesterday."

"Nah, we're starting right now. C'mon!"

"One second," Shane said, picking up the phone. "Hey, Dad, I'm staying in town after work. The guys are playing softball *today*. It's a whole day later, Dad!"

"Like Fritz says, it's a different pace of life."

. . .

Foremost on Paul's mind was the craft show in Rapid City, now only a couple weeks away. He put the boom box smack dab in the center of the kitchen table. "Wha'd ya think, Nikki? This isn't the best sound system, but it'll have to do."

"Oh, Dad," Nicole sighed. She sauntered up to the table in knit pants and a T-shirt. "Is that what you're going to use?"

"Hey, now…I'll rent a keyboard too," he said with air of confidence.

The look on Nicole's face couldn't hide her concern. "Dad, if you write down the music for me, I'll go with you and play the flute lines," she offered.

"Are you feeling sorry for me?" Paul teased.

"Maybe a little," she laughed, sliding onto a chair

"All right," he said, giving her a squeeze around the shoulders. "Want to give it a try?"

"Sure, I'll get my flute." Nicole retreated to her bedroom to find her flute case. Before long Kathy could hear Paul and Nicole practicing songs in the bedroom that served as a studio. It warmed her heart to see father and daughter laughing and making music together.

A few days later a UPS truck followed the school bus up their long driveway. Nicole stepped off the bus and ran to the front door. "Dad!" Nicole exclaimed. "The CDs are here, you need to sign for them."

Paul stepped outside to sign for the delivery. First the bus, then the brown delivery truck made a U-turn in the yard and headed back down the driveway.

"Wow, how many did you order?" Nicole inquired, holding the screen door open for Paul.

"A whole box load," he said, carrying it upstairs to the table. "Be careful," he added. "There's a lot of money tied up in this one box."

"This is so cool, Dad." Nicole smiled, looking up at Paul. "Everyone's gonna love your music."

"Kathy?" Paul called.

"In here," she answered, washing dishes at the kitchen sink.

"It's official now. Are we all set for Rapid City?"

"I think so," she said, brushing her hair back. "I typed up an order form and your artist profile. We'll need to make copies when we get to Rapid City. I think people need to know what's behind the music."

"Good thinking." Paul dug out a phone book to find out where he could rent a keyboard. He couldn't sit in the mall and sell his music without a live sound to draw people in.

Kathy wiped the counters and dried off her hands. "Cheryll gave me Grandma Toni's phone number. She is going to let us stay in her house in Rapid City so we won't have to get a hotel," Kathy advised, moving a stack of paperwork aside. More often, the kitchen table served as a desk than a place to eat meals.

"Did you find something to use for a cashbox?"

"Got it. I also borrowed a folding table to bring along." Kathy slid onto one of the chairs, lowering her voice. "I don't know if we have enough cash for meals and the change we need. It's pretty tight."

"I know," Paul sighed. "But we're *this* close," he said, holding his forefinger and thumb barely a quarter inch apart.

"Do you think the tribal council would help us out?" Kathy asked. "Something to get us started?"

Paul considered Kathy's suggestion. The community as a whole had been very supportive and encouraged them in their new venture. "It's worth a try…I'll go to the next council meeting and ask. They're supposed to help people in certain financial situations."

Paul followed procedure and requested to be heard on the next agenda. It took all his courage to drive to the tribal headquarters on the appointed day. Paul brought along a written proposal even though he was still required to verbalize his request.

Just as he reached the front doors, Paul lifted his face toward the sky and closed his eyes. "If we can just get our music out there," he whispered. "I want at least one chance, God." Paul took a deep breath and went inside.

Five council members were present plus tribal chairman, Mike Jandreau. "Good evening," Paul said, when it was his turn. He smiled nervously and made eye contact with each individual. "I'd like to share a little about my background and what brings me here today..." Paul shared a shortened version of the full story, including the music and trying to establish a new business venture. He stressed he was looking more for a business loan that could be paid back rather than a handout.

The council politely listened as Paul spoke, but in the end they had to turn him down. "Sorry, Paul, we'd like to help you out, but there are other needs in the community that are more pressing at this time. If we assist you with your business, then we open the door to everyone else. We certainly wish you the best."

"Sure," Paul said, nodding.

• • •

On Thursday afternoon Paul carried the box of precious cargo out to the Oldsmobile. The keyboard and speakers barely fit into the back seat, but with a little maneuvering he managed to get the doors shut. Paul, Kathy and Nicole climbed in the front seat and headed down their long driveway, a trail of dust rising behind them. Nerves on edge, no one spoke the full seven miles into Lower Brule.

Everyone they passed in town waved a friendly gesture of good luck. Word had spread that Paul was going to play his new music for the first time professionally. They had already played one event in St. Cloud, Minnesota, but it involved multiple performers without financial compensation. *This* was the real deal.

"Hey, there's Fritz's truck at the casino," Paul noted.

"They said they'd be eating supper and we could stop and pick up the key for Grandma Toni's apartment."

Paul pulled into the parking lot. "Be right back," he said, dashing toward the casino entrance. In a few moments, Paul exited the same door.

"Hey, Paul!" called Mike Jandreau. "Wait up!" He caught up to Paul in front of the car. "I know the council couldn't give you any money for your trip this weekend, but I'd like to help you out. Here's a little something that'll hopefully help." He handed fifty dollars to Paul. "Good luck, this weekend."

Paul looked at the money, speechless.

Nicole nudged Kathy in the front seat. "Did you see that, Mom?" she whispered.

An answer to prayer, it was just enough to cover their gas expenses. "Thank you, Mike," said Paul. "You don't know how much this means."

"Well, I've been following your story through Cheryll and I really respect what you're doing."

"This makes all the difference in the world, Mike. Thank you."

Paul tucked the money in his jeans pocket and slid into the driver's seat. "Can you believe that, Kath?"

The extra fifty dollars almost felt like a thousand. The mood immediately lightened as they started the three-hour drive to Rapid City. West of Lower Brule farmers harvested corn and wheat in some of the large fields. The dry, warm fall afternoons gave South Dakota ranchers much needed time to prepare for the upcoming winter.

"How many people will be there?" asked Nicole.

"I have no idea," Kathy answered. "I haven't been to a craft show in ages. The woman I spoke with said they get a ton of traffic though."

"What if there's like five people?"

"Then hopefully we'll sell five CDs," laughed Paul.

Grandma Toni's apartment was small, but they were thankful to have a place to stay right in Rapid City. Paul made sure the car was securely locked for the night.

Friday morning the butterflies were distributed equally among Paul, Kathy, and Nicole. "Now I know how you felt pulling up to work in this car," Paul mumbled as they pulled into the parking lot at the civic center. "Maybe we should park back here so no one sees us."

"See what I mean," Kathy said.

They carried their equipment and supplies through the doors marked Vendors. Other crafters were busy wheeling in boxes, crates, and tables. People smiled a friendly hello and kept going, finding their spots in the long rows of temporary booths.

"Right through here," a woman said, glancing at the assigned number. "There's your location." She pointed to an out-of-the-way site under a stairway going to the upper level. "If you need anything else, just holler at one of us," she said before disappearing.

"Under a stair well?" Paul complained, glancing at the undesirable site.

"I didn't know," Kathy said with a shrug of her shoulders.

It didn't take long to set up the keyboard and table. They waited in nervous anticipation for the shoppers to filter through the aisles. Kathy stood next to the table with the CDs and order forms, ready to

greet their first customers. Paul sat behind the keyboard with Nicole next to him, flute in hand, waiting for his signal to begin.

"Let's start with 'Brave Hearts,'" Paul said to Nicole.

"Wait—I need to switch sheets." She pulled out a different page and nodded to Paul.

Women and children strolled along the long rows of vendors. A few men were scattered in the mix of people. Paul smiled broadly and nodded to Nicole, letting his fingers touch the keys in harmony with the background music from the boom box. Nicole came in at just the right time, hitting the notes perfectly.

Kathy tossed her hair behind her shoulders and with a friendly smile watched as the people filtered in. Almost in sync, they'd stop walking and turn their heads to see who was playing the unique music. Then they'd take a few steps, intending to keep walking, but they'd retreat and come back to listen for several minutes, like an invisible force pulling them back. Some stepped in close, heads nodding with the beat of the music.

When Paul and Nicole finished the first song, they were met with an unexpected round of genuine applause. "Good morning," Paul said to the small crowd gathered. "My name is Paul LaRoche." He snuck a quick glance at Kathy and smiled to the audience. "It's good to be here with you this morning," he continued, making eye contact with the listeners. "Let me share just a little background of what we're doing here today…"

The craft show organizer was right—there was plenty of foot traffic. Before long the aisles were jammed. Midway through the morning Kathy turned to Paul with a helpless expression. "That's the last CD, Paul," she half-cried.

"Now what?" he asked with a look of desperation.

"We're scheduled here for the whole weekend," she said. "I'll hand out order forms to everyone else. Just keep playing!"

"This is amazing," he whispered to Nicole. He never dreamed he could sell a full order of CDs in two hours. Maybe they were onto something…

• • •

Encouraged by the response at the craft show, Paul had no hesitation when it came to his music. Something inside him was driving to jump from the frying pan into the fire, taking his wife with him.

"A Christmas concert?" Kathy asked. "That's less than two months away."

"I know."

"Are you sure we can handle this?"

"I'm *absolutely* sure," he said with fervor.

"This isn't a craft show like we just did, stuck in a little corner. You're talking about a full-scale concert with dancers and a traditional drummer—the whole works?"

"Exactly." Paul got up from the keyboard and handed Kathy the draft of his song and dance repertoire.

She glanced at the titles. "But *One Holy Night* hasn't even been released yet."

Paul's eyes beamed with enthusiasm. "That's what marketing is all about, Kath. Getting a jump on it. Getting people interested and enthused so they'll want to buy it when it does come out." He took a deep breath, his emotions surfacing. "Oh, Kathy, this is what it's all about. The blending of the two worlds...it's what I've pictured since we first stepped foot in Lower Brule."

"It makes me nervous, that's all," Kathy said, holding her breath.

"I met with Lakota George last week, he's a local flutist, and Maza Oyate has agreed to play the traditional drum. I can get Steve Lynn to play percussion and Max Elg guitar. I'd like the whole family to be involved, I already asked Shane to play guitar. We can invite dancers from Lower Brule. The people have been so supportive; wouldn't it be great to get them involved?"

"Well, yeah..."

"I think it'll create something positive in both communities."

Sizzz—the frying pan was scorching hot! During the next several weeks neither Paul nor Kathy had time to think while working to ensure a flaw-free, first-ever Brulé concert. Two performances were scheduled at Worthington's Memorial Auditorium in mid-December. Kathy was overwhelmed juggling arrangements for the Friday and Saturday night shows. Finding places for everyone to sleep, rides, and coordinating schedules for all the performers and invited guests became a formidable task.

Bessie Estes, better known to everyone in Lower Brule as Grandma Bessie, was a Lower Brule elder who graduated from college at 65 years of age. She also taught the Lakota language and brought her supplies for making homemade soaps and medicines. Paul asked her husband, Johnny Estes, or Grandpa Johnny, to give the invocation. Johnny and Bessie were also going to make appearances at Worthington schools and give demonstrations.

Headlines in the *Daily Globe*, the local Worthington newspaper, read, *"Summers hopes concert will bridge cultural gaps, Native American performers to visit Worthington Friday, Saturday."* The full piece highlighted Paul's message in the concert and the new album, *One Holy Night.*

Inwardly Paul was thrilled to perform in the very auditorium he'd visited many times as a young student. Long, dark-red velvet curtains graced the old-fashioned wood stage until opening. Aside from a few behind-the-scenes dramatics, the concerts were a hit. Those who had traveled from Paul's ancestral home enjoyed sharing their cultural history with the locals where Paul had grown up. All told, a spirit of oneness was present throughout the holiday season.

. . .

Come January, Old Man Winter stormed in with a furor, burying the Dakotas and western Minnesota in record snowfalls.

"Man, did we pick the year to move out here," Paul said, eyeing the ever-growing drift in front of the house. "Another foot and it'll be higher than the roof."

Kathy watched the deepening snow with apprehension. "What if we can't get shoveled out?" She'd been listening to the weather reports from Rapid City all day.

"We'll be okay," Paul said reassuringly.

The wind and snow battered the windows on all four sides of the house. The snow had started to fall a full 24 hours earlier, and there was no sign of it letting up. Temperatures dropped to single digits, but with the high winds the windchills were well below zero. The school bus brought students home early before the rural roads drifted shut. The hours passed but the view outside didn't change—an endless sea of white in every direction. The cattle huddled against the round stacks of hay in search of protection from the wind.

"Linda called—they're completely snowed in too," Kathy said.

"It's nice to know we're close enough to watch out for each other when it gets bad like this," Paul said.

The blizzard dumped several feet of snow, drifting up to six feet in places. The LaRoches and Thompsons had to wait three days for the plow to make a path all the way out.

"That was Linda," Kathy said, hanging up the phone. "The snow-plow just went by their place so she is going to make a run into town with the pickup for supplies. Do you want to go along?"

"Yeah," Paul said. "Guess we better get in while we can."

"We need *food,* Mom," Shane suddenly piped up. "Get some chips and pop. And how 'bout some of those good sausages. I've been hungry for pancakes and sausages."

"When does he eat all this?" Paul asked.

"About ten o'clock every night I hear him in the kitchen," Kathy advised.

"Don't forget Frosted Flakes. And oh, we're out of frozen pizzas," he said, rubbing his stomach.

"Okay, Hungry Man, get your coat on and help me shovel out the door," Paul said. They had to literally fight and push the door open wide enough in order to squeeze through. They shoveled a narrow path from the steps to the yard where the plow had turned around. The wind had blown the snow in a huge drift against the lilac bushes creating a white wall.

About a half hour later Kathy spotted the pickup coming up the driveway. "Here she comes, Paul." They put on their boots and coats and climbed into the Thompson pickup.

"We're gonna make a quick trip," Linda said, turning the pickup around. "Last time we stayed too long and the road drifted shut before we could get home."

"I've never seen anything like this," Kathy said.

The sky was clear and blue, the sun's rays almost blinding against the white snow. Fences, vehicles, and farm equipment were buried somewhere underneath. Linda took her time, making sure the tires stayed in the center of the roadway.

"Look up there!" Paul exclaimed, pointing straight ahead. Linda slowed the truck as they passed through an area where the drifts were over the hood and now closer to the top of the truck. The drifts were so high the plows could only open the road one lane wide, giving a tunnel-like effect for almost a full mile. Linda swerved slightly and the side mirror rubbed the hard-packed snow. In town the streets were plowed, but the going was slow because cars were buried with only parts sticking through the snow. It was like a scene from a movie.

Before January ended, three full-blown blizzards hit the Northern Plains. Day after day, high winds and blowing, drifting snow filled the view out every window. In parts of South Dakota, icy winds had buried entire homes under 15-foot snowdrifts and had closed the interstate for a time. The Dakotas and Minnesota were reeling from record snowfall. Even after the snows stopped, strong northwest winds caused near zero visibility, extending each winter storm.

The second blizzard brought a surge of arctic air with 40- to 60-miles-per-hour winds that created deadly wind chills approaching 80 degrees below zero. The bone-chilling cold froze cattle in their tracks, devastating many local ranchers.

As January rolled into February, Kathy continually searched for information about malls and art fairs, anywhere that included space for independent vendors.

"Good news…I talked to Don McGlaphlin, manager of the Empire Mall in Sioux Falls. He said we could play there," Kathy announced at the dinner table. "The guy hesitated a little because he doesn't know anything about us or who we are. But he's willing to give us a chance."

"We haven't played in a mall yet," said Nicole.

"Good chili, Mom," Shane said.

"Except the kidney beans," said Nicole.

"Geez, Nikki. You still pick out the beans?" asked Shane.

"Leave it alone," she advised her older brother.

"Anyway," Kathy continued, "I've found they don't take me seriously as a manager if I have the same last name as yours," she said, glancing at Paul, "so I'm going to keep using Summers."

"That's fine with me."

"Can I have more?" Shane asked.

"Go ahead," Kathy answered.

"Ready to practice for a while, Nikki?" asked Paul, pushing his chair back from the table.

"Sure, Dad."

"And you can help clean up the kitchen," Kathy instructed Shane.

"Maybe Dad wants me to play guitar."

"Shane…"

After the kitchen was cleaned, Shane laid on the couch, watching TV. Kathy returned to her notebooks, going over the proposed expenses for the trip to Sioux Falls. As she added it all up, a sickening feeling rose in the pit of her stomach. Another gig meant placing another large order of CDs. Could they sell another full order? It was so much money and there was no guarantee.

She got up from the table and walked to the bedroom, leaning against the door frame. Paul and Nicole were still practicing, going over the song lists. Paul glanced up at Kathy and smiled, then returned his focus to the music.

"It'll be easier the second time," Paul advised his daughter.

"I thought it was fun, Dad." Nicole picked up her flute and played part of "Dream Shield." "Last time I messed up a bunch. I'm not going to make any mistakes this time."

"No one knows any different."

"I want to get it right though." Her eyes reflected the serious tone in her voice.

"Just be yourself," Paul said. "That's all I ask."

"Where are we staying this time?"

"We can stay with Mike," Kathy said, looking over the song sheets.

"Mike who?"

"Mike Spears, Dad's cousin. He lives right in Sioux Falls."

"Cool." Nicole rested her flute in her lap. "My mouth is getting tired, Dad. Can I quit for now?"

"Sure, Nikki. I can see improvement already. You're doing really well. I'm proud of you, sweetheart."

"Thanks, Dad." Nicole took her flute apart and put it in the case. "Tomorrow night again?"

"Sure."

"Night, Mom. Night, Dad." Nicole retreated to her bedroom and shut the door.

"I've been meaning to ask you something," Kathy whispered to Paul, eyeing the hallway to make sure they were alone.

"What's up?"

"How come when Shane's buddy was here last weekend, he spent more time with Nicole than Shane? Didn't you notice?"

"I guess I didn't."

"This kid drives all the way out here from Eden Prairie to see *Shane*, in a winter like this?"

"They played baseball together, they're good friends."

"Not that good of friends," Kathy said, shaking her head.

Paul shrugged his shoulders and turned back to his notes.

"Maybe we should talk to her."

Paul was already absorbed in his playlist.

"Never mind," Kathy sighed and crossed the hall. She changed into her nightgown and robe, sensing the start of another headache. She took some ibuprofen and laid down on the bed. Some days it felt like she was the only one keeping up with the kids. Or worrying about forking out the money for another order.

Just then soft, soothing melodies floated from across the hall. An hour later when Kathy got up to watch the news, Paul was still at it.

She was amazed at his dedication and determination. She walked in and sat beside him on the bench, watching his fingers slide over the keys. She closed her eyes and rested her head on his shoulder, listening to the melodious notes.

"Tired, hon?" he asked.

"I had a headache," she said. "But it's better now."

He reached the volume button and slid it down. "I should probably quit for tonight."

"Don't stop," Kathy said. "I love watching you play."

Pure joy beamed in Paul's eyes. "All right," he said, "this one's just for you."

She immediately recognized the notes—"The Greatest Gift," the song he had composed for their wedding.

First thing the next morning, Kathy placed the call to SOAR. When the Sioux Falls appearance rolled around, Paul loaded the keyboard, CDs, and bags into the Oldsmobile. It was just getting dark when they pulled up to the curb in front of the Spearses' house. Mike had just gotten home from work and he walked down the driveway to greet them, newspaper in hand.

"What is this?" Mike asked, pointing to the front end. "One headlight?"

"Yeah, I haven't been able to get it fixed yet," Paul offered, rubbing his chin.

Mike Spears was a big man with broad shoulders and long hair that he combed back into a ponytail. He crossed his arms and tilted his head. "That is the most pitiful sight I've ever seen, man!" he exclaimed. "You know what they're saying on the rez, don't you?"

"What's that?"

"That you're making the rest of 'em look bad with that car," he laughed. "Man, you and Kathy take my pickup this weekend! You can't show up to play in this wreck."

Paul patted him on the back. "You sure?"

"That's what family is for, bro."

* * *

They weren't exactly overflowing in money, but they were making enough at each event to carry them through to the next one. "Do you think you can make it all the way to St. Cloud?" Kathy asked Paul. "I found a little indoor art festival up there that will let you play." St. Cloud was a college community 90 miles northwest of the Twin Cities, a long haul from Lower Brule.

"I don't know if the car will make it that far, but we'll give it a try."

"I don't have much cash, but it should be enough."

With more determination than money, Paul would find a way to get to the next gig. "By hook or crook, we'll get there," he said to Kathy. It was working. People *liked* the music, he could feel it.

This time just Paul and Nicole piled into the Olds with the equipment. Just as they crossed the state line into Minnesota, the car began to act up. "Hear that, Dad?" Nicole asked.

"It doesn't sound good, does it, Nikki." He slowed his speed a little. "If we can make it to Worthington, I can have someone take a look at it there." As soon as he reached the Worthington exit, Paul pulled into a service station.

"It'll run you about fifty bucks," the mechanic said after a look under the hood.

"Go ahead," Paul said. "We have to get to St. Cloud by Saturday."

"I called Grandma Shirley." Nicole leaned on the desk, watching the mechanic unscrew the bolts. "She said she'd pick us up so we don't have to sit here and wait."

"Good," Paul said, smiling. "I'll bet she has something good to eat for us too."

By the time the car was fixed, Grandma Shirley had given Paul and Nicole a nice home-cooked dinner, along with $50 to pay for the car repair. "Thanks, Shirley," Paul said with a deep hug. "You are something special, you know that?"

"Just let me know that you made it up there okay, will you?" she asked.

"You got it."

Paul and Nicole got back on the road and headed north. "If we cut over to Highway 71 and head up to Morton, there's a casino there called Jackpot Junction. The guy there told me we could play any time we wanted," Paul said, watching the highway signs. "This might be a long shot, but if we can get to Morton, maybe they'll let us set up somewhere and play for a while."

"Go for it, Dad," Nicole said.

Later that night, Paul closed up their equipment and packed it back in the car. "How about that? We made enough money to pay for the hotel, with a little left over for gas. We should get to St. Cloud in plenty of time."

Nicole grinned. Playing music and traveling made a nice break from high school.

· · ·

In keeping with the snowy winter, March, too, had its share of storms. By April, folks were desperately looking forward to any sign of spring.

"I figured it out, Paul," Kathy said one Sunday morning.

"What?" he asked.

"The name Brulé doesn't bring people in because no one knows us. But wherever we've played, people buy the music. As long as I can get us into places where there are a lot of people, we'll be able to sell it." Kathy had started a notebook to log their locations, income, and expenses. Slowly she gained a grasp of the art fair and craft show circuit. And now that they had a little experience, she at least could offer some references when asked.

A few weeks later Fritz and Cheryll stopped over for a cup of coffee. "Oh, any business is hard to run," Cheryll said when the conversation switched from the terrible winter to recent events. "Some days we can hardly get people to show up at the store when they're scheduled to work. So then Fritz or I have to run into town and fill a shift. We never get a break," she sighed.

"I don't know if we should have bought the Squeaky Door when we did," Fritz said. "I thought it would be good for the town, but people in Brulie don't seem to shop there all the time."

"Where do they go then?" Kathy asked.

"Oh, all the way to Chamberlain or maybe Pierre," he said.

"Someday when things slow down I told Kathy I want a couple of those wooden rockers out back where we could sit and watch the sun set each day," Paul said.

"Ooh!" Cheryll exclaimed, raising her hands. "That would be perfect. Wouldn't it, Fritz?"

Fritz merely smiled and nodded.

Cheryll loved Paul's idea. "We could put them on that back porch I want you to build, Fritz. Oh, that'd be so nice. I can picture it already."

Fritz chuckled. "I know what I'll be building this summer."

"I could sit out there with my coffee, and I'll plant lots of pansies to look at," Cheryll said dreamily.

"Purple ones, right?" Kathy asked.

"Of course."

"How's it going with the craft shows?" Fritz asked Paul.

"It's going pretty good, enough to get by," Paul said. "We had a little car trouble this last time, almost didn't make it."

"We have to get you a different car, bro. Even the folks out here are embarrassed for you," Fritz laughed.

"Maybe you're right," Paul said.

● ● ●

On Sunday, April 6, 1997, one final blizzard descended upon the Northern Plains, a real doozy. Once again drifts of 5 to 15 feet developed, along with sustained winds over 45 miles per hour that ripped across the area for nearly 24 hours straight. Peak winds included gusts of 69 miles per hour in Rapid City. Almost all roads were blocked or closed and other forms of travel were banned in most areas. Problems were compounded by the heavy rain and sleet that fell before the blizzard developed, causing widespread power outages. Hardest hit by the blizzard were local ranchers, who suffered major livestock losses as calving season was underway. Less than four days later, another late-season storm produced an additional foot of snow.

Unable to play many places because of the horrific winter, Paul used the days to plan out his strategy. Stranded in the house yet again, he scribbled down thoughts and ideas in a notebook. From his days at the theater in Minneapolis, he figured out a budget for the next several months, whatever it took to bring his dream into reality.

By mid-April, the deep snows were finally melting, causing major flooding along the Red and James rivers in the Dakotas and Minnesota. Now the seven miles into town was pure mud, thick and deep. Paul found it necessary to go into town early in the morning when the road was still frozen hard with ruts rather than go during midday and slip and slide from side to side. It was certainly one for the record books, but Paul, Kathy, Shane, and Nicole had survived their first winter on the rez.

ELEVEN

A Great Gathering

"The more I learn about my culture, the happier I become."

—Linda Thompson

Paul knew his music had a message. With his pure passion burning brightly, he felt compelled to seek larger venues for his music and his story.

"I wonder about Mount Rushmore?" he mumbled, half to himself, half to Kathy.

"Huh?"

"I was thinking Mount Rushmore would be a good place to contact."

"They certainly attract huge crowds all summer," she said. "What are you thinking?"

"Maybe a concert? I don't know." He looked up from the map.

"Either there or Crazy Horse," she suggested.

"We can try there, too, I suppose," Paul said, crossing his arms. "For whatever reason, I have a stronger sense to approach Mount Rushmore. Maybe because of the history between the non-Indians and the Native Americans. After all the injustices that were carried out by the U.S. Army against the local bands, they took away the very land that was sacred to the Lakota and built their own monument.

Maybe I can sell the idea of a Native American performer there, to offer a reconciliation of sorts, to start the healing in the very center of the controversy."

"It's worth a try," she said.

"Want to take a drive out there? I can present *We the People* not only as a CD, but as a full stage concert."

Brulé Live at Mt. Rushmore
Concert for Reconcillation of the Cultures

Treatment
for Proposed Spring/Summer Concert 2002

Prepared By: Paul LaRoche

"Sure," she said. "The summer tourist season is still a couple months away. Maybe this would be a good time to approach them."

"I'll prepare a business plan, something real professional looking."

After Nicole got on the school bus, Paul and Kathy packed the car for a little day trip and took off toward the Black Hills. "When I was a kid, we took a long vacation out west and we came back through the Black Hills," Paul told Kathy. "I wonder now what Mom and Dad were thinking when they drove right past the exit to Lower Brule."

Kathy nodded in agreement. "They probably didn't know your biological family was from Lower Brule, but they certainly knew you were from one of the reservations out here."

When they reached the Hermosa exit, Paul turned west on Highway 40 toward the national monument. The open prairie gave way to dark, pine-forested bluffs that rose unexpectedly and mysteriously out of nowhere. Paul followed the twists and turns of the scenic highway.

"It's so beautiful here," Kathy said, looking at the mix of tree-covered hills and unusual rock formations.

Suddenly the granite mountain loomed in full view, the four presidents' faces centered between sections of bookend natural formations.

The sheer size of the mountain evoked a sense of wonder. Pieces of rock blasted from the mountain in the 1920s flowed downward with a few pine trees poking between the fallen rocks on the steep slope.

Paul found a parking spot on the edge of the lot. "Do you have the CDs?" he asked.

"Yup, I've got everything in this bag," Kathy answered.

They walked up the cement pathway to the visitor center. "Here comes a couple park rangers," Kathy said, smiling as the two men approached.

"Good afternoon," Paul said, reaching out for a handshake.

"What can we do for you?" one of them asked. Both men stood with their arms folded, looking at Paul, their faces stern and unfriendly.

"We're looking for an events manager," Kathy said, surprised by their demeanor.

"What about?" the taller man asked tersely.

"Actually," Paul began, now a little nervous as he began to explain. "I have some music that I think would be perfect for visitors at the park." He shared a little bit of his background and explained their intentions. "So we're wondering if there is someone to talk to about possibly playing here." He pointed to the *We the People* CD in Kathy's hand.

The first man started shaking his head slowly. "No," he said, "I don't think that will work here in the park. Besides, we already have entertainment booked most of the season."

"Sure. I understand," Paul said. "Maybe you could book us for one of the weekends they're not scheduled. Just to see how it goes."

"Nope," he said before Paul finished speaking. "Your music wouldn't sell here. Sorry." With his hands perched firmly on his hips, the man spoke very matter-of-factly. "Our show is very patriotic."

"That's perfect," Kathy interjected with enthusiasm. She handed the CD to them. "Take a look. That's exactly what this music is all about."

The two men glanced at the drawing on the CD cover and then at Paul's long hair. "Umm, I don't think it'll work. Sorry, folks." He thrust the CD back in Kathy's hand. "Maybe you could try somewhere else, but not here." They remained with feet planted, preventing Paul and Kathy from entering the visitor center.

Mouth ajar, Kathy was stunned. For the first time in her married life, she had witnessed racial discrimination against her husband. "I can't believe this!" she cried under her breath as they walked away. "It's like we're being kicked off the mountain."

Paul hurried his step. "Maybe they get people coming here all the time and they have to do that."

"No, Paul. It was plain as day—they could see you're Indian and didn't want any part of it, for that reason and that reason alone. They branded you as 'trouble.'" Her words echoed in the mountain air as they crossed the parking lot to the car.

"Welcome to the other side, huh." Paul slid behind the wheel and shut the door.

"Now what?" she asked, still at a loss for what to say or think.

"As long as we're this far, let's head up to Deadwood. It's a tourist trap kind of town. Maybe we can find something there."

. . .

Nicole followed through on her assurance and graduated from high school in Lower Brule. Paul and Kathy couldn't have been prouder. The class was dramatically smaller than Shane's graduating class, but both kids now had diplomas. It was great to see young people who had overcome particularly tough obstacles walk across the stage and receive their diplomas and congratulations.

Shane decided he needed to do something with his life besides hunting and playing softball. He registered at the Vermillion Campus of the University of South Dakota for the fall semester. In preparation, he joined the Chamberlain amateur baseball team as their starting pitcher. Another player's dad was the baseball coach at the university. He helped Shane accumulate a record in order to be eligible for the U's team.

The family was in a comfortable groove, acclimated to Lower Brule and the South Dakota prairie, and their fledgling business was slowly gaining momentum.

"I can't get over the connection with the fans," Kathy said one evening. She unfolded a piece of handwritten stationery. "Listen to this lady from Yankton. 'I can't tell you how much your music means to me. What a difference it's made in my life! I cherish the times I can see Brulé in person. Your music gives me peace and contentment all day, it's touched me like none other...' It goes on and on, Paul. Letter after letter." She held up a handful of envelopes. "'Your music inspires me, peace to your journey.' Or this one, 'I am thrilled to meet such wonderful people. I am blessed by your warmth.'"

The post office had three stacks of rubber-banded envelopes waiting for Paul on his last trip. "It's so humbling. I never imagined it would connect with people so deeply. I think you should book us in as many places as possible."

"I'm trying," Kathy said. "I've been making tons of phone calls."

"By the way, I started looking at pickups in Sioux Falls. We can't keep renting a truck and trailer, it's too expensive."

"I agree, Paul. We've gotta keep this thing going."

• • •

In mid-June Paul, Kathy, and Nicole were on their way home from northwestern Minnesota. Kathy's sister Cindy had gotten married and they had driven to Fergus Falls to be part of the wedding celebration. It was a beautiful, warm weekend with a chance to catch up on news from family and friends on the Frisch side that they hadn't seen in a long time. Paul and Kathy had gotten more news than they bargained for: Nicole confided to a cousin that she'd just found out she was a few months pregnant.

The baby's father was from a good family and lived in Minneapolis, but marriage didn't appear to be the right option. In fact, Nicole hadn't seen him since his midwinter visit to Lower Brule. Never something parents are quite prepared for, the news caught Paul and

Kathy completely off guard. Side by side, they sat down with Nicole and offered their love and support which she gladly accepted.

. . .

The first full year promoting Brulé had given Kathy a good grasp on the craft show and mall circuit in South Dakota and Minnesota. Little by little she expanded to bigger shows. By the summer of 1997 she had events scheduled in Wisconsin and Iowa as well. They were close to selling out their inventory at each event and breaking even on the travel expenses. Paul had purchased a used pickup and a 5x7 trailer to haul their expanding inventory and equipment. It was the most cost-effective way to operate their new livelihood. The Oldsmobile hung on for a while, but eventually it cost more to fix than it was worth. Paul drove it behind the house and parked it next to the pasture. He got out, keys in hand. Something about the car represented that moment in time when Paul changed within. He wasn't sure what to do with it, but for now he didn't want to let it go.

"I booked us a spot at the Sturgis bike rally in August," Kathy noted, pointing her pen at Paul. "You wanted a place with a lot of people…"

Paul grinned. Bikers. At this point, they were willing to do whatever it took to keep it going. "Perfect," he smiled.

. . .

Linda's pickup rolled up the long driveway just before dusk. Although nearly ten o'clock, the sun had just dipped behind the distant horizon. The western sky was all aglow in rich, vivid colors. In a colorful whisper of truth, each sunset in the quiet South Dakota skies declared a unique work of art. Streaks of lavender, salmon, and red painted a wondrous tapestry, calling out to all within view to stop for a moment and acknowledge the Creator's sovereign artistry.

Paul walked from behind the house when he heard the vehicle approach. "Hey, Linda. How's it going?" he asked through the open driver's window.

Linda opened the door and stepped down. "Good. How are you?"

"Couldn't be better," he smiled, wearing his usual blue jeans and a sleeveless T-shirt. He brushed some dirt off his backside. "Just came from a long walk along the river's edge." Paul leaned on the tall walking stick he had taken along. "I love it there, so peaceful and reflective. Just sitting, listening, thinking."

Linda rested her eyes on Paul's frame. "Coming home has been good for you. I'm so glad you're here. This is where you came from, where you belong."

"Mmmm, I could say the same for you."

She nodded and a smile slowly evolved. "Yes, moving back home has been good for me too. I feel like I'm rediscovering my culture and heritage, learning more about myself. It seems the more I learn about my culture, the happier I become. Life is good on the home place these days." Linda turned around and grabbed a buckskin shirt from inside the cab. "I finished your new war shirt," she said, handing it to Paul.

Paul took it from her and held it open with both hands. Completely hand sewn, it was quite stunning. It was made from white buckskin with beautiful hand-beaded accents on the triangle at the neck, and long fringe on the arms and across the back with periwinkle and beads here and there on the fringes.

"See the buffalo tassels? And I put little hawk bells here on the fringes," she said, pointing to the sleeves.

"Oh, Linda…it's beautiful," he said. "What a gift you have."

"Thank you," she smiled. "The elders told me among our people long ago, the *Wicasa Yatapika*, or shirt wearers, were men who had earned the right to wear painted scalp shirts. Demonstrations of great sacrifice and bravery were required in order to rank this high in traditional Lakota society. I think some of those elders who are in the spirit world, my ancestors, their spirits come to help me, guide my hands when I create these things. I know they do. I feel them when they're here."

"It'll be an honor to wear it at our next event," Paul said. He gathered the soft leather between his fingers and together they walked toward the front door.

"Are you gonna be home for the Pow Wow next month?" she asked.

"Wouldn't miss it," Paul answered.

•   •   •

Main Street Sturgis during the infamous bike rally lived up to its purported reputation. The annual event ran during the first full week of August. Thousands upon thousands of motorcycles were parked in rows on Main Street while the riders strolled from shop to shop or bar to bar. Every single square inch within blocks of downtown was flooded with people looking to sell, buy, or hang out.

Brulé was booked in the heart of downtown for the full week. Paul was thrilled to see the endless sea of potential buyers streaming past their booth day and night. Their site was in a little courtyard, half inside and half outside, a perfect way to draw in the people walking past. Paul borrowed a traditional drum to add to the live sound and arranged for a couple guys to play drum throughout the week. The hot, sticky days drained the band members physically, especially Nicole, who was not feeling well because of her pregnancy.

In between sets on the second day, a tall man with broad shoulders approached Paul. "Hey, man, Chuck Davis," he said, reaching for Paul's hand.

Paul shook his open hand. "Nice to meet you." He took a bandana and wiped the sweat off his forehead. "Sorry, man, it's steaming out here today. And we get so hot playing."

Chuck nodded. "I understand, it's a killer out there. Say, I really like your music. I heard you were looking for a drummer." He had a friendly face and long, dark hair pulled back in a ponytail that fell all the way down his back. His brown, deep-set eyes and distinctive features clearly indicated Native American heritage.

"Yeah, actually," Paul said, glancing at the empty drum. "We are. Do you play?"

"Sure do. I'm from Pine Ridge, been playing for years." He put his hands on his hips and smiled a friendly, eager grin. "Should I go get my sticks?"

Paul liked his easygoing nature and outward enthusiasm. "Sure, man. Want to play the next set?"

Chuck retrieved his sticks and joined Paul and Nicole for the next set. He was a natural at drumming and immediately sensed the timing and rhythm for Paul's music. The week was a huge success. Paul and Kathy may have come to Sturgis as greenhorns, but by the end of the week they had enough sense to recognize Brulé's market potential. Chuck Davis proved to be exactly the type of band member Paul was looking for. He was from the Bad Wound family on Pine Ridge and had a very traditional background. They mutually agreed that Chuck would live with Paul and Kathy for logistical reasons, rather than have to drive all the way out to Pine Ridge between gigs. As long as their houseguests pitched in with household chores, Paul and Kathy didn't mind.

After he joined the group, oftentimes Paul and Chuck sat up late talking. Paul could ask questions about the culture, the lifestyle, things he didn't have a chance to know growing up. Chuck was familiar with the traditional ceremonies, and he'd been a Pow Wow singer. He had even participated in the Sun Dance, the most revered traditional ceremony in Sioux culture. Paul admired Chuck's ways. As a single father of two boys, he fit in nicely with the Brulé family. After all, that's what Brulé had become—more a family than a band.

* * *

Patches of puffy white clouds dotted the otherwise bright blue summer sky. The normal population for Lower Brule held steady around 1,300, but during the second weekend in August the town exploded with three large festivals running simultaneously: the Pow Wow, the Professional Indian Rodeo, and the biggest softball tournament of the year. By Friday afternoon the dry, dusty grounds were beginning to fill with vendors and coordinators working the annual three-day extravaganza. Paul could hardly find a place to park with all three events in full gear. He found a narrow opening on a grassy area near the Pow Wow grounds.

"Wow, Dad! I've never seen so many people in Lower Brule," said Nicole.

"Never thought you'd see a traffic jam, did ya?" he laughed.

Paul, Kathy, and Nicole followed other groups of families heading toward the center of activity. Grandparents, parents, children, strollers with babies—every generation was well represented. Many spectators looked of Indian ancestry, but quite a few looked white, *wasicu,* or a mix of the two races. Those heading to the Pow Wow wore the traditional regalia while others came in regular street clothes, shorts, jeans and T-shirts. A young boy, barely four or five years old, dressed in long fringed yarn of blues and aquas sucked on a snow cone flavored the same shade of blue as his regalia.

"What a cutie," Nicole commented as the boy looked up and grinned.

Across the way, the young men and women participating in the rodeo stood out in Wrangler blue jeans, crisply ironed western shirts, and cowboy hats. Softball players crowded the benches on either side of the field between posted games. Several crafters set up inside the perimeter with tents to shade them from the strong August sun. Most of the food vendors used the small buildings while the self-contained dealers lined up inside the fence surrounding the Pow Wow grounds. Smells of fry bread, the infamous Indian taco, and corn and tripe soup wafted through the late afternoon air. Kathy and Nicole stopped to admire some of the Native American crafts made of beadwork—earrings, necklaces, barrettes and bracelets—plus blankets and carvings. Because of the heat, organizers made sure there was plenty of cold water available.

Ever since Paul had witnessed his first Pow Wow, he couldn't wait to experience it again. In the center of the arena the flags flew tall and stately, waiting for the Pow Wow director to announce the order of dances. Each morning began with a flag raising ceremony. The local Native American military veterans, and anyone else who wanted to be present were on hand to raise the American flags. Some were memorials representing deceased Native American veterans who were members of the Lower Brule Sioux Tribe.

Spectators placed extra lawn chairs around the inside of the arena, in addition to the bleacher seating. The Missouri River offered the perfect backdrop to the arena that was painted in the traditional colors. With no alcohol allowed, it presented a welcoming environment for all ages. Little kids were everywhere and it was commonplace for all the adults to keep a watch over them. Drum groups set up chairs in circles in assigned spots around their drum, practicing parts of their songs prior to the official start.

"Fritz and Cheryll are over there," Kathy said, pointing. "They brought some lawn chairs and blankets."

For many Lakota people, the Pow Wow was the true essence of a great family gathering. Several of Cheryll's siblings and their extended families stopped to stay hello or find a place close by to sit. Many of the Thompsons were also planning to attend throughout the weekend. "Linda said she'll be dancing with one of her granddaughters," announced Kathy.

"How are you feeling, Nicole?" Cheryll asked.

"Better today," Nicole said, rubbing her belly. At seven months along, her round tummy now protruded underneath her crimson cotton blouse. "I had a tough time in Sturgis last week. It was so hot during the late afternoons."

"Yeah, I heard. You better take care of yourself and that little one."

"I will," Nicole said, lowering herself into a lawn chair. "Mom kept a close eye on me."

"How's Shane doing?" Cheryll asked.

"He's having a great time playing baseball; their team is undefeated. He starts at USD in a couple of weeks," Kathy said.

"Good for him," Cheryll said.

The Friday evening festivities kicked off with a feed for the dancers and spectators before the Grand Entry, when the dancers enter the ring and are first seen in full regalia. Grouped according to age, hundreds of dancers lined up, standing patiently as they waited for the designated time to enter the arena.

The *eyapaha,* or announcer, began. "Good evening! Please stand in honor of our veterans," he said into the microphone. The *eyapaha* then named the drum that would play for the Grand Entry. Everyone complied while veterans carrying the Eagle Feather Staff and national, state, tribal, and veterans' flags entered the arena first.

"The Eagle Feather Staff is the most important flag because it represents all Native Americans," Cheryll explained. It displayed eagle feathers, beadwork, and buffalo fur, and the carrier carefully secured it in the center.

"Now we'll have a Giveaway," said the announcer.

Paul leaned over to Cheryll. "What's a Giveaway?"

Just then several older women seated nearby giggled, including Cheryll's mother, Violet. "Oh, we sure have a lot to teach this one!" they laughed.

Cheryll grinned and answered Paul's question. "People can have a memorial for someone at the Pow Wow, with a Giveaway. And then that family will sponsor the meal for that part of the Pow Wow, like this family did tonight. You watch, they'll have some people get up and talk about the person, a type of honoring, then they'll give away something to everyone here."

"Everyone?" Kathy inquired.

Cheryll nodded. "Oh, yes. See all the star quilts over there? Plus all the gifts in the center of the arena? The family will hand out all of them."

"What's the meaning behind it?" Paul asked.

"The Giveaway is done to teach that giving things away in our everyday life is good. Years ago they taught that an act of giving will return to you. It's part of a healthy, spiritual life," Cheryll continued. "To detach from materialism and over abundance, sort of a natural process of equalization."

Paul nodded in understanding.

"After the prayer and honor song, they'll start the Giveaway," Cheryll advised.

Soon family members of the honored person dispersed the gifts to every person present. Paul was mesmerized as the ceremony unfolded before his eyes. As soon as the Giveaway ended, the Grand Entry began. The dancers entered by category and danced in single file keeping time with the drum beat, following the sun, moving clockwise around the arena in rhythm with the drum.

"Dancing Feathers," Paul thought, the song title he'd chosen after first viewing a Pow Wow dance, *beautiful dancing feathers*. He watched them step and bob into the arena in order of male traditionals first, seniors, men, and youth, followed by grass dancers, and then the male fancy dancers. They were followed by the women traditionals, the elders first, women, teens, and little girls, then the jingle dancers and finally the fancy shawl dancers.

After all the dancers had entered, the announcer's voice echoed loudly, "Now please join me in prayer." He began in Lakota, "*Tunkasila, Wakan Tanka, unsi malakaye leunpetobe omakeyayl*. Grandfather, Great mystery, take pity on me—on this day help me. *Leanpetukin*, today is a good day. To God, who gave us our ways, to thank you for the items that fulfill the way our elders lived. We are all your children, all your tribes. Bless our people. We are proud of our elders at our celebration." Next the flag and veterans songs were sung, followed by words of welcome. Visiting dignitaries were also introduced, followed by the royalty, princesses and junior princesses from home and other communities.

"See how the dancers create a welcoming circle of fellowship?" Cheryll asked Nicole.

Entranced, Nicole nodded. "Explain what the outfits are," she said. "What are they called again?"

"Regalia," answered Cheryll. "Okay. See that man right there with the eagle-feather bustle, ribbon shirt, and breechcloth who looks like a hunter or warrior?"

"Yeah," Nicole and Kathy nodded.

"He is a Traditional Dancer," she explained. "Notice some of their faces are also painted. Sometimes you'll see a large headdress of feathers with long trailers in a plume. Years ago, the men were showier than the women, like wild birds. Now over there, those men with the long fringes of yarn or ribbons, they are Grass Dancers."

A group of young boys all wore the fringed regalia in bright blues, greens and reds, with bandanas on their heads. Many of the male dancers carried an item of significance, a weapon trimmed in animal fur or a shield painted and decorated in feathers. One dancer's knife was held in place near his waist with a beaded sheath.

"Want some water?" Cheryll asked Nicole.

"Thanks." Nicole twisted open the top and took a drink. "Are you and Fritz coming back tomorrow?"

"For a while," Cheryll answered. "The store sponsors one of the softball teams, so we have to make sure we're at the field when their game is scheduled. And tomorrow night my cousin is in the horse races after the rodeo, so I want to see him, too." Cheryll shook her head. "I wish we didn't have all three events running at the same time, and then the rest of the year—nothing!" she laughed. "They could spread our fun out a little bit."

Paul and Fritz sat next to each other in lawn chairs, chatting as they watched the dancers. "See the bone chokers?" Fritz asked.

"Yeah," Paul nodded.

"Those were worn years ago by the men to keep their throats from being cut."

"Really?"

"And the breastplate too."

"Notice how the men's are different from the women's? The men's bones go across and the women's are up and down."

A heavyset man in his forties with a somber expression danced past them wearing a beautiful breastplate of bone and buffalo horn hairpipe, with deerhide ties and horsehair tassels. Like a kaleidoscope of ever changing prisms, the circle of dancers was a literal splash of color and sound, their side-step and twirling movements pure rhythms of grace.

"*Oloway,* songs, bring us together," the *eyapaha* said, introducing the host drum group. As the evening progressed, the drum groups took turns, each one singing and drumming at the appointed time. One man held a microphone close to the drum to maximize the song and beat. Some drum groups were local, but others had traveled a great distance to perform. It was a great honor to sing and drum at the Pow Wow.

"It's kind of hard to talk while they're playing," Cheryll shouted. "When they stop again, I'll finish…"

They listened to the chanting and drumming, *boom, boom-boom, boom, boom-boom,* like a heartbeat loudly echoing from the speakers.

"Look up," the *eyapaha* suddenly announced. "Many times when the people are gathered together, the *wanbli,* eagle, soars. There he is…maybe this will be a *anpetu waste,* a good day." Most spectators glanced upward into the deep blue sky as the eagle continued to circle, gracefully gliding high above the arena.

The stunning visual of the bald eagle soaring overhead sent shivers down Paul's spine. With a wingspan up to seven feet, the white head and tail feathers were clearly visible as it hovered in flight. Paul's eyes followed the symbolic bird until it was out of view. Since coming to Lower Brule there were moments where he felt completely overwhelmed with emotion, and this was certainly one of them.

After a short break the announcer introduced the next drum group. "Open your hearts to the drum, ladies and gentlemen. Somebody is going to get a blessing. Let the spirit come in."

Boom, boom-boom, boom. "Yi, ya! Yiah, ya, yi, oh yeah, yi..." The young men began their next song.

"Here come the traditional women dancers," Cheryll said.

"Look—there's Linda and Dani," said Nicole.

Linda's dress was made of navy blue trade wool, edged in yellow ribbon with courie shells sewn all over the top. Dani's buckskin dress was made from the hides of antelope that her great-grandfather had shot years ago. The dress has been handed down to Dani by her Gramma Linda.

"Linda looks so stately and dignified," Kathy commented, snapping a few pictures. Her hair was neatly braided with colorful accessories, wrapped with long river-otter fur strips. Other women left their hair untouched; while their moccasin leggings were covered in pretty beaded Native patterns. The women dancers stepped lightly and bobbed slightly up and down with the beat of the drum. The traditional women's dancing looked easy to the eye, but Linda had said it was quite difficult and very tiring to dance in place.

"The regalia for Jingle Dancers are covered with sewn-on, wrapped tin cones that jingle in time with every step and movement," she noted. The jingle dresses sounded like rushing water...*whoosh, whoosh, whoosh...*the dancers' movements were smooth and fluid, feet barely touching the grass with each beat.

"I love watching them," Kathy noted, as they passed in front.

"Oh, I never get tired of the Pow Wow," Cheryll said. "Year after year, it's the same, but I wouldn't miss it for the world."

"See that girl?" Cheryll asked Nicole. She pointed to a teenage girl coming toward them, probably 14 or 15 years old. Her hair was divided in two longs braids with mink pelts tied onto the end of each. She wore a long red skirt, red leggings, and she held a red shawl with long white ribbons. "She's called a Fancy Shawl Dancer." The girl spread out her arms and twirled in a full circle, opening the shawl to show the pattern of ribbons lining the back.

"Throughout the weekend they go through a whole list of dances... the Traditional Dancers, Fancy Dancer, Fancy Shawl, Flag Song, Honor Song, Veterans Dance and various levels of competition dances," Cheryll said.

"I love the little kids," said Nicole. "Look, Mom—it's as though dancing is as natural as walking." Sure enough, a cluster of little girls only two or three years old stepped and bobbed in time, full of smiles and laughter as they made their way around the arena. Many of them had been first introduced to the sound of the drums as infants. A blonde girl in a pale lavender jingle dress stumbled, but quickly recovered and kept right on dancing, barely missing a step.

Paul leaned back in his lawn chair, watching and absorbing yet another new part of his heritage. He was so moved he didn't want the evening assembly to end. The colors, the pride, the history—this culture amazed him at every turn. Was it his imagination or was his heart in sync with the pounding drum beats. *Boom, boom-boom, boom...*

If people from my other world could only see this—how rich, how wondrous, how embracing—they would not be afraid of our people. But they will never come here. How can I bring them to this world? How can I bring this to the white world?

TWELVE

Paha Sapa
Sacred Land of the Lakota

A cool wind and intermittent showers hung over the South Dakota plains for the third day in a row, coating the grass with a heavy mist. Paul threw on a hooded sweatshirt and stepped outside to unlock the back door of the trailer. Much to his dismay, his relatively new trailer was already a bit crowded with the ever-expanding equipment—drum, keyboard, speakers, microphones, tipi with poles—plus their music inventory carried in large plastic tubs. He recently added a white nylon covering on poles to help protect them from the elements during the outdoor events.

With Chuck's advice, Paul had purchased a traditional drum for Brulé. Made from a hollowed out cottonwood tree trunk, it was covered in stretched buffalo hide and hung on a four-legged wooden stand. Kathy found a crafter to paint *Brulé* on a long piece of fringed buckskin with bead and feather accents which she hung along the front of the keyboard. Little by little they were collecting a fair amount of paraphernalia to enhance the Native elements of the band.

Kathy pulled two large travel bags from her bedroom to the top of the stairs. "Nicole!" she called. "It's time to go. Is your suitcase in the trailer?"

"Five minutes," Nicole called back from her room.

Chuck brought his duffle bags out to the trailer and helped Paul reorganize some of the equipment.

Kathy pulled one of the bags down the stairs and opened the screen door half-way. "Paul, did Nicole bring all her stuff out?"

"Not yet," he called from inside the trailer.

Kathy shook her head and started out the door with the bag.

"Hold on, Kathy. I'll get those." Paul jumped down from the trailer and hurried to help her. He grabbed both bags and carried them to the trailer.

"I still need to grab that little cooler," Kathy said, pulling up the hood on her nylon jacket. "Otherwise, that should be everything."

"I'll get it." Chuck went inside and grabbed the cooler. "Are we set?"

"Just about," Paul said, glancing at his watch. He wanted to be in Milwaukee, Wisconsin, by eight that night.

"It's really turned cold," Kathy said, stepping outside into the dreary, wet morning. "We better bring the leather jackets along."

"Good idea," Paul said. "There's room back here."

Just then Nicole charged out the door at full speed, one bag slung over her shoulder, another small one in her hand, and a bagel in hand. "I'm ready!"

The drive from Lower Brule to Milwaukee was 663 miles, meaning ten hours on the road, allowing three stops for gas and food. Through trial and error they were adjusting to life on the road and traveling, much like a 1997 version of the Partridge Family.

Eleven long hours later Paul pulled into the motel parking lot an hour behind schedule. The rear tires on the trailer kept leaking and he had to stop several times to fill them. Paul contemplated buying two new tires while they were in Milwaukee as he eyed his options for a parking spot.

"Hurry up, Dad," Nicole said with urgency from the back seat. "I need some air."

"Two seconds, I just need to find a spot big enough for this trailer," said Paul, making a full circle with the large rig.

"Dad, I'm serious. I need out, now." Nicole leaned forward and grabbed the door handle. She flung open the door and took a deep breath, still occasionally nauseous from riding.

"Are you okay?" Kathy asked.

"Yeah," she said, holding her hand on her stomach.

"Come in with me, maybe there's a vending machine with some crackers to help settle your stomach," Kathy suggested.

Paul and Chuck checked the load; a few things had shifted, but overall everything was still in place.

"When are we setting up?" Chuck asked.

"In the morning. I don't want our stuff out overnight," Paul replied.

After dinner, they retreated to their rooms for the night. Kathy stretched out on the bed while Paul reviewed his play list.

The Indian Summer Festival in Milwaukee began in 1985 and was growing in popularity each year, drawing tens of thousands each day. Designed to showcase American Indian musicians, crafters, and entertainers, the outdoor festival offered both traditional and contemporary formats. Held at lakeside Henry Maier Festival Park, the three-day event captured a multitude of Native American sights and sounds. Kathy was thrilled to get Brulé booked as one of the musical entertainers. Paul had heard good things about Indian Summer and wanted Brulé to make a fine first appearance.

Early the next morning the group reassembled and drove to Henry Maier Park to unload. The trick, he'd learned, was to park as close as possible. Each item had to be unloaded from the trailer in sequential order, one piece at a time, and hooked up accordingly. Early on Paul decided there was no need to join a health club since carrying the heavy pieces and bulky speakers was a complete physical workout. Within time, it became second nature to follow an exact procedure: check the PA system, troubleshoot, and work out any technical problems, all before the designated performance time. Often any number of things could—and did—go wrong. Extension cords that didn't reach far enough, fuses that burned out, stage positions that were too high or too low—the list was endless.

On this September morning all went well and the band enjoyed a little down time before the first set. By midmorning, the clouds cleared and bright sunshine spilled across the park grounds. Festival goers seemed to enjoy the musky crispness of the fall morning and didn't mind the cool breeze coming off the lake. Indian Summer proved to be everything Kathy had been told. The event was geared toward family fun and everyone in attendance thoroughly enjoyed the multitude of activities. Brulé was an immediate hit, with large crowds watching each performance throughout the full three days. During breaks Paul and Kathy had a chance to chat with other people connected with the festival, increasing their network of organizers and participants. Come Sunday, Kathy was tickled when organizers invited Brulé back for next year's festival.

From Milwaukee, Paul drove to an apple festival in La Crosse, Wisconsin, before returning to South Dakota for another craft show in Sioux Falls. The steady schedule gave Paul and Kathy great peace of mind. As September rolled into October, Kathy and Nicole began preparing the house for the baby. On weekend gigs in Sioux Falls or other larger cities, they made stops at the shopping centers for infant essentials. With Shane in college, the family swapped bedrooms and the smallest was now filled with a changing table, crib, and baby necessities.

When Nicole reached the final month of pregnancy she developed a bladder and kidney infection. The doctor in Lower Brule recommended Nicole transfer her care to a larger medical center. After being treated in Sioux Falls, doctors ordered Nicole on bed rest for the last four weeks.

"Now what do I do, Mom?" she asked. A worried expression covered her young face. She sat sideways on the exam table, legs crossed and swinging slowly, hands in her lap.

"It's okay. This is the best thing for you and the baby," Kathy advised. She brushed back the hair from Nicole's temple, soothing the worried look from her face. "Mike Spears already said you're welcome to stay at their house so you can be close to the hospital. They'll make room for us like always."

Kathy and Nicole returned to the waiting room. "Dad, I won't be able to play at the gig next weekend," she said, blinking back tears.

"That's okay, sweetheart. It won't be the same without our pretty girl front and center. We'll just have to make do with the ol' boys," he said with a gentle hug. "It's more important for you to take care of yourself."

"I know," Nicole sighed. She rested her head on Paul's shoulder, cherishing the feel of her dad's arm around her.

• • •

In 1997 SOAR records officially released *One Holy Night*. Paul's marketing and creative senses were hard at work. "We need to book more Christmas concerts," he said, glancing up from his studio equipment.

"Paul! Can we just take it one step at a time," Kathy pleaded. "We've got enough on our plate."

He stood up and smiled. "C'mon, we're ready to take it to the next level," he said, turning Kathy around by the shoulders to face him. "A large video screen, maybe a second tipi, lighted evergreens on stage, our own regular dancers in full regalia."

"Don't you have big ideas?" she asked.

"The one in Worthington was a smashing success, as they say."

"That's because everyone we know from both Worthington and Lower Brule were there! No one else knows Brulé."

"They will in time," he said with confidence.

"The concerts are *so* expensive to put on," Kathy said. "We're safer doing the art fairs and craft shows."

"Since when have we ever played it safe?" Paul's expression turned more serious. "We can do this, Kathy." His steady gaze penetrated her eyes, waiting for her response. He couldn't do it without her approval, her belief.

"I don't doubt you, Paul," she said, her sapphire eyes meeting his gaze. "I've said it many times, I believe in what we're doing or I wouldn't be zigzagging all across the country in a pickup every week-end." She kissed him on the lips, a deep passionate kiss. "You win, Paul Summers LaRoche."

. . .

On November 21, 1997, Paul and Kathy were summoned to the hospital in Sioux Falls. Following a smooth labor and delivery, their first grandchild arrived, a little girl named Jade Marie. The shape of her face and her tiny nose reminded Paul and Kathy of Nicole when she was first born. An air of excitement filled the house with the little addition as friends and family stopped by to see the new mom and baby. Even at a young age, motherhood fit Nicole and she eased into her new role comfortably.

Jade's presence in the house, the sweetness and innocence of a tiny newborn somehow brought a balance that they had been missing. For Paul, on days when all went wrong in the big, bad world, one look at Jade's sleeping face erased all his troubles. He'd gently pick her up and watch helplessly as one tiny smile melted his heart.

. . .

In preparation for their concerts, Paul and Kathy wanted to keep adding to the stage presence. Only video could give the audience a true picture of Lower Brule and the South Dakota prairie, enhancing the music with a powerful visual.

"Let's get some footage at Fort George," Paul suggested. "Or what's left of it." In truth the only building still standing was the church, now weathered and windbeaten, the windows broken out. A simple wooden cross perched high on top the cupola proclaimed a message of hope and restoration from the days of long ago.

The land all around the church and cemetery was now pasture. Separate fences had been erected around the church and cemetery to keep cattle from causing further damage. Remnants of a stone path led from the church to the cemetery where the parishioners lay in rest. A narrow row of cedars lined the entrance to the cemetery, angled perfectly with the tallest in the center. A single wooden cross stood between the trees and the markers.

Holy Name Chapel

Paul and Kathy hadn't been back to the cemetery since Fritz first brought them a couple of years earlier. The mild January day was clear and windy as Kathy turned on the video camera, ready to capture the peaceful setting. Paul stooped to read the headstone on his mother's grave. *Bessie Arlene LaRoche, August 2, 1918 – January 7, 1969.* Part of him wanted to know her, to love and understand her, but he would never have that chance. The cancer took her when Paul was only 14, completely unaware of her pain and suffering. Did she think about him then, during her last days? He could only wonder as he stood before his mother's final resting place.

Stone markers also stood at the resting spot of Arlene's parents, Ben and Ruth Thompson. There were even ones dating back to Ben's parents, Joseph and Mary Thompson. Joseph's simply read, *Joseph Thompson, 1863 – 1949,* with no sign of his Indian name, *Hotanka.*

Paul and Kathy followed the path over to the church. It was here his ancestors found peace, inside the tiny sanctuary of Holy Name Chapel, where Mary loved to sing the hymns in Lakota, and Ruth played the organ for many years.

Paul and Kathy stepped inside the doorway, walking with caution as some of the floorboards were deteriorating. The wind blew through the broken windows, a remnant of a lace curtain caught in the weathered opening. Signs of animals that had found their way inside were visible. The interior was empty other than a few scattered pews and sections of the altar. Pieces of the ceiling were hanging, exposing the peaked roof line.

"Can't you just picture it?" Kathy asked. "Years ago when they all gathered here?"

Paul nodded and stepped into a side room. "Kath—look! The organ is still here!"

"Oh, my goodness!" she said, looking around his shoulder at its dilapidated condition.

"Someone should get it out before it gets ruined," Paul said. "This is priceless."

"You're right, it'd be a shame to let it sit here and ruin."

"We'll have to talk to Fritz or Uncle Bill," he said. "This is the very organ that Grandma Ruth used to play," Paul said, touching it gingerly. "Oh...imagine the songs coming from this ol' church, the voices singing the old hymns. How precious..." He closed his eyes, recalling the voices of the Comanche elders who had recorded the hymns down in Albuquerque that night, how beautiful they had sounded. He could almost hear them again in the wind.

● ● ●

Thankfully, the winter of 1997–98 proved to be much milder than the previous, record-setting year. Before long, Nicole was playing with the band once again and little Jade accompanied them to almost every gig. By spring of 1998, Brulé was performing on a consistent basis all across the Upper Midwest: South Dakota, Minnesota, Wisconsin, Iowa, Kansas, Nebraska, and into Colorado. Whenever there was a long enough break between gigs, they were happy to turn off the freeway at Highway 47 and head north to Lower Brule. Everyone in town always waved a friendly hello as the pickup and trailer passed through town and headed down the long gravel road to their house on the bend.

Just like when they first dated, Paul and Kathy were on a long hike. Now they merely had to climb through the fence behind the house and follow the shore along the Missouri River. An unusually warm April afternoon pulled them outdoors, as a fresh, moist sense filled the spring air.

"It's fun to be on the road, performing and meeting fans, but it's always nice to come home, isn't it?" Kathy asked, watching her step.

"Boy, I'll say," Paul agreed. "It feels good to make a living with music. To be honest I don't even think about the long hours. I can live with the motels and fast food."

"Funny how the hard work doesn't seem so bad when you believe in it."

"Here, hon, I'll help you." Paul reached Kathy's hand to guide her across a crevasse along the bluff's edge. Hawks took to the sky overhead.

"Remember how I always admired Lorie Line back in Minneapolis and how she developed such a successful career simply playing piano?" he asked.

"Didn't she start out at Dayton's downtown during the holidays?"

"Exactly. Serenading shoppers. And now she's a household name in Minnesota. She wrote her own music, added other instruments, and *voila*, a new career. That's why I don't mind working the shopping malls or the art shows." Paul stopped in his tracks. "Watch out, Kath, it's muddy here." He pointed to a gully that dipped down.

"The malls are a bit trickier," Kathy acknowledged.

"I agree. We have to do it just right. Can't be too loud or too soft. It has to fit the environment, complement the surrounding retailers. But as long as we know and understand that, it'll help us be successful in our own right."

"We've come a long way this year," Kathy said, stepping over a large patch of clumped grass.

"Besides learning the circuit, we're finding our own dedicated and loyal fans. You know what I love about what we're doing now?"

"What's that?"

"We're up close to the fans. It gives them a comfortable way to approach us, talk to us. It's a positive end result, both ways. We grow as artists and they feel connected to us and our music. I'm committed to always talking to the fans between sets and signing the CDs. That's what makes the difference."

"Oh, I see that at every event," Kathy acknowledged.

"Plus I think they perceive it as something special when they see we're a family organization. They can see it comes from the heart."

Paul and Kathy continued walking along the bluff's edge rather than down below. The river was high from the spring melting, not leaving enough shoreline to walk until the water level retreated.

"Let's sit for a while," Paul said, pointing to a grassy ledge that faced the river below. "Here's a good spot."

They found a dry ridge and sat together, sharing their thoughts and admiring the vista before them. The whole prairie was coming to life after another long winter, meadowlarks singing their pretty songs. Here, the Missouri River cut a path between the bluffs on either side as it wound its way south.

"You know what I dream about?" Paul asked so softly that Kathy barely heard him speak.

"What?"

He hesitated for a moment, eyes fixed on the distant horizon. "You'll probably think I'm crazy, but I'd like to have a permanent place, somewhere in the Black Hills, for our concerts. I've written an entire script for a ninety-minute show I titled *We the People*, just like the CD. It includes a full orchestra, choreographed dances for certain songs, smoke, fog, colored lights, the works. That's what I've been working on late every night, a script to correlate with the concert theme, 'Native Wisdom.'" Paul turned to Kathy to further his point. "I want a place where we can share our life journey, like we do now but on a larger scale. Maybe at Mount Rushmore—"

"We weren't exactly welcomed last time we tried there," Kathy interrupted.

Paul shook his head in agreement. "I know, I know. To the Indians, Mount Rushmore is an ignominy of our sacred lands. But what better place to bring healing?" Paul pulled up one knee and rested his arm, playing with a blade of long, prairie grass. "What can I say, Kathy? That's my dream."

Kathy took his hand and squeezed it. "I like your dream."

• • •

Even with all the traveling and multitasking, Kathy tried her best to maintain a few close friends, including Morgaine Avalon. Off and on they'd talk long-distance or plan a time when they could see each other. So when Kathy saw Morgaine's number light up on her cell phone, she merely expected another conversation to catch up on things.

"Hey, Kathy," Morgaine said.

"Hi, Morgaine. Good to hear from you again," Kathy said. "I've been meaning to call you. We've been so busy again this summer— but that's a good thing," she added with a laugh.

"Well, if you're not too busy," Morgaine said with a hint of excitement, "I've got a proposition for Paul...."

The simple conversation led to an opportunity of a lifetime. Through her continued involvement in worldwide cultural events, Morgaine was now working with The Hague Appeal for Peace planned for The Hague, Netherlands, on May 11–16, 1999. Billed as an event of the century, the global conference was expected to draw close to 10,000 participants. Members of nongovernmental organizations from around the world were meeting to discuss and share ideas and initiatives being developed for peace in the new century. The conference was timed to coincide with the hundredth anniversary of the First Hague International Peace Conference held in May 1899.

"So," Morgaine said, taking a deep breath, "would Paul be interested in coming to speak and perform as a musical ambassador?"

Paul accepted—his head and thoughts reeling to be part of such a momentous occasion. In need of a guitar player for the performance, Paul and Kathy asked Shane to join Brulé on the overseas journey so the whole family could experience it together. They fully realized the significance—an international event with the presence and voices of many Nobel Peace Prize Laureates, famous leaders, and moral authorities from around the world. It was almost surreal.

The quest for world peace was shattered momentarily closer to home when Shane and Nicole clashed one evening in their hotel room. After the fireworks, brother and sister worked through their issues, resuming a peace-filled family trip in conjunction with the conference theme.

• • •

As usual the Burnsville Center was overflowing with weekend shoppers as Memorial Day weekend neared. Located on the southern edge of the Twin Cities, the popular mall consistently maintained a high volume of traffic. Brulé was set up in the large rotunda on the lower level in front of Dayton's, the premier Minneapolis-based department store.

Nicole stood with her flute on one side, Chuck played drum right in front of the tipi, and Paul stood at the keyboard on the other side, with large speakers on both sides. The fringed piece of painted buckskin hung prominently so everyone could see *Brulé*. Kathy had worked things down to a science at the CD table. She had ordered customized holders for the CDs and cassettes and whichever song Paul played, Kathy set that CD on the top so people would know which one was currently playing.

The unique look of the tipi and traditional drum drew people's interest like a magnet. Shoppers crowded the railings on the second level to observe the unique band below and throughout each set many descended the open staircase to get a closer look. As usual, they'd stop and listen for a song or two, eyes smiling, toes tapping, before moving on. Many times they'd retreat, and come back to listen for a full set.

Nicole had worked hard to develop her position as lead instrumentalist. She crafted her own flute style and was comfortable performing, even when the audience was up close. Eyes closed, she could let her whole self feel the music as she played, still committed to her goal of flawless performances. Traditional (wood) flute players were typically male, so Nicole kept her classical flute and fleshed out a unique sound that made her stand out among Native American flutists.

As soon as the music stopped, people moved in, asking questions, sharing comments, eager to purchase a cassette or CD. Paul, Nicole, and Chuck politely chatted with new fans, explaining the meaning behind the music, sharing their backgrounds, and signing CD covers.

An older woman in brown slacks and a flowery, polyester blouse approached Kathy. "Oh, I love this music!" she said. An abundance of wrinkles gave away her age, but her posture was spry and lively. "Who is this band?" she asked with enthusiasm, her curled hair held in place with bobby pins.

"The band is called Brulé," Kathy started.

"Are they Indian?" she inquired, eyes fixed on Paul's long hair and fringed vest.

"Yes, both Paul and Nicole are enrolled members of the Lower Brule Sioux tribe in South Dakota," Kathy explained. "And the drummer, Chuck, is from the Pine Ridge Reservation."

"Hmm," she said, nodding. "Well, I think it's beautiful, truly beautiful."

"Thank you," Kathy smiled.

"Can I buy this music in a store?" another woman interrupted.

"No, it's very hard to find in stores." Kathy handed her an order form.

"Are you from around these parts?" an elderly gentleman asked, arms folded, head cocked as he studied Paul.

"Three of us are originally from Minnesota and the drummer is from South Dakota," Kathy explained.

After a short break Paul, Nicole, and Chuck went back to their instruments, ready to start another set. Suddenly a tall man with a big, round face approached Kathy. He appeared in his early 30s, and his eyes were strikingly large and wide. "This music is awesome. Nothing like I've ever heard before," he said, his face erupting in a broad grin. "I'm in the music scene here in the Cities. I don't think I've seen you guys around before."

"We've played several places around the area," Kathy said. "What do you play?"

"Lead guitar and drum," he said, handing her a business card. He stayed for the entire set, chatting with Kathy between songs.

Brulé's next performance was only days away at the Ordway Theater in downtown St. Paul for a concert called *Without Reservation.* Nationally known as a premier performing arts center, the Ordway was considered the "crown jewel" of St. Paul. Paul really wanted to include a guitarist for the special performance, but Shane was in the middle of finals at school. As the day wound to a close, Kathy told Paul about the musician she had met.

"I think he might work for the Ordway show," Kathy offered.

"We don't know anything about him."

"It sounds like he's got a lot of experience."

"He might, Kathy," Paul said. "But this isn't how you pick up a guitar player. *Without Reservation* is a big deal."

"I have a good feeling about him." Kathy tossed her long hair behind her shoulder and bent down to pack the CDs and cassettes into a plastic tub.

"We need to go through an audition process if we're going to add a guitarist." Paul made his statement with all the great knowledge and authority he had gained from his years in the music industry.

"I think you should at least talk to him," she pressed, snapping the lid shut.

Paul bit his lip and stood with his hands on hips. "Okay, all right. You win." To humor his wife, he would agree to meet the guitarist. "Say, as long as we're in town, we should get together with Mark and Lori."

"Yeah, Lori left a message for us to call them. They're super busy right now with all the kids' sports schedules. She did say Mark is planning to meet his biological family soon."

"Hmm, every journey is different," Paul said. "I hope it goes well for him. Call her and see when we can drive over."

"Sure," Kathy said, making a mental note.

"So—are we going to meet this guitarist?" he asked, still patronizing his wife.

Kathy picked up her purse, determined not to give up. "I've got his address right here," she said. "Let's go."

A first-generation Greek, Vlasis was very likable and his dark eyes and black hair blended in nicely with Brulé's Native American presentation. More important though, he had a way with the guitar and his level of talent was just what Brulé needed. Before Paul and Kathy left the apartment, Paul invited Vlasis to join Brulé for the Ordway performance. Like a good husband, he had to admit Kathy's instincts were right—again.

. . .

In one of her many searches, Kathy got word of a popular bar on Main Street in Deadwood, South Dakota, looking for live nightly entertainment. Limited-wage gambling had been legalized in 1989 in the historic town to rejuvenate tourism, attracting large crowds throughout the summer season in the Black Hills. The Buffalo Stockade was a large bar and restaurant that opened onto the sidewalk where tourists strolled day and night.

Every evening the newly renovated Main Street in the mythical Wild West town came to life with a reenactment of Wild Bill Hickok's murder at the famed No. 10 Saloon. Tourists jammed the boulevards night after night to watch local actors portray the legendary people of the Wild West. Additional open-air second-story seating at the Buffalo Stockade gave their patrons an advantaged position to watch the scene unfold, drawing even more customers into the bar.

Thrilled to have Brulé booked in one place for six weeks straight, Kathy rented a two-bedroom apartment in Lead, the little gold-mining town next to Deadwood. Although roomier and more affordable than a motel, even a two-bedroom apartment proved to be short on space for the whole entourage. Paul, Kathy, Nicole, and Chuck did their best to make it work, taking turns sleeping on the floor or in hallways, along with making room for Jade and Chuck's two boys. Hot summer days with no air conditioning shortened tempers. Nerves became frayed. So much for the glamorous life of a band.

Over the weeks Paul and the band members developed a good relationship with the owner of the Buffalo Stockade. Tourists were friendly and Brulé felt a welcome atmosphere in the little cowboy town. Paul enjoyed spending quiet time with Chuck as their friendship deepened. With his background on the Pine Ridge reservation, Chuck was well versed in Lakota culture. Paul treasured the times when Chuck shared stories of the elders.

Spending time in the heart of *Paha Sapa,* the Black Hills, at times Paul felt the power of the sacred land surrounding him. One afternoon Paul and Chuck drove over to Rapid City to replace some extension cords and pick up supplies. On the way back to Lead, Paul took a back road, winding through the scenic Nemo Road that cut between the pine-covered bluffs. A small creek gurgled along the narrow gulch, birch trees thriving near the low, cool ground.

"Look!" said Chuck. "There's *wanbli.* I love to watch them soar across the sky, so graceful and majestic." He glanced skyward, still following the eagle's movement. "Do you know about the eagle dancing with our people?"

"No, I don't."

At the next curve Paul pulled the truck over to the shoulder. Both men got out and walked to a couple large boulders a short distance from the guardrail. The afternoon sun glistened through the long pine needles. High on the hillside, boulders rested against the trunks of the tall pines, preventing them from rolling farther down the steep side. It was here, amidst the abundance of creek-carved canyons and alpine meadows, the scenic wonders stirred ones senses.

"Tell me about it," Paul said, breathing in the pine-scented breeze. "I'd like to hear the story."

"Oh, it's not a story, Paul." Chuck shook his head and raised his hand to emphasize his point, his long black braid hanging down his back. "This *really* happened."

"I'm listening," Paul said in anticipation.

"It wasn't too long ago," Chuck began, lifting his face slightly, feeling the warmth of the sun on his face. "One of our last great Lakota leaders was considered to be a chief—it was a different era back then, when the chief carried more of a leadership quality. Much different than today; today it's more about politics." He paused, taking his time. "Years ago men became chief because of the important things they had done in their life; they earned the title through demonstration. Like a war bonnet where they earned an eagle feather every time they did something significant," Chuck explained, setting the stage for what he was about to share.

"Sure," Paul said, nodding in understanding.

"Frank Fools Crow was Lakota, from Pine Ridge. Shortly after the massacre at Wounded Knee in 1890, he traveled to the rez. He was a very humble man, quiet and soft spoken. Back in the 1950s and 1960s kids were losing the old, traditional ways. He was worried about the young people and the struggle between generations." Chuck lifted his boot to a smaller boulder in front of him and rested his elbow on his knee.

"Frank was able to do things that people don't do anymore in ceremonies, back when they always had a strong connection to the Creator. He told everyone to pass the word that he was conducting a ceremony in the Pow Wow arbor and there was something powerful to see. As the people gathered, he asked for a certain drum song. Everyone watched, wondering what was going to happen. The kids were getting restless, waiting. 'What's gonna happen?' they asked. The drum group played another song and some of the dancers came out. People whispered, 'Frank must be crazy.'" Chuck paused for a moment, reflecting.

"Then the eagle dancer came out and started dancing around. Just like that an eagle flew down and circled the arbor and landed by the flag pole—with all these people still around." Chuck raised his hand and swooped it downward, like the eagle. "The drummers kept playing and the eagle dancer danced with the eagle. This went on for about ten minutes. On that day about a hundred people witnessed it."

"Wow," Paul said softly.

Simply retelling the stirring event filled Chuck with great emotion. "This was a real thing, Paul. It really happened with our people. Frank died in 1973, we don't have anyone to make the connection anymore, but it's still there. Someday Paul, you will have to visit *Mato Paha*."

"What is that?"

"It is where many of our ancestors fasted and prayed because it is sacred and spiritual. Notable leaders like Sitting Bull, Red Cloud, and Crazy Horse prayed there. It is a single butte—called Bear Butte—that sticks up from the ground covered in cedar and pine trees. At times the top is shrouded in a mist of clouds, other times a thunderstorm appears confined to the top of the mountain."

Paul's interest was piqued. "Where is it?"

"Over near Sturgis. You must go there someday."

Paul's eyes swept across the valley below, an emerald oasis of ponderosa pines and granite spires that stuck up from the ground, some towering fifty feet or more. One rock near the top of a spire tilted at an angle as though ready to tumble, yet it remained in place as it had no doubt for generations. No wonder his ancestors felt close to the Creator in this land called *Paha Sapa*.

• • •

With Brulé's growing popularity many of the large-event coordinators invited the band back year after year. Paul and Kathy were also discovering groups of faithful fans at each location, thrilled to see their favorite band return. The continuity gave Kathy a better picture of what to anticipate, both travelwise and financially. By September 1999, she knew exactly what to expect at Indian Summer and looked forward to the large festival.

Just before they packed to leave for Milwaukee, Kathy received a surprise phone call. "You won't believe this!" she said, hanging up her cell phone.

Kathy was watching Jade late one morning while Nicole ran over to Chamberlain to do some errands. Paul and Chuck were discussing 1960s rock-and-roll bands while Chuck's boys scrounged in the kitchen for a late breakfast.

"What?" Paul asked, surprised at the elevated excitement in Kathy's voice.

"That was the producer for *Live with Regis and Kathie Lee*, the television show! You won't believe this!" she squealed again. "Regis and Kathie Lee are doing a show from Mount Rushmore and they're looking for a Native American band to perform. Another Native American band already turned them down—of course because it's Mount Rushmore—so someone gave them our name."

"What did you tell them?" Paul asked. "When is it?"

"It's right after we're done with Indian Summer. We'd literally have to drive through the night from Milwaukee to the Black Hills to get there in time. Do we still want to do it?"

"National television? Absolutely!" Paul exclaimed, slapping his thigh.

"For real?" asked Chuck.

"Yes, it's the real deal," Kathy insisted. "It'll be our first national television performance. Oh, I've got work to do!" she squealed. "I want Brulé to make a statement."

"This could be big," Paul said.

Kathy started toward her office and turned around. "This could open doors for us, who knows! Maybe we can give Regis and Kathie

Lee each a star quilt. It would demonstrate the very purpose behind Brulé, for us to give the star quilt as a gesture of healing and reconciliation—and what better place than Mount Rushmore."

"Perfect," Paul nodded.

"I better call Cheryll and ask about ordering a couple of quilts."

The days leading up to the show were both hectic and exciting. Kathy scrambled day and night to make sure they were ready for their debut television performance. It required driving all the way from Lower Brule to Milwaukee to play for three full days at the Indian Summer Festival, only to load up all the equipment and head straight back west, all the way to the Black Hills. They drove all through the night in order to make it across Wisconsin, Minnesota, and South Dakota in time. When Paul pulled the rig into the lot, he and Kathy were almost too tired to think about the last time they'd been in the national park. This time, however, they were greeted warmly by both park personnel and the show's staff.

Thankfully, Fritz and Cheryll had let Jeremiah go along as an extra hand on the road and they needed every set of hands to get the equipment set up in time. Paul and Nicole hurried to change into buckskin regalia; Chuck looked especially handsome in his beautiful

traditional ribbon shirt. Like all television shows taped in front of a live audience, a tight time schedule took precedence over guests that included Randy Travis, Richard Simmons, and Brulé. Paul only had a brief time to chat with Regis and Kathie Lee on air and play parts of two songs.

Kathy had advised the show's producers ahead of time about the quilt presentations and they loved the idea. It went wonderfully and both Regis and Kathie Lee seemed genuinely to appreciate both the gesture and the gift as Paul explained the meaning.

Late that night Paul and Kathy crawled into bed, exhausted from the grueling week but still beaming from the incredible day.

"Isn't it interesting how things come full circle?" Kathy whispered in the darkness.

"Hmm," Paul said close to her ear. "We couldn't have scripted it any better ourselves."

THIRTEEN

On Tour
Ancestor's Cry

By 1999 both *We the People* and *One Holy Night* were selling very well at each event, but Paul knew it was time to give the fans something fresh and new. He talked to Tom Bee and they agreed to release *One Nation*, one of the albums from his initial trip to Albuquerque. J. D. Challenger came up with another cover drawing that blended nicely with *We the People*. The up-tempo arrangements on *One Nation* went a step beyond *We the People* in its world flavor and driving dance rhythms. Vlasis had officially joined Brulé full time as both guitarist and drummer.

While Paul was busy with Tom preparing for the release, Kathy flew to Phoenix to visit her sister Renee. Although many of the craft shows and art fairs came to a halt or moved indoors in the Midwest during the winter months, Kathy was surprised to see a number of large-scale outdoor events still running in the Southwest. Her manager's instincts took over and she placed a call to the organizer, asking questions about crowd size and vendor prerequisites. She couldn't wait to call Paul with the news.

"Here's what I found out," she started. "There's a collection of artists in the Phoenix area that host six large events from January through March, plus they have more scheduled in November and December. It sounds like they do plenty of advertising. They're all outdoors and they pull in artists that are billed as world class. Designers, painters, sculptors—I think we'd fit in wonderfully. Native American artists apparently have a huge following across the Southwest."

"It'd certainly keep us busier through the winter," Paul agreed.

"I called and got us booked for one event in February, sort of a tryout. If we do okay, they'll book us for the rest. What do you think?"

"Sure," Paul said. "We can drive down for it and see how it goes."

Kathy flew home, mentally preparing for what this expansion could mean for Brulé's status in the industry. First and foremost, however, December was just around the corner and she had to help Paul prepare for their scheduled Christmas concerts.

As manager, Kathy was on duty 24/7, her cell phone with her at all times. Some days it rang nonstop as one week's urgencies were resolved one by one, only to uncover new and different concerns the next week.

When time allowed, Paul and Kathy did their best to replenish supplies and copy new order forms and promo materials. Driving home from an office supply store in Pierre, Kathy's phone rang for the umpteenth time.

"Hello, Kathy speaking," she said.

"Hi, Kathy," said a woman's voice. "I'm with the First Americans In the Arts and we're calling to let you know that Brulé has won a performance award for 1999."

Kathy motioned for Paul to turn down the music. "Who is it?" he whispered.

With swift hand gestures Kathy tried to emphasize the importance of the call. "First Americans," she mouthed while listening. "Yes, oh, that's great. When is the ceremony? Yes, we'll plan to be there. Uh-huh. Thank you," she said, hanging up the cell phone.

"Who was it?" he asked, curious to know what was going on.

She slid her sunglasses up like a headband. "Remember the nomination and review process we went through for the First Americans in the Arts for *One Nation?* You got it, Paul!" Kathy's excitement magnified the blue in her eyes. "She said you've been selected for a performance award for Outstanding Musical Achievement."

"Are you serious?" he asked.

"Yes," she said emphatically. "The ceremony is February 26, 2000, in Los Angeles. Thank goodness it's after the Christmas concerts."

The award was being given by the prestigious First Americans In The Arts (FAITA) at their eighth annual awards ceremony honoring Native Americans in all branches of the arts. Many great names from the entertainment field were expected to participate and attend, along with tribal leaders, elders, and dignitaries from all over the country.

Paul was well aware that award shows may at times have political undertones, but in his eyes the fact that Brulé was being recognized was truly significant. To be selected from all the great talent in the world and be recognized by their peers was indeed something special.

When they pulled into the yard, Paul carried the boxes of printed materials into the house. Kathy rushed to her desk and pulled out their tour schedule.

"I don't believe it!" Kathy cried, holding up the three-ring binder.

"What now?" Paul asked, opening a can of soda.

"The award ceremony is scheduled the same weekend of our tryout performance in Fountain Hills."

"No, way!" he shouted.

Kathy had been informed that they couldn't miss any of the three days or they wouldn't be invited to return. Both Paul and Kathy could see the potential for growth for Brulé with getting their foot in the door in the Southwestern market.

"Wait now, let's think this through," Kathy said, pen in hand.

"Man, of all the luck!" Paul complained.

"Hold on—Los Angeles isn't that far from Phoenix."

Paul took a deep breath and exhaled slowly. "You're right, Kath—there has to be a way."

"How about this?" Kathy suggested. "The whole band can play on Friday, just like normal. Then on Saturday, you play until around noon. I'll book a flight from Phoenix to LA for the two of us so we can get to the awards ceremony. Chuck and Nicole will keep playing through the rest of the day without you. Then we'll make sure we're back before Sunday," she said, looking up at her husband. "I don't know how else we can be in two places at once—and they're both important."

"It'll have to work."

As the end of February neared Paul prepared the pickup and trailer for the long trek from Lower Brule to Phoenix, roughly 1,400 miles or 23 hours—maybe more with pulling a trailer. Chuck made arrangements for someone to watch his boys while the band was in Arizona. As feared, the drive in mid-February turned a bit treacherous through the northern states and higher elevations, slowing their travel. After an unplanned stop in Colorado due to icy, snow-packed roads, they were thankful to arrive in the desert area the day before the start of the festival.

The Fountain Hills Chamber of Commerce was just one of several area communities that hosted the Thunderbird Artists festivals. Less than twenty miles northeast of Scottsdale, the area had a slightly higher elevation than Phoenix, subsequently becoming an attractive destination in the sprawling desert communities.

Paul, Kathy, Nicole, and Chuck set up their site early Friday morning, just one of 500 artists lining the Avenue of the Fountains Boulevard. With a name like Fountain Hills, of course, there was a fountain nearby in the middle of a man-made lake. One of the world's highest fountains, the 560-foot tall plume of water shot to the sky periodically, visible for miles.

Enhanced by stunning desert vistas and mountain views, the picturesque backdrop added to the festive mood. Brulé played several sets throughout the day, once again drawing large crowds. It was always the same, people were first lured by the captivating music and then further fascinated by the bits and pieces of Paul's story that he shared between songs.

Sometimes individuals had a connection, an adoption story that they wanted to share with Paul. Other times people pulled Paul or

Chuck aside to ask questions about their Native American heritage, or even sometimes, to offer an emotional apology for the wrongs that were done years ago. Time after time, Paul was taken aback by the impact of the music and the message everywhere they played.

Saturday morning the whole entourage returned to the art show to set up for the day. Kathy rechecked the details for their quick trip to Los Angeles. No flights were available to come back that night, so she reverted to Plan B: She and Paul would have to rent a car and drive back to Phoenix.

About 11:45 a.m. a blue passenger van with bright, yellow lettering drove slowly down the street, looking for commuters. "Paul!" Kathy called from the side of the stage. "Here's the shuttle." She waved at the driver and he pulled over near the curb. Kathy grabbed her travel bag with their change of clothes for the formal event, while Paul gracefully exited the stage.

Nicole and Chuck nodded good-bye and started another song. A friend arrived to take over Kathy's spot at the CD table. Saturday, of course, was the busiest day of the festival. Nicole and Chuck kept the music going even though it meant Nicole now had to play flute along with the songs via a CD player hooked up to the speakers. In between songs, she had to literally jump over the drum to push Stop or Play. It didn't allow the music to fade in or out without Paul playing the keyboard live, but it was the best they could do under the circumstances. They kept at it, working up a sweat in the heat of the afternoon, and by six o'clock they were drained from the warm temperatures and playing dual roles.

Meanwhile, Paul and Kathy hopped a flight to Los Angeles, rented a car, and drove over to the prestigious Century Plaza Hotel, located on Avenue of the Stars, on what was once the back lot of Twentieth Century Fox Studios. Set in the vibrant heart of West Los Angeles, the award-winning urban resort combined the glamour of Hollywood's Golden Age with contemporary grace and style. Referred to as the "Western White House," the hotel often served as the West Coast residence to many presidents as well as the home to numerous star-studded events.

Paul and Kathy found their way to the right area and checked in with the evening's hostess. She welcomed them and directed them to the proper table. Paul and Kathy were "wowed" by the number of famous entertainers gathered for the evening's formal occasion. Wes Studi, a well-known Native American actor, was the host of the eighth annual event. Studi had roles in such star-studded movies as *Dances With Wolves, Last of the Mohicans, Heat,* and *Geronimo* to name a few.

"This is amazing," Kathy whispered, her eyes glancing around the impressive banquet room.

"I'll say," he whispered back, scanning the crowd. "There's some big-name people here."

They slipped into their chairs among the honored guests and stars, and struck up a conversation with their tablemates. Both Paul and Kathy tried to relax and appear as if this was old hat, even though the butterflies were threatening to make an appearance. In the back of their minds, they couldn't help wonder how things had gone back in Fountain Hills.

As the ceremony started, it both humbled and honored Paul to be included. He thought back to Brulé's first gig under the stairway in the Rapid City Civic Center with just him and Nicole, a rented keyboard, and a cassette player.

Look how far you've come, Paul thought as his name was called and he walked to the stage. Kathy beamed, watching her husband accept the award in front of so many talented performers.

Rather than stay and mingle with the crowd, as soon as the event concluded Paul and Kathy got back in the rented car and drove through the night back to Phoenix. They barely had a few hours to crash before getting ready for the final day of the Fountain Hills Art Show. When all was said and done, Brulé claimed a prestigious award from FAITA and the Thunderbird Artists invited the band to perform at two more festivals in March.

Kathy now had another daunting task at hand: living arrangements for the extended time in Arizona.

"There's a little community north of Phoenix called Cave Creek with a fairly decent house for rent. I can drive up there and look at it," she suggested. "Long term I think it'll work better than a motel, especially if we expand to the November shows, plus January through March."

"Sounds good, hon." The cramped quarters of the hotel didn't allow for any extra space. "It'd be nice to have a little room to spread out." His boot caught on an open suitcase on the floor. "See what I mean?" he growled.

Kathy rolled her eyes and flipped the suitcase shut. By the time March rolled around, she had rented the house and started furnishing it with the basics. It wasn't very big, but the price and location were right. At least they could unload more of their equipment in the garage and use it as a makeshift studio. The little desert community offered a comfortable setting and easy access to their events.

She set her folder of notes aside and grabbed her phone. It was time to place her weekly call to her mother. "Hi, Mom," she said.

"Are you down there already?" Shirley asked.

"Yup, we got in a few days ago," Kathy replied.

"You sound tired."

"It was a long drive. Our second time to Arizona in only a couple months."

"Oh, dear. I should have known," Shirley said as though holding something back.

"What?"

"Remember how your father and I were living in Sacramento when you were born?"

"Yeah…"

"We moved back to Minnesota when you were only eight weeks old. You traveled in a car-bed with this, this bird mobile," she giggled, "hanging over your bed for two thousand miles, all the way across the country. I swear that must be why you don't mind all your traveling and being on the road," Shirley sighed.

Kathy laughed. So that explained it.

．　．　．

When spring rolled around, the Brulé entourage loaded up the studio equipment, stage props, all their gear and headed north. By now Kathy had found a few places in Colorado, Nebraska, and Oklahoma to play on the way back to their home base, ensuring a solid, year-round schedule.

Early one morning in mid-June, Kathy got another surprise call.

"Hi, Kathy. This is the entertainment director at Mount Rushmore," a woman began. "We're planning a new presentation for our Fourth of July show and we would like to invite Brulé to be a part of it."

The invitation caught Kathy off-guard. She took a deep breath and held it, then felt instant warmth pulsing through her. "We'd love to," she breathed.

Reconciliation. That's exactly what the music and passion of Brulé was all about. Maybe—just maybe—it was coming through. The long hours, the cramped living quarters, the hard work—this is what kept them going.

The following week Paul tried several gigs at Crazy Horse, the large monument and park near Mount Rushmore. Started in 1948 by sculptor Korczak Ziolkowski in honor of the Lakota warrior, the ongoing mountain carving drew in thousands of visitors. Paul set up their stage near the Indian Museum and Cultural Center outdoors, but the unpredictable weather conditions on the mountain always seemed to work against them, so they returned to their old hangout in Deadwood.

Brulé had another six-week stint scheduled at the Buffalo Stockade, and Paul looked forward to spending some additional time in *Paha Sapa.* He had grown to love the rocky hills and thick pine forests of the hills.

One afternoon Paul suggested a visit over to Bear Butte, the sacred hill of the Lakota known as *Mato Paha.* Paul and Kathy took the drive from Lead/Deadwood to Sturgis, through downtown on Main Street. During the week of the infamous bike rally, Main Street would be blanketed in two-wheeled cycles of chrome. Throughout the rest of the year, Sturgis was just another small prairie town.

Sure enough, on the other side of town, a single butte rose up from the ground, poised proudly where the dark hills suddenly rise out of the golden prairie. Paul and Kathy parked the pickup and walked up one of the two mile-long trails that wound around the slopes and up the mountain, a lonely and majestic outcropping. Now a South Dakota state park, its interpretive center stood at the base of the mountain and provided insight into the historical and cultural significance for park goers unfamiliar with Sioux traditions.

As Paul and Kathy neared the summit, they discovered a breathtaking view that looked down on the valley below. There were no other hills around, just this single peak protruding above the western South Dakota prairie in the middle of nowhere. The summit itself was a relatively confined area and Chuck's words came to Paul's mind. *This is where many of our ancestor's prayed, leaders like Red Cloud, Crazy Horse, and Sitting Bull.*

As Paul stood on the grassy crest, it suddenly occurred to him that he could be standing in the exact same spot where Crazy Horse had once stood, or possibly his own ancestors. The thought of crossing the same path of so many of the great leaders moved him deeply. He drew a deep, cleansing breath and scanned the panoramic view, turning slowly in a circle, trying to imagine what they must have experienced.

Desperate to save their people, it was here they came looking for answers, knowing their beloved way of life was fast disappearing. They came with heavy hearts, he knew, often staying for days. After all, this is where they found a connection to the Creator.

Suddenly his heart beat a little stronger and faster. Paul's being there, standing in that same spot, was not a coincidence. There was something deeper happening, a profound moment in knowing that the God who keeps the heavens and earth in order was the same God who put purpose to chance. Paul was here for a very real reason.

After a short while Paul and Kathy walked back down the mountain. Much like his first view of Lower Brule, this, too, was a profound moment in Paul's life, another one of the little dots connecting him back to his roots. The thoughts and feelings from Bear Butte lingered in Paul's mind for several days, and he carried that heaviness with him.

. . .

After three years at USD–Vermillion, Shane and his girlfriend, Heather Naser, decided to do something "really exciting"—move to Hawaii. Heather had just graduated with a Bachelor of Science degree in English education and Shane had applied to the National Student Exchange Program. Shane was accepted and Heather soon found a job teaching middle school and high school English in Honoka'a, Hawaii. Shane, who was on the all-too-common five-year plan and had two years of school left, transferred to the University of Hawaii. In the fall of 2000, Shane and Heather happily relocated to beautiful Hawaii.

Between performances, Paul used any and all spare time to begin another musical collaboration, this time with the single other band member who had been at his side from the beginning—Nicole. He and Kathy could see how she had taken ownership in Brulé over the years, further developing her unique, passionate style of flute playing and building her own fan base.

Paul created a production company called Buffalo Moon Productions with the intent to feature Nicole's flute playing on the tracks of the next CD. Always eager to express her creative talents, Nicole jumped at the chance to craft music alongside her father.

As they worked together, oftentimes Paul came up with a rhythmic idea, a basic chord or melody, and Nicole would take it from there. "Dad, I hear this…" and she'd change it to fit her own musical interpretations. Hour after hour they kept at it, often late into the night, deciding on song titles and graphics.

In the end, Paul and Nicole created a new series of CDs, simply titled *Nicole*. The first one, *Passion Spirit*, was recorded and released in late 2000 with a whole new look. This time a close-up of Nicole's face graced the cover and they included one of Nicole's poems on the back. One of the songs particularly close to the entire band was a selection titled "Ancestor's Cry," a musical interpretation of Paul's experience on Bear Butte and what his ancestors might have felt when they crested the top of *Mato Paha*.

Paul felt strongly that he couldn't take credit for the song; the emotion and feelings were borrowed from long ago. He simply rearranged the notes and somewhere, his own heaviness pushed the dramatic, emotive compilation forward, as though pleading to share it with the world. Nicole's hauntingly beautiful flute captured the essence of the story behind the song and visualized the anguish of the people.

• • •

A true bundle of energy and joy, little Jade loved being with Grandma and Grandpa on the road. She was still young enough that she could travel everywhere without missing school. Her light-brown hair and sweet smile garnered attention everywhere they went.

Chuck's boys, however, were older and during the school year it became more complicated with the group's extended travels. Now that Brulé was scheduled in the Southwest in the months prior to and just after the Christmas concerts, it presented an even bigger issue for Chuck.

As much as he wanted to keep playing with Brulé, Chuck knew in his heart that the boys needed him at home. The time had come to move back home and finish raising his sons. Everyone hated to lose him, but they knew it was the right thing.

"We can use Vlasis to help out on drum temporarily, but we will need a full time drummer," said Paul.

"It's too bad things didn't work out for him," agreed Kathy.

"He brought a lot more to Brulé than just his drumming," Paul said, thinking of his many extended talks with Chuck.

He would miss his friend.

• • •

Throughout the months and years Paul continually drafted and fine-tuned the script for his concert presentation, *We the People*. He spent hours creating the perfect outline of song selections, dances, lighting, fog, smoke, and stage props. He had everything down to the minute details of music and dance repertoire, script vignettes, cast members, along with promotional material, both written and video. He spent additional time putting it all in order with color graphics to create a top-notch, professional package to present to various venues.

Only one question remained: Were mainstream audiences ready for such a musical presentation?

FOURTEEN

Hope and Healing
The Seven Lakota Concepts

Paul and Kathy had just finished another successful three-day performance at Indian Summer in Milwaukee. Once again they enjoyed a warm reception from fans, and they loved the festive atmosphere at the Native American celebration. Monday morning they drove to Chicago for a scheduled record promotion. They arrived at the record store in downtown Chicago only to find out all outdoor music performances had recently been banned on the plaza near the base of the Sears Tower. Unaware of the new policy, the store owner apologized for the mix-up. With the unexpected cancellation, Paul and Kathy decided to spend the night and head for home the next morning.

Tuesday morning, September 11, 2001, dawned bright and clear as they hooked up the rig and headed across Illinois toward South Dakota. Then came the awful news. Words couldn't describe the horror as radio broadcasters relayed reports and images of the two towers collapsing, knowing so many people were still inside. To their disbelief, that news was followed by the devastation at the Pentagon and the horrific ending of Flight 93 in a Pennsylvania field. Paul and Kathy grieved along with the rest of America as details of the horrific morning unfolded over the airwaves. The shock, the anger. The question, why?

Throughout history prejudices and tensions have separated races, religions, and cultures. Blacks and whites. Catholics and Protestants. Kurds and Turks. North and South. No place or country is exempt from such conflicts. Statistics make the horrors distant and impersonal. Often though, one person's story can touch people's hearts and begin the healing process.

In the days immediately following September 11, Paul heard the enraged and angry comments aimed at people of Middle Eastern descent. He wondered how such people living in America would come to terms with the outrage now aimed toward their culture. He imagined they must feel anger on this side and sorrow on both sides. The whole ugliness of it hit home for him as he envisioned once again the unprovoked massacres of the American Indian tribes in the nineteenth century. Native Americans were no longer subject to such cruelties, but the after effects lingered for generations. It seemed only fitting for Paul to include the current focus on the Middle East when he spoke of cultural healing.

. . .

Now a consistent draw in the Southwest, Brulé was back in Arizona for the 2001–02 winter season. Paul, Kathy, and the band had settled into the house in Cave Creek, ready to take part in the outdoor festivals that showcased some of the world's most gifted designers, painters, sketchers, and sculptors. Brulé and everything it represented was a perfect match for the venue. Kathy also found a few sites in New Mexico and San Diego for performances between the Phoenix area art shows. Brulé's ensemble now required two trucks and two large trailers to haul all the equipment and inventory.

The long awaited follow-up to *We the People* was released in November 2001. *Star People,* a melody-driven CD, was listener friendly and radio ready. *Star People* featured 14 original compositions that crossed genres, becoming one of the first Native American recordings to emerge in the mainstream music industry. Fans warmly received the blend of ballad, medium tempo, and dance tracks interwoven with traditional and contemporary Native American instrumentation.

One evening in Cave Creek Kathy made an announcement at the dinner table. "Remember Camille, the gal here in Phoenix? She called this morning and her friend from Tennessee is flying down to audition for drummer," Kathy said, setting out dinner plates and silverware.

"It'd be nice to have someone on board before January," Paul said. "Pass the ketchup, could you, Nikki?"

Nicole handed over the Heinz bottle. "Is there more pasta salad?" she asked.

"On the counter," Kathy said.

After a lifetime of Minnesota and South Dakota winters, Paul rather enjoyed grilling burgers outside in 70-degree weather on a November evening with the sun slipping behind the desert horizon.

"Mmm," Vlasis said, nodding. "Good burgers."

Nicole and her boyfriend, Roy Hampton, had moved into their own apartment with Jade in Fountain Hills. Next year Jade would start kindergarten, so Nicole needed to have a home base and get her registered for school. Nicole liked the desert climate and arts-minded community. It was far enough from Phoenix to have a small-town atmosphere, with easy access to the airport when she needed to fly to performances.

Three days later, John Lone Eagle knocked on their front door. Slender and trim, he stood about 5'10" with long dark hair that fell passed his shoulders. Kathy welcomed him inside and introduced Paul, Nicole, and Vlasis.

"Nice to meet ya'll," he said with an unmistakable Southern drawl. "And call me Eagle. I just go by Eagle."

Everyone greeted Eagle and welcomed him into the kitchen.

"Glad to have you," Paul said.

"I just want ya'll to know," Eagle began. "I'm a big fan of ya'lls. I've been listening to your music ever since it came out, I even sell it in my store."

"What kind of store?" Nicole inquired.

"I own a gift shop in Jackson, Tennessee—where I live—called Native American Legacy. It's in the Casey Jones Village tourist area, about an hour east of Memphis. I've got all the Brulé music, man. We play *We the People* all the time," he said, smiling. "'Buffalo Moon' is my favorite."

"Tell us a little bit about yourself," Kathy suggested.

"Let's see," Eagle said, wiping his hands on the thighs of his blue jeans in a nervous gesture. "I graduated from Baylor University in Texas back in the 80s. I played a little major league baseball for the Padres, tried a few things over the years, I guess," he said. "Still own my business, use to do rodeo and bull ridin' until I got hurt. But I love playing the traditional drum, man. If that's what you're looking for. I mean, I'm part Apache, part Cherokee, so I know what's behind the traditional drum and how to play it right."

As soon as the discussion turned to the drum, Vlasis offered to show Eagle the drum Brulé used. Kathy glanced at Paul and locked eyes, not saying a word. Her instincts were at work again—she had a good feeling about John Lone Eagle.

Shane and Heather flew home for Christmas break. When they returned to Hawaii, he brought his guitar back and started practicing Brulé music. Even though he didn't verbalize it, Heather knew exactly where it was leading. Shane had a great admiration for his father and the passion he displayed for his music. If there was any way Shane could help his dad, he would be there in a heartbeat.

By the following summer, Shane had made up his mind and he wasted no time in catching up to Brulé. He graduated from the University of Hawaii in June 2002 with a Bachelor of Arts degree in anthropology. Three days later, he and Heather left Hawaii and Shane was at his father's side on stage in Wisconsin for his first official gig. Now the full-time guitarist, Vlasis helped Shane get set up with the right guitars and equipment. Without any formal training, his musical genes took over and he quickly learned the ins and outs of the guitar.

• • •

For all that Paul loved performing in front of people, sharing his story, and watching fans enjoy the music, sometimes the pace and long hours on the road caught up to him. "Time to go home again," he'd tell Kathy. Spending quiet time on the South Dakota prairie stirred his spirit and rejuvenated his soul.

As soon as he and Kathy had made the move, there was no looking back. No regretting—even once—the move to tiny Lower Brule. Six years later they still lived in the same little house on the Little Bend. The only difference was now there were three full-sized trailers parked in the yard between gigs. The eight miles of gravel took a toll on the equipment, the dust penetrated every tiny crack, coating their sensitive electronic equipment. Paul was thinking about getting a place closer to a paved road.

Once again, he took his walking stick and crawled through the fence in jeans and a T-shirt, heading toward the bluff's edge along the riverbank. He stooped down to pick a sprig of sage. Back on the bend, only the female variety of sage grew, with a shorter, more delicate stem. He twirled the herb in his fingers, studying the leafy texture. The South Dakota prairie also produced a low-growing cactus with a beautiful yellow flower, similar to a rose.

Initially the land had been selected for an Indian reservation because the terrain was nonagricultural, basically barren and useless. *Good enough for the Indians.* The Pine Ridge Reservation—which shared land with Badlands National Park—was a good example, still one of the poorest areas in the entire United States. But as Paul scanned the surrounding view, to him it was some of the most beautiful land in the whole country.

He climbed down the angled bluff to the shoreline along the river. Paul walked along the sandy shore toward an archeological site that had been studied a few years earlier. He thought about the rich history he'd learned from people in the community, great insights from the likes of Grandma Bessie, Emet Eastman, and brothers Altwin and Noah Grassrope.

Traditionally an oral heritage, American Indian elders held a goldmine of knowledge within, wisdoms that needed to be shared. Many things he'd been told by the elders contradicted the things he'd been taught in mainstream America his whole life. For example, corporate philosophy was linear, existing daily to get from Point A to Point B. The pace is ever increasing and individuals strive to accumulate, materially, as much as possible along the way. Since Point B ends such a great distance from Point A, it is easy to ignore much of what is in between. The biggest house he and Kathy ever owned was the one on Darnell Road in Eden Prairie, yet it was probably the unhappiest they ever were as a family. Now they lived in an unassuming rambler on the rez and his soul was undeniably fulfilled. It brought a peace that surpassed material possessions.

He remembered too his parents' auction and seeing all their belongings stamped with price tags. If he'd have known of the give-away concept, he would have given it all to those in need, and at the same time, given a remembrance of Clarence and Irma.

Paul hiked the narrow shoreline where the water lapped against the small rocks lining the edge. Here the bluff was a vertical wall 20 to 30 feet, sometimes as high as 50 feet, but across the river it was a gentle slope upward to the plateau. Numerous cottonwood tree trunks lay along the shore, washed up whenever they broke loose along their base. Now barkless and smooth, they presented a reminder of the land lost to the damming of the river.

Paul continued until he reached the site that had been excavated. He poked his stick around the water's edge, loosening a couple rocks that were wedged into the sand. His eyes caught a log floating mid-river and a story that Altwin Grassrope once told him came to mind.

When I was about 12 years old, they took me off the rez and told me I had to go to boarding school in Fort Pierre. I didn't want to go, but my parents told me, "you must go or they'll make it difficult." I didn't want to leave my home and family, but I didn't have a choice. I had a bad teacher and they made me cut my hair. They didn't treat me real nice, so I escaped three different times.

Paul pondered Altwin's choice of words: "escape," one usually associated with something much harsher than a school.

The last time I escaped, I snuck out of my room at midnight and went down to the river. It had just rained and the Bad

River was running pretty swift, but I didn't care. I stepped into the black water until it was chest high and I let the current carry me away in the darkness of night. I could hear someone out looking for me, but they didn't come down by the river.

The Bad River flows into the Missouri and there I caught a log and hung on through the night. When the sun came up, I was tired and didn't know how far I had floated. I looked up and saw some trees that looked kinda familiar, so I started swimming for the shore. By the time I reached the shallow water, I was exhausted and could hardly pull myself onto dry land.

Just then I saw a rider on horseback. I ducked down in a thick grove of sandbar willow, worried they'd send me back to boarding school. I glanced back at the swift current, but I was too tired to swim any farther. Then I heard a voice and turned around to see Fred LaRoche. It was your dad on the horse, and he gave me a ride home. Your dad was a real nice man.

The words floated across the river as though Altwin had just said them. *"Your dad was a real nice man..."* Paul closed his eyes, imagining his father riding up on horseback to save the young Grassrope boy, dead-tired and half-drowned. Paul knew that the Bad River entered the Missouri at Fort Pierre, a good 60 miles from Lower Brule. How desperate Altwin must have felt to be swept away in the river's current rather than remain at the school.

Had Paul yet reached a point where he understood the foundations of his people? An elder named Emet Eastman once noticed Paul's uncertainty about life's complexities and told him to follow the Seventh Direction, one of the Seven Concepts of the Sioux Nation. Paul had read them, studied them, and contemplated the truths within. The concepts went deeper than mere words on a page. Rather, they expounded an entire way of life.

Hours passed as he poked around the ruins of the archeological site where Indian relics were more than likely still buried far beneath the soil. He heard a low rumble and glanced to the west where a thundercloud was beginning to form.

Follow the Seventh Direction...

. . .

Concept of the Seventh Direction

The medicine wheel shows the four colors of the human race and their daily acknowledgement for a balanced life. Red is east, to remind us of the setting and rising sun, bringing a new day and a new beginning, no matter how difficult the previous day has been. Yellow is south, to remind us of the warm spring winds, a time of renewal. White is north, a reminder of the long winter to come, a time of reflection and cleansing snows. Black is west, to remind us of the nighttime approaching and to live out each day as best as possible. Above is the sky, the awesome universe, and it keeps us humble. Below, the earth, to keep us grounded and connected.

The Seventh Direction is the most important of all for it is within. It is the direction to follow in times of difficulty for it never lies. Follow the heart, for it is the truest direction of all, but the most difficult to follow.

Concept of the Brotherhood

Observe the animals, for they are the innocent ones, the truthful ones who follow obedience as God intended. See here what the Creator has made, behold how these truthful ones live in harmony among and with themselves. Notice that they care for their young and never abandon them. Notice that they do not overpopulate their world. There is much to learn from these humble creatures; teach the children to observe them.

The winged ones, the four-leggeds, the finned ones, and the crawling ones. The animals always obey the laws of harmony, balance, and truth. They never take more than they need and respect others of their kind. We, too, could still learn, if we only look around us.

Concept of the Giveaway

It is believed that the love of possessions is a weakness to overcome. It appears the material part of life, if allowed its way, would disturb one's spiritual balance. Therefore, children should learn early the beauty of generosity. They are taught to give away what they prize most, that they may taste the happiness of giving.

Our people, in their simplicity, give away all that they have to relatives, to guests of other tribes, and above all to the poor and the elderly from whom they could hope for no return.

Concept of the Circle

All of Lakota life is viewed in a circular philosophy, emulating the creation. The circular line ends where it begins. All is connected in between and the line is unending, teaching respect of all things and all others along life's way. The power of the universe works in circles. The medicine wheel symbol is a circle with a cross through it, dividing the circle into four sections. The four cardinal directions, north, south, east, and west, and the four colors represent the four races of the two-leggeds, red, yellow, black, and white. The circle connects all and all are related. Mitakuye Oyasin, "We are all related."

Concept of the Elders

Those who came before us are important in the making of this great nation. The elders are the most important and respected members of the family, community, and tribe. They should be consulted on all activities regarding the well-being of the

tribe. Great respect is given for their accumulation of knowl-
edge and wisdom.

Concept of the Pow Wow

The Pow Wow is an event that draws together and unites an
entire village or band. It draws and holds everyone, from the
little children to the elders and everyone in between for sev-
eral days and nights. It is a time where all can participate and
enjoy friendship and food. Song, prayer, and dance all add to
the social event.

Concept of the Vision Quest

Only a few understand the importance of the Vision Quest. It is
simple, really. A person goes off alone to a quiet place, away
from all distractions for several days and nights to fast and
pray. The solitude and tranquility provide time to think, to
observe nature, and to rest. Many answers to life's problems
will come this way.

Until they moved to Lower Brule, Paul rarely went off to a quiet place alone. Now he did it with great frequency, and he felt restored each time. Maybe the most important treasures from the past weren't the artifacts buried beneath the soil. No, the real treasure was in the depth and meaning of the Native Peoples' concepts, often shared in a soft voice from one person to the next through simple, uncompli- cated words.

Paul's eyes studied the large thundercloud across the plateau. The massive head towered thousands of feet straight up, dark and churn- ing at the bottom, but snowy white at the top. Just then another deep rumble rolled across the wide open prairie. It was still a good 45 miles away and Paul figured he had roughly an hour to get home before the storm hit. He followed the shoreline back, his own single set of foot- prints still visible in the wet sand.

By the time Paul neared the pasture behind the house, loud cracks of thunder accompanied each jagged, dancing flash of light. The thunderous roars were deep enough to shake the ground under his boots. The dry, dusty pasture thirsty for the drenching rain was now barely a half mile away. A gust of wind blew his hair in front of his eyes and he brushed it back, daring one last glance at the approaching storm.

Boom-Crack! the sky roared again, like the mighty voice of *Watan Tanka,* God the Creator. *Follow the Seventh Direction...*

. . .

"Paul!" Kathy called from the back bedroom/office. "We did it! I just checked the Web. *Hurry!"*

Paul rushed from the kitchen down the hall to the bedroom. "What?"

"The Native American Music Awards, Paul," she said, pointing to the computer screen. "Brulé has been nominated in four categories," she squealed. "Look—Duo/Group of the Year, *Brulé, Star People.* Best Instrumental Recording, *Brulé, Star People,"* she read proudly. "Record of the Year, *Brulé, Star People,* and—oh, Paul, Songwriter of the Year. Isn't that wonderful? I can't wait to update our promotional material. *Four categories!* You're bound to win at least one of them, don't you think?"

"Who can say, Kathy. You know how these things are," Paul said scrolling the cursor down the screen. "Look at all the big names, wow..."

"The NAMAs are going to be held at Indian Summer in Milwaukee in September. At least we'll be there."

The next week Paul, Shane, Kathy, Nicole, Vlasis, and Eagle gathered around the kitchen table for a meeting. As business manager for Brulé, Kathy held meetings periodically to discuss issues that cropped up. Outside, another soft blue sky filled the July backdrop. They'd just finished a successful weekend at the art festival in Spearfish, South Dakota, a remarkably beautiful canyon in the Black Hills.

"We've talked about this before...Eagle, I think you should stand up rather than sit behind the drum," Kathy said. "It's just a suggestion, but I think it'll help the fans be able to see you better if you're standing."

"Stand through the whole thang?" Eagle asked, head cocked. His chair was pushed back from the table, his cowboy boots perched on the chair legs.

"Actually Paul should too, rather than sitting on a stool behind the keyboard. I'm talking about the concerts, not the art fairs where we play all weekend," she added.

"Hmmm," Eagle said, leaning back in his chair. "I guess if ya'll want, I can give it a try."

"Good," Kathy said. "Paul?"

"Yeah," he said, nodding. "We can try it."

"I'll see if there's a different reaction from the audience," Kathy said, marking a check on her list of topics.

"Mom!" Jade said, running into the kitchen. "Fix this," she ordered, handing over a broken Barbie doll.

"What do you say?" Nicole asked.

"Peeze," she immediately responded.

Nicole popped the arm back into place and adjusted the skirt and jacket. "There you go," she said, handing her the doll. "Now play with your things for just a few more minutes. Mommy's almost done." Nicole took a drink of her bottled water and twirled back on her chair.

"Hey, Shane," said Eagle.

"Yeah?"

"It's been a month…how you doin'?"

"Yeah, I'm sure Mom told you. I had a little stage fright," he admitted. "My nerves, man, it just gets me when I step on stage."

"It'll get easier," Eagle reassured. "Man, when I first started, I sat back there on the drum and let my hair fall right over my face so I wouldn't have to look at anyone. Now I just wear sunglasses," he laughed. "I close my eyes and get into the beat, man."

"Yeah, I'm trying…"

"Don't worry about it. Not everyone can be like Vlasis here, getting right to the front—"

"Or even into the crowd," laughed Nicole. "Working the audience."

"Some of them love it," Vlasis stated. "But hey, we can't all do that."

"Each of us has our own style," Nicole said flatly. "It's as simple as that."

"Let's see," Kathy said, looking over her list. "That's it for now. Up next is a school performance down at Rosebud, day after tomorrow." Paul and Kathy made a point to include the surrounding schools in their tour schedule whenever time allowed.

The group dispersed and a few minutes later Shane approached Paul outside by the trailers. "What are you doing now?"

"I need to look at the lights before our next concert. I noticed one section was shorting out." Paul unlatched the back door, lowered it to the ground and then stepped inside.

"Dad, you work too hard," Shane said, ducking as he followed him inside the trailer. "Let me help you with the concert prep. I've been working on some new lights and how to run them. You and Mom are getting burned out, I can tell. This is a tough schedule to keep going."

"That's the way it is, Shane," Paul said, juggling the heavy crates in order to find the right one.

"Can I show you what I'm working on?"

Paul moved another crate aside, already working up a sweat in the confines of the trailer. "Sure, I'll take a look at it." He smiled and patted Shane on the back. "It'll be nice to have some fresh blood in this."

Three days later the Brulé entourage traveled two hours south and west from Lower Brule to the Rosebud Reservation, to their sister tribe of the *Sicangu*, or Burnt Thigh band, of the Lakota. Much larger than Lower Brule, the Rosebud Reservation bordered a corner of the Pine Ridge Reservation on the west and Nebraska on the south, although the gentle rolling hills of southern South Dakota were quite similar in landscape.

After they finished setting up, Paul chatted with several staff members at the small school before it was time to begin playing. Groups of children filed into the gymnasium led by their teachers, their enthusiastic voices echoing in the large room as they scrambled for seats on the bleachers.

A middle-aged man with a broad, gentle face approached Paul. "Hello, Paul. I'm Roy Stone. Welcome! We're delighted to have you here." A tribal elder and spiritual leader on the Rosebud Reservation, Roy Stone was well known and respected in the Sioux community.

Paul extended his hand and shook hands. "I'm delighted to be here," Paul answered in all honesty. "We really enjoy coming to the schools. This is my daughter, Nicole, and our drummer, Eagle. Vlasis plays guitar, my son, Shane and my wife, Kathy."

Roy shook hands with each one. "Nice to meet you all, welcome to Rosebud."

Just then Jade ran up to Paul and hugged his leg. "And we can't leave out this little one," Paul said. "My granddaughter, Jade."

"Come here, sweetie," Kathy said, picking up Jade. "You can sit with me until Grandpa and Mommy are done."

"Everyone's here," a teacher said to Roy, nodding to the students.

Nicole, Eagle, Shane, and Vlasis took their places as Paul stepped behind the keyboard. Roy took the microphone to introduce Brulé to the school kids. "All right, if we can have your attention…" He waited a moment for the kids to quiet down. "We have someone special with us today. Someone who's had a most remarkable journey," Roy said to the young crowd gathered. "His name is Paul LaRoche. He grew up far away from here and did not know of his people, his family. When he discovered the place of his birth, he came back; he came *home*."

Roy turned to Paul and continued. "On behalf of the Rosebud community, we would like to extend a welcome home to you, Paul LaRoche, and to your family."

A small group of children came forward dressed in traditional regalia, smiles on their faces, and danced while two high school age boys kept time with small, hand-held drums.

Roy picked up an eagle feather and brought it to Paul. "For you Paul," he said. "Take this feather and carry it proudly, wherever your footsteps take you in this world." Next two young girls came forward carrying in a star quilt. Paul looked at Kathy in complete surprise, but her expression matched his own. Neither of them anticipated this special observance.

"As you know, both the eagle feather and the star quilt are gifts of honor for the Lakota people," Roy continued. "Your journey is a circle. In the sacred hoop of life, we give you these gifts, so you will know that you are welcome in our community as well."

Outwardly Paul smiled, touched by the surprise ceremony. Inwardly, it struck him deeper than he could share. To think that this sister community 120 miles from Lower Brule would plan a welcome home ceremony made Paul feel like he belonged all the more. The inclusive nature of the Lakota tribe to extend the family structure was demonstrated once again, and it warmed his heart.

       •   •   •

Brulé had double-duty at Indian Summer during the September 2002 festival. Not only were they playing regular performances throughout the day from 10 a.m. to 6 p.m., but also they had an hour-long concert scheduled for 7 p.m. that night on a different stage.

"Okay, guys, let's get at it," Paul said after their last set. "We don't have much time to tear down and get set back up for the concert."

The band members and road crew scrambled into motion. "Grab that cart!" Eagle shouted to Shane. "I'll start moving the drums."

"Whoa," called Vlasis. "Watch out for the mic, it's still plugged in." He immediately began unplugging various cords.

"Hey, you guys coming to the awards tonight?" one of the organizers asked.

Paul picked up a speaker and carried it to a cart. "Planning to," he said, slightly out of breath.

"Great," the young man said and disappeared.

Shane caught his dad's eye. "That's the second person who's come over and asked," he advised with a slight grin.

"Either way, we gotta keep at it," Paul said, hoisting another speaker.

With great teamwork, they took down the entire set and reassembled it on the larger stage. Everyone worked like crazy to get the additional props and speakers in place for the concert. At seven o'clock sharp they started the performance to a full house. Paul knew the awards ceremony was already in progress and his plan was to trim the concert by fifteen minutes in order to make it for the second half.

Following the last song, Paul bid farewell, thanking the fans for their enthusiasm and loyalty. Once again the band members and crew rushed to break everything down and put it in storage for the night before racing to the Marcus Amphitheater, trying not to disrupt the ceremony as they took their places at a table. All the other nominees were already seated, enjoying the special evening. Before they barely had time to catch their breath, the presenter announced the nominees for Duo/Group of the Year.

"And the winner for the 2002 Native American Music Award for Duo/Group of the Year goes to Brulé!" the emcee said, followed by an eruption of applause.

Paul, Nicole, Shane, Vlasis, and Eagle all walked up to receive the black-and-gold award amid cameras flashing.

"Thank you so much," Paul began, speaking into the microphone. "Whew!" he laughed. "We barely made it." He took a second to gather his thoughts and then continued. "I've always said we have one of the hardest working bands in America and tonight is a perfect example. We just finished a concert and got here a little late, but I'm thrilled to accept this award on behalf of the entire Brulé group. Thank you so much!"

Paul and the group returned to the stage one more time to receive the 2002 Best Instrumental Recording. It had been a killer day, but one they'd remember for a long time.

Walking back to their truck for the ride to the hotel, Paul wrapped an arm around Kathy. "Group of the Year was the best award to receive because it truly reflects the relentless efforts of the whole band," he whispered, holding the award in his hand. "Including you."

• • •

"Shane said he's not coming again tomorrow," Kathy announced, the disappointment evident in her voice. She closed the motel room door and kicked off her shoes. "He said it's because he doesn't feel well, but I know him, Paul. It's because we're in the mall. He doesn't feel comfortable that close to the audience."

The motel suite offered a living area which gave them a little extra space. Since their business was literally on the road, everything went with them from city to city, hotel to motel. Kathy opened one of the cases and pulled out the calculator and order forms. She sat at the small desk and started tallying up the day's proceeds and expenses.

"He's fine when we play the concerts," Kathy explained, pointing her pencil.

"I know," Paul said, nodding. "But I don't want to push him."

"I don't either," Kathy agreed. "He's just like me. I used to struggle with stage fright, remember? I suffered from real anxiety. I know exactly what he's going through."

"Maybe he's not cut out for it," Paul sighed. "I don't know."

"He loves playing with you Paul, we both know that. I need to sit down with him and tell him, he's either in the band all the time, or he should choose to do something different."

"Just be careful how you say it," Paul instructed.

"I will," Kathy said. "But you heard how many people came up to us between sets at Rosedale today asking about Shane. He can't pick and choose when he wants to play and when he doesn't." She put down her pen and turned to Paul, tucking one leg under the other. "What I want to tell him is he can get over this fear."

"Well, this is our last mall venue for the year," Paul said, glancing at the schedule. "Next week we start the Christmas concerts. Did I tell you Shane and I spent one afternoon brainstorming. He's got some great ideas for next year…adding more colored lights, more video."

"Yeah, I heard him talking to Vlasis and Eagle about it."

"I'm glad he's on board," Paul said. "What a treat to have both our kids doing this along side us."

"They believe in it the same as you and I."

Staying in Arizona for several months allowed Paul and Nicole to compile the second release for Buffalo Moon Productions. Once again, Nicole put her heart and soul into the new project, allowing her own silent feelings to surface through musical composition. Titled *Night Tree,* the tracks were a combination of more than music. To her it was part art, smiles, tears, joy, and, in her words, *echoes of kind thoughts.* Nicole appreciated the chance to express her artistic creativity, and the fans loved it.

FIFTEEN

A Mission

Sicangu Woileciceya
Advocate for Burnt Thigh

It often amazed Paul to see the thousands of miles they drove in a calendar year. Besides booking and physically getting the band to each event, Kathy also had to work out flight schedules and additional details for dancers who came from all parts of the country. Then to coordinate hotels, timing, and transportation in each city became quite a monumental task. In 2003 they had 70 scheduled dates of performances spread out all across the country.

Brulé 2003 schedule

January 14:	Concert, Mesa, AZ
January 17–19:	Concert / Indian Art Show, Denver, CO
February 13:	Art Show, Carefree, AZ
February 21–23:	Art Show, Fountain Hills, AZ
February 28–March 2:	Fine Art & Wine Festival in Carefree, AZ
March 4:	Concert, Mesa, AZ
March 6:	Art Show, Carefree, AZ
March 21–23:	Concerts / Indian Art Show, Arlington, TX

March 28–30: Phoenix Home & Garden Show, Phoenix, AZ

April 4–6: Concert / Indian Art Show, Overland, KS,

April 8: Concert in Phoenix, AZ

April 26 Concert in Albuquerque, NM

May 10–11: Art Festival, Henderson, NV

May 17: Concert in Bellevue, NE

May 24–26: Art Festival, Denver, CO

May 30–June 1: Art Festival, Edina, MN

June 7: Art Festival, Norfolk, NE

June 21: Grand Opening at Tatanka, Deadwood, SD

June 27–29: Art Festival, Omaha, NE

July 11: International Festival, Worthington, MN

July 12–13: Art Festival, Brookings, SD

July 18–20: Art Festival, Spearfish, SD

August 16–17: Art Festival, Yankton, SD

August 31: Concert, Mitchell, SD

September 5–7: Indian Summer Festival & concerts, Milwaukee, WI

September 13: Concert, Two Rivers, WI

September 22–26: Cruise with Brulé, Catalina Island, CA

October 3–5: Apple Fest, Bayfield, WI

October 11: Benefit Concert at Black Hills State University, Spearfish, SD

October 31–Nov 2: Fine Art & Wine Festival, Carefree, AZ

November 8: Concert, Phoenix, AZ

November 14–16: Art Festival, Fountain Hills, AZ

December 6: Christmas Concert, Yankton, SD

December 10: Christmas Concert, Sioux Falls, SD

December 13–14: Christmas Concert, Deadwood, SD

By fall Kathy more than welcomed Heather aboard as Brulé's new assistant manager and, even more important, as a member of the family. On July 3, 2003, Shane and Heather were married in Mitchell,

South Dakota, Heather's hometown. The summer of 2003 was especially difficult for Heather, as her mother was suffering through the final stages of breast cancer. Sharol Naser was the center of a strong family core, and Heather wanted to stay with her in Mitchell as long as possible. After the funeral and things were settled, she rejoined Shane on the tour.

Frequently Shane or Nicole would harp on their parents. "You work too hard. Slow down, relax a little bit!" But the one constant Paul and Kathy knew in their business was "no play, no pay." Musicians live from week to week with no security, no pension, no retirement—and those facts remained firmly planted in the back of their minds. The rather grueling schedule combined with pulling the big rigs cross-country sometimes through difficult and dangerous road conditions took a toll on Paul and Kathy in some respects. Somehow though, their commitment to the message kept it from being overwhelming.

It didn't take long for Shane's guitar playing to advance, and slowly the fear of being on stage in front of the audience subsided. It took real determination on his part not to let it keep him from doing what he loved most.

Paul often commented during their performances that Brulé was the hardest working band in the country—and he wasn't kidding. Throughout the course of time they'd hit every scenario as a touring band, from best case to worst case: pulling the rigs into a convention center with a heated environment and the stage five feet away to parking the trailer with the event on the third floor and having to carry 500 pounds of equipment up the stairs, unable to work the big pieces around corners, and back down following the show.

The long trailers were loaded in an exact order, one piece at a time. The fifty 100-foot extension cords and the audio cable added up to over 300 connections per concert. This was not a task a brand new roadie could do without being prompted each step of the way. Each and every time it took great teamwork and precise movements.

Fritz and Cheryll were forced to close the Squeaky Door. It tore their hearts apart to give up on their business, but they weren't making enough money to make it worthwhile. They still had the ranch, and began traveling with Paul and Kathy as part of the road crew.

Fritz helped with set-ups and tear-downs, and Cheryll worked the CD table. They didn't mind the hard work and enjoyed traveling with Brulé and meeting fans all across the country. For Paul and Fritz, it helped make up for some of their lost years.

. . .

Good things were happening. The hard work was paying off. Their reputation in tiny Deadwood, South Dakota, opened a door like none other. Movie star Kevin Costner and his brother had owned and operated the Midnight Star Casino on Main Street, Deadwood, for a number of years. Costner also owned a large piece of property just outside of town with the intent to develop. After much debate—and some controversy—with the locals, Costner decided to build a museum that honored the role the buffalo played in the lives of the Lakota Sioux Indians. He was well familiar with Lakota tradition from his role as Lieutenant John Dunbar in *Dances With Wolves.*

The centerpiece of Tatanka…Story of the Bison was a larger-than-life bronze sculpture featuring 14 bison being pursued by three Lakota riders. An interpretive center depicted the relationship of the bison and the Plains Indians through interactive exhibits. The museum included an authentic Lakota encampment where everything from tipis to live Lakota interpreters offered a snapshot of Indian life during the height of the Buffalo Culture around 1840.

Brulé was hired to play for the grand opening in June 2003, including a private showing the day prior to the public opening. The two-day event gave Paul a chance to spend one-on-one time with the Hollywood actor, both in a personal and professional sense.

Costner liked Brulé's music so well that he invited the band to perform in August at the Hollywood premier of his newest movie, *Open Range.* The old-fashioned western of good versus evil starred both Kevin Costner and Robert Duvall as grizzled cowboys in the final years of the Wild West. Filmed in the Canadian Rockies, the scenery was stunningly beautiful and majestic. In typical Hollywood fashion, the grand event was star-studded as guests and honorees mingled throughout the evening. For Brulé though, it was just another gig, because they were there to work. Well, maybe not just another gig because it was the first time they'd been paid to fly to the location instead of driving the rigs across the country. The accommodations were exceptional and the entire band was treated very well. The bottom line was that a business relationship had been established, with room to grow.

Meanwhile, Nicole received four nominations from the Native American Music Academy for her release *Night Tree*. This time the awards were slated for the Isleta Casino Resort Showroom in Albuquerque, New Mexico, in November 2003. Nicole took top honors for "Best Instrumental Recording" for *Night Tree,* but because of scheduling conflicts, had to attend and receive the award alone.

By December Brulé was full swing into another season of Christmas concerts, one of Paul's favorite times of the year. Vlasis, the front-and-center lead guitarist for the past five years, decided it was time to pursue his own musical ambitions and parted ways with Brulé before the 2004 schedule kicked into gear.

· · ·

It was satisfying to sense a degree of longevity in their annual schedule. Familiar faces greeted them at each event, in each city, like meeting up with family. Come spring, the whole entourage made the trip north for the summer season. Eagle flew home to Tennessee whenever the opportunity presented itself. His mother, Fran Astisaga-McManus, had been running the store in Jackson for him ever since he joined Brulé. Without her dedication, he couldn't be doing what he loved most: drumming.

"Fritz and Cheryll have done so much for us, all through the years," Kathy said with great emphasis. "We *have* to be home the weekend of their Giveaway Ceremony."

"When is it?" Paul asked.

"The third weekend in June."

"That's fine. Just don't book us that weekend. It'll feel good to have a few days on the bend anyway."

Kathy turned her back to Paul and grinned. How on earth would she keep it a secret until mid June! Last summer Fritz and Cheryll had hosted a Naming Ceremony for their son, Jeremiah, and Lakota tradition held that the following year the family host a Giveaway Ceremony. The current day ceremony was quite different from the ones of long ago, but the same principles applied. In one sense, it was the opposite of a wedding ceremony where the host family invites all their friends and relatives, and everyone who comes brings a gift for the newly married couple. In this instance, the host family still invites all their friends and relatives and in the reverse, gives each guest a gift.

In keeping with the Lakota traditions, star quilts were an important part of the Giveaway. Cheryll added up the names of people they planned to give a star quilt and came up with a grand total of sixteen. Because of the large quantity, she didn't have time to get them locally and had to order them from a lady on a reservation in Nebraska so she could be assured to have them all by June.

For months Cheryll and Fritz had been collecting various household items to give away, checking sale items every time they shopped in the bigger cities. Friends and family also helped by donating items to the celebration. As the months went by, Cheryll found it a challenge to store all of the gifts until the designated date.

Fritz and Cheryll had also decided to give their sons, Frederick and Harlee, their Indian names at the same time. And the big secret that everyone was ordered to keep from Paul was that he too would receive his Indian name, 11 years after his first visit to the rez.

. . .

On a cool, cloudy afternoon in mid June 2004, over 100 people descended on the *Kul Wicasa Oyate, Akicita Wokiksuye O'tipi*, the brand new community center in the heart of Lower Brule, dedicated in honor of soldiers from the Lower Brule tribe. With a gymnasium and expansive kitchen facilities it was the ideal place to hold large gatherings. Fritz, Cheryll, and a host of helpers had spent all evening setting up the gym for the Naming and Giveaway Ceremonies. The bleachers were pushed back against the wall to make room for the rows of banquet tables. Gifts were stacked along the entire front width of the gym. Many smaller items were placed in plastic baskets or small laundry baskets.

Twelve brightly-colored star quilts hung against the wall, a splash of brilliant blues, yellows, pinks, greens, and reds, a beautifully stirring reminder of the most honored gift in Lakota ceremonies next to the eagle feather. In the open area between the gifts and the tables, three chairs were set up facing the tables. A star quilt was draped over each chair, and next to each one sat a plastic tub filled with gifts. A fourth chair was positioned off to the side, also with a star quilt, for the spiritual leader, Altwin Grassrope.

"Does he know?" Cheryll whispered to Kathy as they passed in the foyer.

"Unbelievably no, he doesn't have a clue," she said with a laugh. "What can I help with?"

"It's all under control," Cheryll said out of breath. "Thanks for all your help last night."

Within another hour, the gymnasium was filled with friends and family. Young and old, they greeted each other with handshakes and hugs, busily chatting with one another at the tables. Cheryll had asked her cousin Scott Jones to emcee the important ceremony. Dressed in black jeans, a blue shirt and vest, and a western style necktie, Scott picked up the microphone and the crowd quieted.

"Welcome!" he began in a warm and friendly tone. "We are gathered here to give names to our young men in the community as part of our ancestral heritage. They are on a narrow buffalo trail, created for those trying to keep the traditions alive in spite of modern technology." He paced a few steps back and forth, scanning the faces in the audience. "We will now call the three young men who will receive their Lakota names."

"Frederick LaRoche, please come to the front and be seated in one of the chairs," Scott announced. Fred grinned and casually walked to the front. "Harlee Langdeau, please come to the front and be seated." Harlee also responded with a broad smile and sat in one of the chairs up front, both brothers fully aware of their honored role in the ceremony.

"The third man to receive his Indian name has had a long journey back home," Scott said, pausing while a toddler cried out in the background. "Paul LaRoche, please come to the front and be seated."

A surprised smile emerged across Paul's face and he slowly stood and walked to the front. When all three honorees were seated, Scott then invited Altwin Grassrope forward to give the opening prayer. Both Altwin and his older brother Noah, who had recently passed away, were well regarded in the community for their knowledge of the Lakota ways. Altwin even had a book published, titled simply, *A-l-t-w-i-n...A Lakota's Tribute with Indigenous Notion*.

Approaching his later years, Altwin was now somewhat frail in appearance, his long gray hair hanging on either side of his weathered face. As a spiritual leader and respected elder, he too took a seat of honor. "These young men will receive their Lakota names...given to them through this ceremony," Altwin began in a soft-spoken voice. "It is a responsibility and commitment with the name...to the Indian ways. We must remember those who are alone...and those who have gone on...and the medicine ways."

Next the drum group, Maza Oyate circled the drum, ready to play. The boys were all from Lower Brule and friends of Harlee and Frederick. They performed several songs while everyone from the community was invited to come forward and form a circle, welcoming Paul back home.

After everyone was once again seated, Scott continued. "This is significant in what our grandfathers have accomplished...one of the seven sacred ceremonies...and when given to us, it is for us to carry on through the rest of our lives. We use a large feather to wave smoke from a bowl with burning sage to the young men. Now stand and face the directions," he instructed the entire audience, "west, north, east, south, and west again while Altwin sings."

Next, sponsors for Fred and Harlee each came forward to participate in the individual portion of the naming ceremony. Fred was given the name *Mniwanca Ozuya* or Ocean Warrior, most fitting since his grandfather, Fritz's and Paul's father, had been a Navy firefighter and Fred was now training to become a firefighter in the California forests. Harlee received the name, *Kolayapi* or Friendly Ally, since the prominent characteristic of the Lakota was to be allies with people of any race or color.

Then Paul's sponsor Mike Jandreau was called to the microphone. As Tribal chairman, but more important as a friend and supporter of

Paul's music and mission, Mike accepted the position of sponsor with honor. "Paul has been away since he was very little. He sought and found his way back home to Lower Brule, through God's mercy. He is therefore named Advocate of the Burnt Thigh."

Mike paused between sentences, relaxed and unhurried, a noticeable speech characteristic in the Native dialect. "Put the eagle feather on…become a sacred man of God's creation. Carry the feather proudly among your people, your tribe. Represent a man of dignity, like our forefathers," he said.

Altwin Grassrope then put a dot of red paint on Paul's forehead. Next he tied the eagle feather to the back of Paul's hair as the drum group played another song. "Be loyal to the most important person— yourself. Once you take a name, it changes your outlook," he said with conviction. "You reflect your responsibility. You are now rooted into a group of people. Learn to accept and understand. Commit to know love…respect…deal with the beauty of who you are. It is a great honor to have a name bestowed…and a great honor to accept."

All the guests were then invited forward to congratulate each of the three men, followed by a side-step dance around the gym while Maza Oyate played and sang. Scott then announced a short break before a special performance.

Soon Paul, Eagle, and Richard Edwards returned, all three men dressed in traditional regalia. In another surprise, Kathy commissioned Linda Thompson to make the regalia and then arranged for Paul to receive it several months earlier at a Brulé concert. The shirt was bright red with buckskin fringes on the cuffs, adorned with a buffalo horn hairpipe breastplate. A dark blue breechcloth hung over the front of his buckskin leggings. He had received the handmade hawk dance stick from Eagle, and the moccasins from Linda, both as gifts. Paul stood with an air of pride that came in the significance of the moment, unable to hide the sparkle in his eyes.

Eagle and Richard prepared to join Paul for the special performance. Richard was a dancer for Brulé from the Rosebud Reservation and also worked for Paul and Kathy on the road crew. His regalia was a beautiful mix of red, white, and black with numerous native accessories. Eagle looked stunning in a shimmering blue shirt and fancy breastplate. Each wore a roach headdress, differing slightly in style.

The men posed for pictures, all three looking especially handsome and dignified. Kathy donned a black silk shawl that flowed to the floor, trimmed with long red fringes. The *Brulé* logo covered the back, a classy accessory for the special occasion.

As the music began, Paul, Eagle, and Richard stepped and bent in response to the beat of the drum and began a wonderful rhythmic dance while Altwin sang a song. Their movements were fluid and effortless as they danced using hand motions, turning in circles and back again, and all too soon the song ended.

Shane was selected to present the prestigious eagle feather bustle to Paul. Worn on the back, it represented an important part of a traditional dancer's regalia and could only be given after a man had received his Indian name. Paul stood before the many friends and family members. "I'm at a loss for words to describe the true feelings of being welcomed back so quickly and honestly. I will live with respect and honor to represent the people of Lower Brule," he said humbly. Paul tipped his head in appreciation and took his seat.

Altwin stood up to the microphone. "The family of Fritz and Cheryll is sharing this bounty," he said. "The spirit of giving…the spirit of sharing…the spirit of receiving. Let us now eat, because the people are hungry."

Helpers immediately stepped forward and began serving two delicious kinds of soups, hot dogs, chips, bakery rolls, fry bread, and *wojapi,* a sweet berry sauce. For dessert, three large cakes waited to be cut, each one bearing the Lakota name just bestowed on the honored guests.

As the Naming Ceremony concluded, the Giveaway Ceremony began. Cheryll and Fritz first gave away the star quilts, one by one, sharing a story of why each person selected was special in their lives. Just like when Paul and Kathy received their star quilt from Fritz and Cheryll, each recipient was invited to come forward and be wrapped in the quilt. Once the quilts were all dispersed, helpers assisted Fritz and Cheryll by distributing the gifts to all the guests until there were none left.

• • •

They said Grandpa Ben was the "elite of the reservation," honest as the day was long. He had integrity, a willingness to help others, and a wonderful sense of humor. Like others on the reservation, he was a farmer and a rancher, which equaled a hard worker. Life for the Thompsons, like many, cohered along the ever-flowing Missouri River.

Grandpa Ben's parents, Joseph and Mary Thompson, possessed great insight and were married for 65 years. Imagine, *65 years!* Did Paul even know anyone else who'd been married that long? Their love must have been true and strong because they died within months of each other, just like Clarence and Irma.

His great-great-great grandfather, Strikes the Ree, the Yankton chief, stood out as a man of great character. When he died in July 1888, his tribe erected a monument at the Greenwood Agency, the very place Lewis and Clark first met with the Yankton Sioux. Inscribed on his tomb were the words, *"Padaniapapi Huhu Tawa Den Wanka Ihanktonwan Iye Tokoheya Christian Wocekiye En Mniakastanpi."* Translated it says, "Here lies the remains of Struck-By-the Ree, the first Yankton to be baptized a Christian. He was in his day the strongest and most faithful friend of the whites in the Sioux Nation."

This was a man born in the year 1804 in the vast and unnamed territory of the Northern Plains, yet he received medals from U.S. presidents Franklin Pierce, Ulysses S. Grant, and James Garfield. Imagine meeting three presidents!

Paul could feel the pride in his heritage overflowing at times. Yet he knew that his adoption journey was unique. Not everyone could return to such a warm and welcoming embrace, Indian or non-Indian.

The truth remained that many families who had grown up on the rez were not as fortunate. Alcohol stole healthy, productive lives and passed the associated dysfunction from one generation to the next. Native Americans struggle to live in areas with high unemployment, and are forced to swallow the bitter belief thrust upon their forefathers that it was better to "become like the whites." As a matter of survival they lost their language and culture, diminishing their self-worth. Other concerns arose for those who were part-Indian and part-white.

Not being full-blooded Indian or white can also be a rough spot to live in. Neither race fully accepts you.

Prejudices were still alive and well in central South Dakota. Whenever students from Lower Brule competed against non-Indian schools, players and spectators could count on name calling and harassment that often led to the police being called. Without fail, law enforcement always approached the Indian side of the bleachers first. Fritz and Cheryll knew firsthand how it felt to be on the receiving end of racial slurs and cruel comments. They heard it 30 years ago when they were in high school, and they still heard it directed at students from Lower Brule today.

There were, however, homes on the reservation that reflected great pride, and people within the community were doing good things to restore the culture. Lakota language classes were available, adults were teaching children how to sew regalia, groups of students from the Boys and Girls Club attended events where they could dance and perform.

Coming home brought great joy for Paul, but a part of his heart cried for the lingering effects of the wrongs from years ago, when darkness entered the Lakota world. Once again, walking stick in hand, he trudged the shoreline of the river, listening to the voices of the past that called out to him in whispered breezes.

There lies a mission, a purpose...take the positive from both worlds and blend it into the music. He could have never created this scenario, only the Creator knew how the pieces would come together. In truth, it was merely his life experiences—he and Kathy, along with Shane and Nicole. Something declared that it had value—and it was worth sharing with others.

Over the years he too had searched and questioned things in life like most people, but now he was privileged to have walked in two parallel but vastly different worlds. Advocate for Burnt Thigh... yes, he would accept it with great pride, and move forward with great purpose.

SIXTEEN

Reconciliation

"When all else fades away, Faith,
Hope, and Love will remain.

Those feelings that are so strong,
so mysterious.

I think of you my relatives,
and I thank you."

—*Paul Summers LaRoche*

One Holy Night, the reworked version of traditional Christmas songs, remained a best-selling CD year in and year out. Paul's Christmas concert presentation, *Red Nativity*, was a fan favorite, growing in popularity each year. Something about the spirit of the season brought an added air of excitement prior to each holiday performance.

All afternoon light snow fell, covering Rapid City and the surrounding hills in a layer of glistening white. Even the dark evergreen branches high on the rocky hills were dressed in white for the special occasion, creating a picturesque winter evening. The enchanting scene was right out of a Hallmark holiday movie. Brushing snow from their jackets, last-minute attendees hurried to their seats. The hustle and bustle of guests settled in anticipation of the start.

Kathy scurried to the front row. It never failed—every large con-cert brought the jitters. The cast had grown to roughly 27 people to present the *Red Nativity* show, including stagehands, light crew, danc-ers, the band, Kathy and Heather. Once again, Fritz and Frederick were along as part of the road crew, while Cheryll helped sell CDs before and after the show. It took the whole day to set up the stage props and new lighting equipment. Shane's choreographed light show was an impressive addition to the Christmas concerts, bringing the performance up a notch in professionalism.

Suddenly spotlights swirled across the audience and settled on each side of the room. There was a hush as people saw Eagle standing on the far right side of the audience dressed in full regalia. His shim-mering blue shirt dazzled under the light, in what appeared as a halo of feathers from his headdress and bustle. With a sparkle in his eyes he lifted his arm in the direction of the opposite side of the room. There stood Paul, also in full regalia, who in turn lifted his arm in response. Together they began down the steps in a wonderful rhythmic dance. Part way down toward the stage, there was a stir, a sensing that this was not just a show but an invitation to share in a very special evening.

Just then the lights dimmed and the curtains opened. The assem-bly quieted and a reverent atmosphere filled the auditorium. Each time the view took Kathy's breath. Evergreens lined the back and sides of the stage, draped in white lights. Two large tipis filled the background on either side of the drums.

"Good evening," Paul began. "And welcome to the Rushmore Plaza Civic Center on a snowy, winter night. It's so good of you to come out on such a night to see us. We thank you for that." Dressed now in a black-and-red leather vest with fringes, Paul looked more handsome than ever. Shane and Nicole also were dressed in their Christmas-concert finest.

Brulé started with "The Miracle of Life," and the audience was immediately captivated by the unique composition. On the left side of the stage, Linda Thompson bobbed and slowly danced toward the center dressed in traditional buckskin regalia, holding an "infant." Soon a male dancer, also in traditional regalia, stood beside her. Then the visitors stepped forward to see the infant, their steps synchro-nized to the music.

The band moved into "Serenity's Child" and "Come Faithful Ones," a mist rising to give a buoyant effect to the stage. Three traditional male dancers appeared on stage for "Three Shaman," and Paul acknowledged the audience's applause for the dancers' wondrous movements. Along with the colorful light show, a video of winter in Lower Brule played on the large screen. In the dim light, Eagle's silhouetted profile drew gasps from the audience as he played the drum as only he can do.

When the song ended and the applause subsided, Paul spoke again. "I'd like to take few moments to share a personal and intimate story. It's about a wonderful, miraculous journey…" And just like every other time he'd performed, Paul shared bits and pieces of his life journey, describing his and Kathy's first impressions of the reservation, pulling off the road, overwhelmed, flooded with emotion.

"Many have asked what Christmas is like on a reservation. They are always surprised to hear the story of our first Christmas on the reservation. Christmas is a holiday of the heart. The observance of Christ's birth is a time for reunion of the family and a season that transcends language barriers, national boundaries, and racial distinctions. It is from this blending of cultures, worlds, and ways of life the Red Nativity was conceived."

Images of beautiful winter scenes came to life on the large screen as Paul shared his story, his message. "Together, the music of the Christmas season and the traditions and customs of Native America can help connect the hearts of people from all countries at this special time of year. Our message is clear: The hope for all nations and people begins with the birth of every child. In the innocence of every newborn, let us see the way to peace on earth and goodwill to all."

The holiday performance ended with "Silent Grace," a blending of "Silent Night" and "Amazing Grace" with an underscore of cultural sounds. The audience rose to their feet, enthusiastically applauding. Many had tears, everyone had smiles.

Paul, Nicole, Eagle, and Shane acknowledged the standing ovation, and joining hands, took a bow. The dancers too filed on stage and took part in the closing. The audience continued applauding with cheers of appreciation echoing into the quiet winter setting outdoors.

• • •

It had been six long months since Paul and Kathy had spent time at home in Lower Brule. Following the winter stint in Arizona they worked their way north with performances in Kansas, Illinois, and Iowa. Since most venues were east of South Dakota, Paul and Kathy ended up staying in Sioux Falls with Shane and Heather for a month. The time in Sioux Falls served two purposes. First, the proximity to their performances, and second, Shane and Paul were collaborating on a new music project.

Just like Paul had produced the *Nicole* series that featured Nicole and her signature flute as the lead instrument, he felt it was time to co-produce material with Shane featuring the guitar. *Tatanka* was the first release of the new AIRO series, American Indian Rock Opera, a completely fresh and new twist to the Brulé sound. The family designed the new entity to include numerous musicians, performers, artists, dancers, and singers from around the globe. He knew the music would sound different from Brulé's repertoire, but it was the direction he needed to follow.

His time in Albuquerque taught him to allow the music to go where it must. In a sense, he was once again following the direction of his heart—the Seventh Direction. AIRO would be the music that shared a common vision of hope, peace, and reconciliation—the next generation of their journey.

Paul knew one thing—he'd beaten the odds. It was rare for a band at any level to survive in the music industry for 10 years. Even Ronnie Dunn, half of the famous country duo of Brooks and Dunn, admitted he was surprised and honored to still be performing regularly after 10 years. Even though Brulé started with a few scattered performances and only two members, the key point to consider was that Brulé was still playing, week in and week out.

Paul also knew it was time for another Christmas project. In one sense, it was a good feeling to know he could never run out of things to do. His creative forces were still thriving, still stirring with ideas and concepts. At 50 years of age it made his heart sing to still touch audiences. Most musicians his age were on the downhill slide, washed up in the brutal world of entertainment or maybe trying to do the oldie circuit. Paul felt like he was possibly at the cusp of his career, ready to take off to the next level at any moment. He considered himself the luckiest man on earth and liked being exactly where he was. Paul had been in music long enough to appreciate the little things. He knew these past 10 years had been something special, and he looked forward to the next 10.

The "kids" were now young adults, settled in their lives and living close by. Shane and Heather had bought a home in Sioux Falls as they prepared to welcome the birth of their first child. Nicole, Roy, and Jade had relocated to Yankton in order to be nearer family and most of the performances. Nicole liked the small-town atmosphere Yankton offered with less stress than the bigger cities. In between gigs, she enjoyed her time at home with Jade, who was now in second grade. Jade loved to travel with the band in the summer months and dance on stage, easily becoming a crowd favorite.

Only weeks earlier Paul and Kathy had celebrated their thirtieth wedding anniversary. Paul wholeheartedly gave the credit to Kathy for being married to a musician for 30 years—that in itself was a triumph. And he loved how she did it with such class and heart.

Their first morning back on the bend, Paul waited as Kathy started a fresh pot of coffee. Relaxed in sweats and a T-shirt, Paul unloaded a box of groceries they'd brought home from Sioux Falls.

"We've got fresh muffins," Kathy said, opening the bakery box.

Paul leaned back in his chair and stretched. "Mmm…feels good to be home." He glanced around the small living room, the framed family pictures rested on the end table, a favorite star quilt hung on the wall. And centered along the north wall stood Irma's intricately carved writing table with the curved legs, the desk that held the secret for so many years. He would never know the details of Arlene's circumstances or what prompted her decision long ago. Maybe it was better that way. Opening the drawer and discovering the envelope uncovered a wondrous world he couldn't imagine being without, and he was grateful for that alone.

Still in her pajamas and robe, Kathy pushed opened the windows in the kitchen and dining area. The house still had that closed-up feeling even though they'd had someone come in to clean and get it ready for them. "Whew," she said. "We need a little fresh air in here." She crossed her arms and stood in front of the window. "Look at that view, Paul."

Paul rolled the chair from the table closer to the window. "Never realize how much I miss it until we get home."

Nothing had changed. The river bluffs were visible in the background, a bluish-aqua filled the morning sky. A pheasant ran across the back yard and disappeared into the pasture. The trilling call of a redwinged blackbird sang his morning song, followed by a chorus of cheery meadowlarks. The cattle still meandered in the pasture, chewing their cud, blurting out a few random bellows. New and bigger rolls of hay were stacked in rows along the corral, freshly rolled from the summer's first cutting.

The sun's rays reflected brightly on a piece of metal, catching Paul's eye. The Oldsmobile. It was still parked in the back next to the hay. He looked at the old car, dented, rusted, and undrivable. He could've gotten rid of it a long time ago. Something inside made him keep it, a reminder of how far he'd come—or how easy it would be to end up right back where he started.

Paul hadn't given up on his dream to have a permanent venue in the Black Hills. He had some options, possibly at *Tatanka...Story of the Bison*, Kevin Costner's museum in Deadwood. Through Kevin's experiences in the Black Hills, he too had come to appreciate the legacy of the Lakota people and everything they'd been through. Kevin had even included these sentiments at the dedication of the museum. "Despite all that we have thrown at you, all that you have been through, all that we have done to destroy you, you are *still standing.*"

Paul and Kevin had discussed ideas for an outdoor amphitheater positioned into the hillside overlooking the valley, with musical and stage presentations to further edify the Lakota way of life. Who knew where this journey would next lead? Wherever, though, he was willing to go.

The coffee dripped the last few dark drops into the full pot, the aroma stimulating their senses. Kathy walked to the counter, slippers swishing on the linoleum floor, and poured two cups.

"Thanks, hon," Paul said.

She pulled up a chair next to him and took a sip of the steaming, brown liquid.

"Maybe next year we'll get those rocking chairs and put 'em out here in the back," Paul said.

"You keep saying that, Paul." She crossed her legs and pulled her robe over her pajamas. "In the mean time, we still have a tour to finish."

Her blue eyes still held a sparkle that captivated Paul's heart. "One of these years, Kath, it'll be you and me, watching the sun set over the bend, from right here in the back. It won't get any better than that."

. . .

On a bright July morning Paul and the crew drove back from a hotel in Hill City to Mount Rushmore. The grounds were still empty except for park personnel preparing the visitor center for another busy summer day. The last time Brulé played at Mount Rushmore for the Fourth of July show, they barely had time to enjoy the wondrous setting of the park. This time they were scheduled for four consecutive days with performances off and on throughout the day, much like an art fair setting.

As Paul entered the plaza he glanced up at the familiar faces carved in stone that rested high above the mix of pine, spruce, birch, and aspen covering the surrounding hills. Even for Paul their sheer size brought a sense of awe, visible for miles from their elevated position. The Avenue of Flags that represented the 56 states and territories drew visitors from the concession building to the Grandview Terrace for viewing the epic sculpture of the four exalted presidents. Open year round, Mount Rushmore National Monument averaged 3.8 million visitors per year, and anywhere from 10,000 to 40,000 in a single day. And this July day would be no different. Rain, snow, or sunshine, people came to witness the great carving that represented the facets of Americans throughout the generations: courage, dreams, freedom, and greatness.

Paul had discovered that the park itself was in a transition of sorts. For the first time in history, an American Indian was serving as park superintendent. From the Mandan-Hidatsa tribe in Fort Berthold, North Dakota, Gerard Baker arrived at the park in June 2004. His approach at Mount Rushmore was to bring reeducation to the Black Hills through various programs including American Indian interests so people in general can know who the American Indians are as a people. With a new promoter operating the concession area, Gerard felt the timing was perfect to reintroduce the local culture, and subsequently Brulé was invited to perform at the park.

With the stage area set and in place for the week, Nicole and Heather opened the side covers of the nylon vendor tent they used for the CD and T-shirt sales table. The morning breeze managed to rustle the edges even though the sides were tied and secured in place. At seven months pregnant, Heather was in need of a place to sit and lowered herself onto one of the large plastic tubs.

"How's that baby this morning?" Paul asked.

"Kicking," Heather sighed, rubbing her firm belly that protruded underneath her white cotton blouse. "And pushing into my rib cage." She leaned back, trying to find a comfortable position.

For this event Paul planned to feature the new AIRO series *Tatanka* and *Tribal Rhythm*. Heather already had multiple copies of both new CDs in the tabletop showcase ready for purchase.

Eagle uncovered the large drum and performed a tobacco ceremony to honor the drum, a ceremony he carried out before each performance. He hung the tobacco pouch on the side of the drum and organized his percussion instruments.

"Everything set?" Paul asked Shane.

"Two minutes, Dad," Shane answered, checking the connections on the electric guitar.

Kathy opened one of their many black totes and took out the 35-millimeter camera. "I'm going to get a few shots before it gets busy," she said.

"Great," Paul said.

"Where's Jade and Roy?" Kathy asked Nicole.

"Jade just finished breakfast. They'll be here in a few minutes," Nicole said.

"I can take her later," Kathy offered. "She can hang out with Grandma this afternoon if she gets tired."

"Okay," said Nicole.

Gerard Baker passed by in his gray park uniform, headed toward the concession building. "Mornin' folks!" he called, stepping swiftly in a half-run.

"Good morning," Paul answered. He thought back to his dinner with Gerard the other evening when they'd had a chance to share each other's backgrounds.

"How'd you end up at Mount Rushmore?" Paul had asked.

"I started by cleaning toilets at Theodore Roosevelt National Park," Gerard answered with a chuckle. "This is my eighth national park. I've done it all—law enforcement, back country, interpretation. Through the years my wife and I raised our four kids in the national parks." Gerard's long braids were now mostly gray, but his eyes held an astuteness that came from a long, sometimes challenging, career in the park system. His easygoing nature and smile automatically drew people in.

Paul's eyes widened in amazement. "Wow, what a cool experience."

Gerard nodded in agreement. "It's been great. To be honest, much of the park philosophy goes hand-in-hand with the Native American culture: respect for the land, animals, and conservation."

"Yes, there are many similarities," Paul agreed.

"I like your approach, Paul," Gerard stated. "Where someone like you or me, in our positions, can choose education and cultural awareness, rather than anger and guilt, to accentuate the Native American culture, both in the traditional sense and in contemporary aspects." He paused for a moment and tipped his head to Paul. "The Great Sioux Nation wants their story told…"

Paul crossed his arms, studying the panoramic view, and took a deep breath of the cool morning air. Here he was, standing before Mount Rushmore in 2005, ready to share his own message of reconciliation in the very place the White world and the Native world collided when the Whites claimed the Black Hills, *Paha Sapa*, sacred land of the Lakota, for themselves. Through his ancestors who propelled him to this role, the transition was complete. Strikes the Ree, the Yankton chief, had been a formidable ambassador of peace for his generation. Hotanka, who later became Joseph Thompson, learned the White man's trades, bringing that knowledge home to the South

Dakota prairie. Ben Thompson embraced the lessons of his father and became a successful rancher and farmer. All those forces were at work, deep within his soul, even though Paul had been taken off the reservation at birth. Destiny brought him to this place and time, of that he was sure.

Paul's eyes scanned the horizon, soaking in the surrounding scenery with a humbled admiration. The massive granite monument loomed in the background as the visitors began strolling across the plaza. Only a few wisps of feathery white clouds were visible in the otherwise blue sky. The outline of the light-gray granite carving cut a stark contrast against the deep blue backdrop.

In his signature black jeans and black vest, Shane readied his guitar and gave his dad the thumbs-up. Eagle was already in position behind the drum, Grandmother to the People. Kathy stood nearby, camera in hand, ready to capture another momentous occasion in the Brulé/AIRO journey.

Already curious about Brulé, several visitors crowded around the CD table, asking questions about the band and the music. Just then Roy came walking toward the stage area with Jade in hand.

"Hi, Grandma," Jade said to Kathy.

"How's my sweetheart?" Kathy asked, reaching for a hug.

"A little sleepy," Roy answered.

"Dad…" Nicole's voice snapped Paul back to the present.

"Yeah?" Paul asked.

"Are you ready?" Dressed in jeans and a long, flowing turquoise blouse with sequined accents, Nicole studied her dad with a quizzical look, flute in hand, the mountain breeze blowing her hair behind her shoulders.

"Yes, I am," Paul said. "I'm more than ready."

As Paul let his fingers slide across the keys, his long black hair spilling over his shoulders, faces turned toward the sound. Once again, his leather vest and bone choker highlighted his Native American features. "Good morning, everyone, and welcome to Mount Rushmore," Paul said, eyes beaming. It was more than circumstantial joy that brought his smile on this day. It came from deep within, a peace-filled, purpose-driven joy. "What a beautiful place to be this morning."

References:

Electronic References

Travel South Dakota official Web site. "Mount Rushmore"
http://www.travelsd.com/parks/rushmore/ (accessed September 2, 2005)

Mount Rushmore National Memorial, National Park Service
http://www.nps.gov/moru/ (accessed September 2, 2005)

Lone Star Quilts – A Quilt with History and Meaning
http://quilting.about.com/libarary/weekly/aa050599.htm (accessed September 9, 2004)

USA Today, Weather
http://www.usatoday.com/weather/wapr0697.htm
(accessed November 19, 2004)

National Weather Service, Storm Data & Unusual Weather Phenonmens
http://www.crbnoaa.gov (accessed November 19, 2004)

PBS – THE WEST
http://www.pbs.org/weta/thewest/program/episodes/six/index.htm
http://www.pbs.org/weta/thewest/program/episodes/six/tatanka.htm
http://www.pbs.org/weta/thewest/program/episodes/six/yellowhair.htm
http://www.pbs.org/weta/thewest/program/episodes/six/goodday.htm
http://www.pbs.org/weta/thewest/program/episodes/index.htm
http://www.pbs.org/weta/thewest/resources/archives/five/
http://www.pbs.org/weta/thewest/places/trails_ter/indian.htm
http://www.pbs.org/lewisandclark/native/index.html
http://www.pbs.org/lewisandclark/native/yan.html
(accessed March 17, 2005)

Journals of the Lewis and Clark Expedition Online August 27–30, 1804
http://libtextcenter.unl.edu/examples.servlet/transform/tamino/Library/
lewisandclarkjournal... (accessed March 17, 2005)

Sioux – Lakota – Dakota – Nakota
http://www.crystalinks.com/sioux/html (accessed March 22, 2005)

Rosebud Indian Reservation, South Dakota
http://tradecorridor.com/rosebud/rosebud.htm (accessed August 21, 2005)

Rosebud Sioux Tribe community profile
http://www.mnisose.org/profiles/rosebud.htm (accessed August 21, 2005)

Press & Dakotan – Making History 08/23/04
http://www.yankton.net/stories/082304/opE_20040823001.shtml
(accessed May 21, 2005)

Press & Dakotan – History of Yankton, South Dakota Struck-By-The-Ree
09/15/99 http://www.yankton.net/stories/091599/bus_struck.html
(accessed March 17, 2005)

Historic Sites on the Yankton Indian Reservation, South Dakota, Yankton Sioux
Tribe http://www.yanktonsiouxtourism.com/historic/htm
(accessed March 17, 2005)

The Yankton Sioux Treaty of 1858. Father DeSmet bicentennial, page 207
http://users.skynet.be/pater.de.smet/pj-e/pagina207.htm
(accessed March 17, 2005)

Notable Dakota Nakota Yanktonai People, Yankton Sioux Tourism Association
http://www.yanktonsiouxtourism.com/yanktonpeople.htm

Untitled, http://65.222.51.24/reehtml (accessed March 17, 2005)

Lower Brule Sioux Tribe Community Profile
http://www.mnisose.org/profiles/lwrbrule.htm
(accessed November 16, 2004)

South Dakota Indian Tribes
http://www.kstrom.net/isk/maps/dakotas/sd.html
(accessed November 16, 2004)

Hampton Institute American Indian Stories
http://www.twofrog.com/hamptonstories2.html
www.twofrog.com/hamptonmale3.txt
(accessed March 17, 2005)

Archives of the Hampton University, Hampton, VA:

Thompson, Joseph (Winnebago)
Hotanka, Loud Voice, Sioux
Lower Brule, SD
November 1878 – September 1881
Trades: Farmer, carpenter, wheelwright, policeman

Standard Published References:

Hirschfelder, Arlene. 2000. *Native Americans: A History in Pictures.* NY: Dorling Kindersley.

Karolevitz, Robert F. 1975. *Challenge: The South Dakota Story.* Sioux Falls, SD: Brevet Press. Bk. 1: 35; bk. 2: 45, 68, 69; bk. 3: 87.

Mails, Thomas E. 1997. *The Library of Native Peoples: Peoples of the Plains.* Tulsa, OK: Council Oak Books.

Marshall, Joseph M. III. 2004. *The Journey of Crazy Horse.* NY: Viking.

Pedigree Report: Laroche, Paul

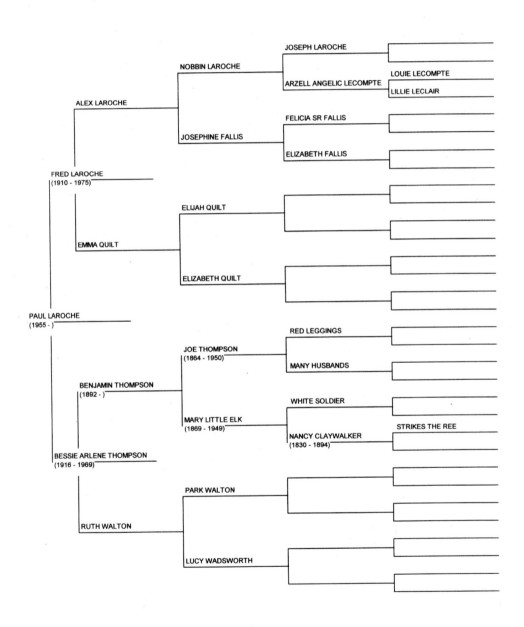

PAUL LAROCHE
(1955 -)

FRED LAROCHE
(1910 - 1975)

BESSIE ARLENE THOMPSON
(1916 - 1969)

ALEX LAROCHE

EMMA QUILT

BENJAMIN THOMPSON
(1892 -)

RUTH WALTON

NOBBIN LAROCHE

JOSEPHINE FALLIS

ELIJAH QUILT

ELIZABETH QUILT

JOE THOMPSON
(1864 - 1950)

MARY LITTLE ELK
(1869 - 1949)

PARK WALTON

LUCY WADSWORTH

JOSEPH LAROCHE

ARZELL ANGELIC LECOMPTE

FELICIA SR FALLIS

ELIZABETH FALLIS

RED LEGGINGS

MANY HUSBANDS

WHITE SOLDIER

NANCY CLAYWALKER
(1830 - 1894)

LOUIE LECOMPTE

LILLIE LECLAIR

STRIKES THE REE

Notes

There are varying reports on the Yankton Chief, Struck By the Ree or Strikes the Ree: According to legend, Palaneapape was wrapped in an American flag by Captains Lewis and Clark and baptized as an American citizen, predicting that he would someday be a great leader and a loyal friend of the White man. Nowhere in the journals of Lewis and Clark do they record such an incident, but the story followed him throughout his life. Even more controversial, however, has been the chief's name. Struck By The Ree is used on the treaty document. One version states he was partially scalped in a skirmish with the Arikara (Ree) Indians, thus the name Struck By the Ree was given him. Another report declares that he avenged his brother's death by killing an Arikara warrior with a spear and thus earned the title Strike the Ree. George W. Kingsbury, who was at Yankton during the village years and knew the chief personally, used the latter name in his writings. Similarly, the Frost-Todd trading post ledger kept by George D. Fiske at the Indian camp in 1859 listed the Sioux leader's account under the heading of Strike the Ree. In early newspaper accounts he was referred as Old Strike. Regardless, historian Harold Shunk reported when the Greenwood Agency was established, Old Strike asked for a flag. "Every day of the year from the establishment of the agency at Greenwood, the old chief would raise and lower the flag without fail. He was…proud of the American flag." When facing the daunting task of condensing 150 years of family history into a single chapter, I was unable to include all this information.

From left to right:
Moses Brings Plenty, Shane LaRoche, Nicole LaRoche,
Paul LaRoche, Eagle
(2006)

Brulé Discography

TRIBAL RHYTHM

Featuring the classical guitar, this unique melody-driven album captures the rhythms and beats of the indigenous people. Containing a mix of both upbeat and more soothing tempos, this album takes the listener on a journey across the plains. *Tribal Rhythm* is a great CD for listeners of all ages.

TATANKA

Tatanka, the first release by AIRO, pushes the envelope to encompass more styles, sounds, and genres of music, thereby bridging the gap between all cultures, nations, and people. AIRO, American Indian Rock Opera, has taken the music of Brulé to the next level. This album is the first release of what is to become a two-part series that will tell the story of the buffalo from before man, to its relationship with the American Indians, and through its near extinction due to the westward expansion across the plains. If you enjoy the fun, up-tempo album *Star People*, this CD is one you will want to add to your collection.

NIGHT TREE

Night Tree is the long-awaited follow-up to Nicole's *Passion Spirit*. This CD includes Brulé and the rest of the ensemble. The music is mainstream ready and contains 12 original songs featuring Nicole's unique style of beautiful and haunting flute playing. If you have enjoyed Nicole and Brulé in the past, this groundbreaking CD is sure to become one of the group's most memorable projects.

STAR PEOPLE

This CD is melody-driven and is best described as listener friendly and radio ready. *Star People* features 14 original compositions that have crossed over from New Age to pop instrumental. This CD is one of the first Native American recordings to emerge into the mainstream music industry. *Star People* was voted "Instrumental Recording of the Year" by the Native American Music Awards in 2002.

PASSION SPIRIT

This is the debut release by Nicole LaRoche, Paul LaRoche's (aka Brulé's) daughter. This CD features Nicole's signature haunting and mesmerizing flute melodies along with other instrumentation. On this CD, Nicole captures the passion of indigenous peoples from across the globe. This contemporary world instrumental recording is bound for its place as a classic among the Native American music genre. Fourteen songs for 61 minutes of beautiful music.

ONE NATION

Released in November 1999, this recording features up-tempo arrangements with heavy Native American vocals (tranquil and medium tempos as well). *One Nation* goes beyond *We the People* in its world flavor and driving dance and club rhythms. This is new ground for Contemporary Native American music.

ONE HOLY NIGHT

Considered the first Native American Christmas recording, this CD blends recognizable Christmas melodies with a unique Native American arrangement and style reminiscent of *We the People*. This CD provides an enjoyable listen any season and is a consistent best seller year round.

LAKOTA PIANO

A tranquil and meditative recording featuring beautiful haunting piano melodies with soft instrumentation. All eight compositions flow and drift with a touch of tranquility that carries the spirit of Native America. This recording is very popular with massage therapists and people who like "soft" music throughout the entire CD.

WE THE PEOPLE

Brulé's best-selling CD features a unique blend of contemporary and traditional Native American instrumentation and rhythms. *We the People* is one of the top-selling Native American and New Age recordings today with over 1 million copies sold worldwide. This CD was composed by Paul LaRoche during his reunion with his Lakota family on the Lower Brule Sioux Reservation in SD. All Brulé CDs are considered instrumental.

About the Author

Photo by Lori Mosby

Barbara Marshak is a freelance writer and author with nearly 100 published articles and stories. Her work can be found in several compilation book series such as *Groovy Chicks*, *Cup of Comfort*, and *God's Way*. She has also written articles for national and regional periodicals such as *Guideposts*, *Minnesota Monthly*, and *Lake Country Journal*. In 2006 she was selected as a featured author in *Bylines*.

A native of Minnesota, Barbara enjoys writing heartwarming stories that readers find rewarding and uplifting. She especially values inspiring, true life dramas and is privileged to bring *Hidden Heritage* to the printed page. Barbara and her husband, John, reside in the Twin Cities and have a blended family of six children.

For further information see **www.barbaramarshak.com**.